Recent Advances in Hybrid Metaheuristics for Data Clustering

Recent Advances in Hybrid Metaheuristics for Data Clustering

Edited by

Sourav De
Cooch Behar Government Engineering College, West Bengal, India

Sandip Dey
Sukanta Mahavidyalaya, West Bengal, India

Siddhartha Bhattacharyya
CHRIST (Deemed to be University), Bangalore, India

Registered Offices
John Wiley & Sons, Inc., 111 River Street, Hoboken, NJ 07030, USA
John Wiley & Sons Ltd, The Atrium, Southern Gate, Chichester, West Sussex, PO19 8SQ, UK

Editorial Office
The Atrium, Southern Gate, Chichester, West Sussex, PO19 8SQ, UK

For details of our global editorial offices, customer services, and more information about Wiley products visit us at www.wiley.com.

Wiley also publishes its books in a variety of electronic formats and by print-on-demand. Some content that appears in standard print versions of this book may not be available in other formats.

Library of Congress Cataloging-in-Publication Data

Names: De, Sourav, 1979- editor. | Dey, Sandip, 1977- editor. |
    Bhattacharyya, Siddhartha, 1975- editor.
Title: Recent advances in hybrid metaheuristics for data clustering / edited
    by Dr. Sourav De, Dr. Sandip Dey, Dr. Siddhartha Bhattacharyya.
Description: First edition. | Hoboken, NJ : John Wiley & Sons, Inc., [2020]
    | Includes bibliographical references and index.
Identifiers: LCCN 2020010571 (print) | LCCN 2020010572 (ebook) | ISBN
    9781119551591 (cloth) | ISBN 9781119551614 (adobe pdf) | ISBN
    9781119551607 (epub)
Subjects: LCSH: Cluster analysis–Data processing. | Metaheuristics.
Classification: LCC QA278.55 .R43 2020 (print) | LCC QA278.55 (ebook) |
    DDC 519.5/3–dc23
LC record available at https://lccn.loc.gov/2020010571
LC ebook record available at https://lccn.loc.gov/2020010572

Cover Design: Wiley
Cover Image: © Nobi_Prizue/Getty Images

Set in 9.5/12.5pt STIXTwoText by SPi Global, Chennai, India

Printed and bound by CPI Group (UK) Ltd, Croydon, CR0 4YY

10 9 8 7 6 5 4 3 2 1

Dr. Sourav De dedicates this book to his respected parents, Satya Narayan De and Tapasi De; his loving wife, Debolina Ghosh; his beloved son, Aishik De; his sister, Soumi De, and his in-laws.

Dr. Sandip Dey dedicates this book to the loving memory of his father, the late Dhananjoy Dey; his beloved mother, Smt. Gita Dey; his wife, Swagata Dey Sarkar; his children, Sunishka and Shriaan; his siblings, Kakali, Tanusree, and Sanjoy; and his nephews, Shreyash and Adrishaan.

Dr. Siddhartha Bhattacharyya dedicates this book to his late father, Ajit Kumar Bhattacharyya; his late mother, Hashi Bhattacharyya; his beloved wife, Rashni, and his in-laws, Asis Mukherjee and Poly Mukherjee.

Contents

List of Contributors

Laith Mohammad Abualigah
Amman Arab University
Jordan

Rishabh Agrawal
VIT
India

Kauser Ahmed
VIT
India

Mofleh Al-diabat
Al Albayt University
Jordan

Bisan Alsalibi
Universiti Sains Malaysia
Malaysia

Mohammad Al Shinwan
Amman Arab University
Jordan

Belfin R V
Karunya Institute of Technology and
Sciences
India

Siddhartha Bhattacharyya
CHRIST (Deemed to be university)
India

Indu Chhabra
Panjab University
Chandigarh
India

Sunanda Das
National Institute of Technology
Durgapur
India

Sourav De
Cooch Behar Government Engineering
College
India

Prasenjit Dey
Cooch Behar Government Engineering
College
India

Sandip Dey
Sukanta Mahavidyala
India

Tania Dey
Sikkim Manipal Institute of Technology
India

Khaldoon Dhou
Drury University
USA

Arnab Gain
Cooch Behar Government Engineering
College
India

Essam Hanandeh
Zarqa university
Jordan

Grace Mary Kanaga
Karunya Institute of Technology and
Sciences
India

Ahamad Khader
Universiti Sains Malaysia
Malaysia

Debanjan Konar
Sikkim Manipal Institute of Technology
India

Suman Kundu
Wroclaw University of Science and
Technology
India

Ruchita Pradhan
Sikkim Manipal Institute of Technology
India

Helio Pedrini
Institute of Computing
University of Campinas
Brazil

Prativa Rai
Sikkim Manipal Institute of Technology
India

Marcos Roberto e Souza
Institute of Computing
University of Campinas
Campinas
Brazil

Essam Said Hanandeh
Zarqa University
Jordan

Anderson Santos
Institute of Computing
University of Campinas
Brazil

Tejaswini Sapkota
Sikkim Manipal Institute of Technology
India

Mohammad Shehab
Aqaba University of Technology
Jordan

Gunmala Suri
University Business School
Panjab University
Chandigarh
India

Series Preface: Dr Siddhartha Bhattacharyya, Christ (Deemed To Be University), Bangalore, India (Series Editor)

The Intelligent Signal and Data Processing (ISDP) book series focuses on the field of signal and data processing encompassing the theory and practice of algorithms and hardware that convert signals produced by artificial or natural means into a form useful for a specific purpose. The signals might be speech, audio, images, video, sensor data, telemetry, electrocardiograms, or seismic data, among others. The possible application areas include transmission, display, storage, interpretation, classification, segmentation, and diagnosis. The primary objective of the ISDP book series is to evolve future-generation, scalable, intelligent systems for faithful analysis of signals and data. The ISDP series is intended mainly to enrich the scholarly discourse on intelligent signal and image processing in different incarnations. The series will benefit a wide audience that includes students, researchers, and practitioners. The student community can use the books in the series as reference texts to advance their knowledge base. In addition, the constituent monographs will be handy to aspiring researchers due to recent and valuable contributions in this field. Moreover, faculty members and data practitioners are likely to gain relevant knowledge from the books in the series.

The series coverage will contain, but not be exclusive to, the following:

- Intelligent signal processing
  a) Adaptive filtering
  b) Learning algorithms for neural networks
  c) Hybrid soft computing techniques
  d) Spectrum estimation and modeling
- Image processing
  a) Image thresholding
  b) Image restoration
  c) Image compression
  d) Image segmentation
  e) Image quality evaluation
  f) Computer vision and medical imaging
  g) Image mining
  h) Pattern recognition
  i) Remote sensing imagery
  j) Underwater image analysis

  k) Gesture analysis
  l) Human mind analysis
  m) Multidimensional image analysis
- Speech processing
  a) Modeling
  b) Compression
  c) Speech recognition and analysis
- Video processing
  a) Video compression
  b) Analysis and processing
  c) 3D video compression
  d) Target tracking
  e) Video surveillance
  f) Automated and distributed crowd analytics
  g) Stereo-to-auto stereoscopic 3D video conversion
  h) Virtual and augmented reality
- Data analysis
  a) Intelligent data acquisition
  b) Data mining
  c) Exploratory data analysis
  d) Modeling and algorithms
  e) Big data analytics
  f) Business intelligence
  g) Smart cities and smart buildings
  h) Multiway data analysis
  i) Predictive analytics
  j) Intelligent systems

Preface

Grouping or classifying real-life data into a set of clusters or categories for further processing and classification is known as *clustering*. The groups are organized on the basis of built-in properties or characteristics of the data in that dataset. The features of the groups are important to represent a new object or to understand a new phenomenon. Homogeneous data should be in the same cluster, whereas dissimilar or heterogeneous data is grouped into different clusters. The clustering of data can be applied in different fields of the world, such as document retrieval, data mining, pattern classification, image segmentation, artificial intelligence, machine learning, biology, microbiology, etc.

Broadly, there are two types of data clustering algorithms: supervised and unsupervised. In supervised data clustering algorithms, the number of coveted partitions and labeled datasets is supplied as the basic input at the beginning of the algorithm. Moreover, in supervised clustering algorithms, it is attempted to keep the number of segments small, and the data points are allotted to clusters using the idea of closeness by resorting to a given distance function. By contrast, prior information about the labeled classes, decision-making criterion for optimization, or number of desired segments beyond the raw data or grouping of principle(s) on the basis of their data content are not required for the unsupervised algorithms.

Metaheuristic algorithms have proved efficient in handling and solving different types of data clustering problems. Metaheuristics is designed to tackle complex clustering problems where classical clustering algorithms fail to be either effective or efficient. Basically, the solving procedure of a subordinate heuristic problem by an iterative generation procedure is known as *metaheuristic*. This is done by syndicating intelligently different concepts to explore and exploit the search space, and the nonoptimal solutions are derived efficiently by the learning strategies that are applied on the structural information of the problem. The main objective of metaheuristic is to derive a set of optimal solutions large enough to be completely sampled. Different types of real-world problems can be handled by the metaheuristic techniques because conventional algorithms can't manage many real-world problems, in spite of increasing computational power, simply due to the unrealistically long running times. To solve the optimization problems, these algorithms make a few assumptions at the initial stages. It is not assured that metaheuristic algorithms will generate globally optimal solutions to solve all types of problems since most of the implementations are some form of stochastic optimization and the resultant solutions may depend on the set of generated random variables. To solve optimization algorithms, heuristics, or iterative methods, metaheuristic algorithms are the better option as they often determine good solutions with lesser computational effort by exploring a large set of feasible solutions. Some well-known metaheuristic algorithms include the genetic algorithm (GA), simulated annealing (SA), tabu search (TS), and different types of swarm intelligence algorithms. Some recognized swarm intelligence algorithms are particle swarm optimization (PSO), ant colony optimization (ACO), artificial bee colony optimization (ABC), differential optimization (DE), cuckoo search algorithm, etc. In recent advancements of the research, some modern swarm intelligence–based optimization algorithms such as Egyptian vulture optimization algorithm, rats herd algorithm (RATHA), bat algorithm, crow search algorithm, glowworm swarm optimization (GSO), etc., are found to perform well when solving some real-life problems. These algorithms also work efficiently to cluster different types of real-life datasets.

During the clustering of data, it has been observed that the methaheuristic algorithms suffer from time complexity though they can afford optimum solutions. To get rid of these types of problems and not depend on a particular type of metaheuristic algorithm to solve complex problems, researchers and scientists blended not only different metaheuristic approaches but also hybridized different metaheuristic algorithms with other soft computing tools and techniques, such as neural network, fuzzy set, rough set, etc. The hybrid metaheuristic algorithms, a combination of metaheuristic algorithms and other techniques, are more effective at handling real-life data clustering problems. Recently, quantum mechanical principles are also applied to cut down on the time complexity of the metaheuristic approaches to a great extent.

The book will entice readers to design efficient metaheuristics for data clustering in different domains. The book will elaborate on the fundamentals of different metaheuristics and their application to data clustering. As a sequel to this, it will pave the way for designing and developing hybrid metaheuristics to be applied to data clustering. It is not easy to find books on hybrid metaheuristic algorithms that cover this topic.

The book contains nine chapters written by the leading practitioners in the field.

A brief overview of the advantages and limitations of the fuzzy clustering algorithm is presented in Chapter 1. The principle of operation and the structure of fuzzy algorithms are also elucidated with reference to the inherent limitations of cluster centroid selection. Several local-search-based and population-based metaheuristic algorithms are discussed with reference to their operating principles. Finally, different avenues for addressing the cluster centroid selection problem with recourse to the different metaheuristic algorithms are presented.

The increasing size of the data and text on electronic sites has necessitated the use of different clustering methods, including text clustering. This may be a helpful unsupervised analysis method used for partitioning the immense size of text documents into a set of groups. The feature choice may be a well-known unsupervised methodology accustomed to eliminating uninformative options to enhance the performance of the text clustering method. In Chapter 2, the authors have a tendency to project a rule to resolve the featured choice drawback before applying the k-means text clustering technique by rising the exploitation searchability of the fundamental harmony search algorithmic rule known as H-HSA. The projected feature choice methodology is used in this chapter to reinforce the text clustering technique by offering a replacement set of informative features.

In the advancement of data analytics, data clustering has become one of the most important areas in modern data science. Several works have come up with various algorithms to deal with data clustering. In Chapter 3, the objective is to improve the data clustering by using metaheuristic-based algorithms. For this purpose, the authors have proposed a genetic algorithm–based data clustering approach. Here, a new adaptive position–based crossover technique has been proposed for the genetic algorithm where the new concept of vital gene has been proposed during the crossover. The simulation results demonstrate that the proposed method performs better compared to the other two genetic algorithm–based data clustering methods. Furthermore, it has also been observed that the proposed approach is time efficient compared to its counterparts.

A social network, used by the human population as a platform of interaction, generates a large volume of diverse data every day. These data and attributes of the interactions become more and more critical for researchers and businesses to identify societal and economic values. However, the generated data is vast, highly complex, and dynamic, which necessitates a real-time solution. Machine learning is a useful tool in order to summarize the meaningful information from large, diverse datasets. Chapter 4 provides a survey of several applications of social network analysis where machine learning plays a critical role. These applications range from spam content detection to human behavior analysis, from topic modeling to recommender systems, and from sentiment analysis to emotion contagion in social network.

Predicting students' performance at an earlier stage is important for improving their performance for higher education and placement opportunities. Early prediction of student grades allows an instructor to detect the students' poor performance in a course automatically and also provides enormous opportunities to the decision-makers to take remedial measures to help the students to succeed in future education. A model predicting students' grades using CART, ID3, and improved multiclass SVM optimized by the genetic algorithm (GA) is investigated in Chapter 5. The model follows a supervised learning classification by means of CART, ID3, and SVM optimzed by the GA. In this study, the model is tested on a dataset that contains undergraduate student information, i.e., total marks obtained in the courses taken up in four years with the respective labeled subject name and a code at Sikkim Manipal Institute of Technology, Sikkm, India. A comparative analysis among CART, ID3, and multiclass SVM optimized by the GA indicates that the multiclass SVM optimized by GA outperforms ID3 and CART decision tree algorithms in the case of multiclass classification.

Significant advances in information technology result in the excessive growth of data in health care informatics. In today's world, development technologies are also being made to treat new types of diseases and illnesses, but no steps are being taken to stop the disease in its track in the early stages. The motivation of Chapter 6 is to help prepare people to diagnose the disease at early stages based on the symptoms of the disease. In this chapter, the authors have used various nature-inspired clustering algorithms in collaboration with k-means algorithms to actively cluster a person's health data with already available data and label it accordingly. Experiments results prove that nature-inspired algorithms like firefly with k-means are giving efficient result to the existing problems.

With the fast development of pattern discovery–oriented systems, data mining is rapidly intensifying in other disciplines of management, biomedical, and physical sciences to tackle the issues of data collection and data storage. With the advancement of data science, numerous knowledge-oriented paradigms are evaluated for automatic rule mining. Association rule mining is an active research area with numerous algorithms used for knowledge accumulation. Chapter 7 focuses on handling the various challenging issues of only demand-driven aggregation of information sources, mining and analyzing relevant patterns to preserve user concerns, and implementing the same association rule mining problem for multi-objective solutions rather than as a single-objective solution for post-purchase customer analysis.

The GA and fuzzy c-means (FRCM) algorithm is widely used in magnetic resonance image segmentation. In Chapter 8, a hybrid concept, quantum-inspired modified GA and FRCM are used to segment MR images. The modified GA (MEGA) enhances the performance of the GA by modifying population initialization and crossover probability. To speed up this classical MEGA and also to derive more optimized class levels, some quantum computing characteristics like qubit, entanglement, orthogonality, rotational gate, etc., are incorporated into the classical MEGA. The class levels created by the quantum-inspired MEGA are employed to the FRCM as initial input to overcome the convergence problem of the FRCM. A performance comparison using some standard evaluation metrics is delineated between quantum-inspired MEGA-based FRCM, classical MEGA-based FRCM, and conventional FRCM with the help of two grayscale MR images, which shows the excellence of the proposed quantum-inspired MEGA-based FRCM over both the classical MEGA-based FRCM and the conventional FRCM methods.

Large volumes of data have been rapidly collected due to the increasing advances in equipment and techniques for content acquisition. However, the efficient storage, indexing, retrieval, representation, and recognition of multimedia data, such as text, audio, images, and videos, are challenging tasks. To summarize the main characteristics of datasets and simplify their interpretation, exploratory data analysis is often applied to numerous problems in several fields, such as pattern recognition, computer vision, machine learning, and data mining. A common data analysis technique, commonly associated with descriptive statistics and visual methods, is cluster analysis or clustering. In Chapter 9, the authors propose a hybrid method based on k-means and the genetic algorithm guided by a qualitative objective function. Experiments demonstrate good results of the proposed method.

The editors hope that this book will be helpful for students and researchers who are interested in this area. It can also prove to be a novel initiative for undergraduate students of computer science, information science, and electronics engineering for part of their curriculum.

October, 2019

Sourav De
Cooch Behar, India
Sandip Dey
Jalpaiguri, India
Siddhartha Bhattacharyya
Bangalore, India

1

Metaheuristic Algorithms in Fuzzy Clustering

Sourav De[1], Sandip Dey[2], and Siddhartha Bhattacharyya[3]

[1] *Department of Computer Science and Engineering, Cooch Behar Government Engineering College, India*
[2] *Department of Computer Science, Sukanta Mahavidyalaya, Jalpaiguri, India*
[3] *Department of Computer Science and Engineering, CHRIST (Deemed to be University), Bangalore, India*

1.1 Introduction

Fuzzy clustering refers to the process of assigning data points to different clusters based on the similarity/dissimilarity of features. This process ensures that items in the same cluster are as similar as possible, while dissimilar items belong to different clusters. The identification of the clusters and the assignment of items to clusters are decided with the help of several similarity measures, which include measures of distance, connectivity, and intensity. The choice of the similarity measures depends on the type of data or the application [1].

Both classical and new algorithms have evolved over the years to address the clustering problem. Notable among them are the k-means [2] and fuzzy clustering [3, 4]. The classical algorithms primarily segregate the data points into completely different clusters while ensuring that the dissimilarity between the different clusters and the similarity of the constituent data points within any cluster are maximized in the process. Thus, these algorithms ensure that there is no overlap between the clusters. However, fuzzy clustering relies on the soft meaning, thereby enabling overlapping between clusters with the constituent data points belonging to more than one cluster depending on a degree of belongingness.

The main limitation in any clustering algorithm lies in the initialization process, which entails an initial selection of cluster center points, which are chosen randomly in most cases. Hence, an improper initialization of the cluster centers may lead to an unacceptable result since the positions of the cluster centers, with respect to the constituent data points, are major concerns in the assignment of the data points to the cluster centers.

1.2 Fuzzy Clustering

Fuzzy clustering, often referred to as soft clustering or soft k-means, is a method that entails a soft distinction of the constituent data points. By contrast, in any non-fuzzy/crisp clustering, each data point is designated to belong to exactly one and only one cluster with no

Recent Advances in Hybrid Metaheuristics for Data Clustering, First Edition.
Edited by Sourav De, Sandip Dey, and Siddhartha Bhattacharyya.
© 2020 John Wiley & Sons Ltd. Published 2020 by John Wiley & Sons Ltd.

overlapping of clusters. The data points, however, can belong to more than one cluster, implying that certain overlaps exist between resultant clusters. The underlying principle behind this partitional clustering technique is the concept of fuzzy soft set theory, which holds that for a given universe of discourse, every constituent element belongs to all the sets defined in the universe with a certain degree of belongingness (also referred to as membership) [3–5]. Fuzzy clustering is often treated as preferable due to the inherent advantages of having a natural affinity of incorporating larger datasets, a simple and straightforward implementation, the ability to handle large datasets as the time complexity is $O(n)$, the ability to produce very good results for hyper spherically shaped well-separated clusters, being robust in design, and the ability to converge to a local optimal solution [1].

1.2.1 Fuzzy *c*-means (FCM) clustering

FCM clustering is one of the most widely used. It was developed by J.C. Dunn in 1973 [6] and improved by J.C. Bezdek in 1981 [1]. The operation of the algorithm is quite similar to the widely known *k*-means algorithm. The basic steps are as follows:

1) Select a number of clusters.
2) Randomly assign coefficients to each data point to label them to the clusters.
3) Repeat until the algorithm converges, i.e., when the change in the coefficients in two consecutive iterations is no more than a predefined threshold ε.
4) Compute the cluster centroids for each cluster. Every data point x is identified by a set of coefficients indicating the degree of belongingness to the kth cluster $w_k(x)$. In FCM, the mean of all the participating points weighted by their degree of belongingness to the cluster represents the cluster centroid. It is mathematically given as

$$c_k = \frac{\sum_x w_k(x)^m x}{\sum_x w_k(x)^m} \tag{1.1}$$

where m is a hyper-parameter that controls the fuzzyness of the clusters. The higher m is, the fuzzier the cluster will be in the end.
5) For each data point, compute its coefficients of belongingness in the clusters.

1.3 Algorithm

An algorithm attempts to partition a finite collection of n elements $X = \{x_1, \dots, x_n\}$ into a collection of c fuzzy clusters with respect to some given criterion. Given a finite set of data, the algorithm returns a list of c cluster centers $C = \{c_1, \dots, c_c\}$ and a partition matrix $W = w_{i,j} \in [0,1], i = 1, \dots, n, j = 1, \dots, c$, where each element w_{ij} tells the degree to which element x_i belongs to cluster c_j.

The aim is to minimize an objective function in the following form:

$$argmin_C \sum_{i=1}^{n} \sum_{j=1}^{C} w_{ij}^m ||x_i - c_j||^2, \tag{1.2}$$

where:

$$w_{ij} = \frac{1}{\sum_{k=1}^{c} \left(\frac{||x_i - c_j||}{||x_i - c_k||} \right)^{\frac{2}{m-1}}} \tag{1.3}$$

K-means clustering works along similar lines. However, it differs from the k-means objective function by the presence of w_{ij} (or the cluster fuzziness) determined by the fuzzifier, $m \in R$, with $m \geq 1$. A large m results in smaller membership values, w_{ij}, and, hence, fuzzier clusters. In the limit $m = 1$, the memberships, w_{ij}, converge to 0 or 1, which implies a crisp partitioning. m is commonly set to 2. The algorithm also minimizes the intracluster variance that often leads to a local minimum. Moreover, the clustering results depend on the initial choice of weights. Fuzzy clustering suffers from the fact that the number of clusters in the given dataset should be known beforehand. It is also sensitive to noise and outliers.

1.3.1 Selection of Cluster Centers

Most of the clustering algorithms require an initial selection of cluster centroids (which is often made in a random fashion) without exception. In fact, the selection of the initial cluster center values is considered one of the most challenging tasks in partitional clustering algorithms. Incorrect selection of initial cluster center values leads the searching process toward an optimal solution that gets often stuck in a local optima yielding undesirable clustering results [7, 8]. The primary cause behind this problem lies in the fact that the clustering algorithms run in a manner similar to the hill climbing algorithm [9], which, being a local search-based algorithm, moves in one direction without performing a wider scan of the search space to minimize (or maximize) the objective function. This behavior prevents the algorithm to explore other regions in the search space that might have a better, or even the desired, solution. Thus, proper exploitation and exploration of the search space are not effected in the running of these algorithms.

The general approach to alleviate this problem is to rerun the algorithm several times with several cluster initializations. However, this approach is not always feasible, especially when it comes to the clustering of a large dataset or complex dataset (i.e., a dataset with multiple optima) [10]. Thus, this section mechanism may be incarnated as a global optimization problem calling for the help of optimization algorithms.

Several global-based search algorithms have been proposed to solve this local-search problem [11]. These algorithms include both local search-based metaheuristic algorithms such as SA, TS, or such as EAs (including EP, ES, GAs, and DE), HS or such as PSO, ABC, and ACO. The following sections provide an overview of the algorithms proposed to solve the clustering problem where the clusters number is known or set up *a priori*.

1.4 Genetic Algorithm

Genetic algorithms (GAs), a popular optimization algorithm, are generally used to search for optimal solution(s) to any particular computational problem. This is done by maximizing or minimizing a particular function, called an objective/fitness function. GAs represent evolutionary computation [12], a field of study, where they emulate the biological processes like reproduction and natural selection to find "fittest solutions" [13]. There exist various GAs processes in the literature that are random in nature. In this technique, a different level of randomization and control are allowed to set for operation [13]. GAs was proven to be a powerful and well-regulated optimization technique in comparison with other random search algorithms and exhaustive search algorithms [12].

GAs are designed to imitate biological process, and a large number of the pertinent terminology is taken from biological science. The fundamental components that are common among all GAs are

- A fitness (objective) function
- A population of number of chromosomes
- Selection operation to produce pool of chromosomes in population
- Crossover operation to produce population diversity in the subsequent generations
- Mutation operation to change the chromosome's property in new generation

A given algorithm is optimized with reference to an objective function [14]. The term "fitness" originated from evolutionary theory. The fitness function is used to test and quantify each individual potential solution. Chromosomes in a population are referred to as numerical values that are used to represent a candidate solution for a given problem, which is solved using a GA [14]. Each of the candidate solutions is passed through an encoding process, which is basically a stream of parameter values [15]. Theoretically, the encoding of each chromosome for a problem having N dimensions is accomplished as an array of N chromosome as given by $[q_1, q_2, \ldots, q_N]$. Here, each q_k represents a specific value of the kth parameter [15]. In general, chromosomes are encoded using a bit string, i.e., a sequence of 0s and 1s. In modern-day computer systems, chromosomes can be generated by including real numbers, permutations, and also other objects.

A GA starts with a number of chromosomes, chosen randomly, which creates the initial population. Thereafter, a fitness function is introduced to evaluate each member in the population. This evaluation is basically accomplished to study how well it can potentially solve a given problem at hand. Afterward, a selection operator is introduced to choose a number of potential chromosomes for reproduction on the basis of a user-defined probability distribution. The selection is done in accordance with the fitness of the chromosomes in the population. The probability of the selection of a particular chromosome increases as the increase of its fitness for the subsequent generations. For example, let f_n be the fitness function introduced for solving a particular problem. The probability of selecting C_n is chosen by

$$P(C_n) = \left| \frac{f_n(C_n)}{\sum_{k=1}^{N} f_n(C_k)} \right| \tag{1.4}$$

It can be noted that the selection operator is used choose chromosomes with replacement. This approach ensures that the same chromosome can be selected a number of times. The is somehow analogous to the biological crossover and recombining them. Two offsprings having different features are created by swapping two chosen chromosomes at a single point or at multiple points. Suppose the parent chromosomes [10010010010011] and [11010011001011] are crossed over at the fifth position. It creates two new offsprings, given by [10010011001011] and [11010010010011].

The mutation operation overturns individual bits to get new chromosome. Basically, bit 0 is turned into bit 1 and vice versa once this operator is introduced. Generally, mutation operation occurs with an exceedingly low probability (such as 0.001). In a few occasions, the order of implementation of mutation operator before other two operators is subject to the matter of preference by the designer. Selection and crossover operators generally prolong the genetic information of better (fitter) chromosomes, which can result in the quick convergence of a given algorithm. This causes the algorithm to be stuck at a local optima much before attaining the global optima [16]. This maintains population diversity by helping the algorithm to protect against this problem. It can also be the cause of the algorithm suffering from slow convergence.

1.5 Particle Swarm Optimization

The concept of particle swarm optimization (PSO) was first developed by James Kennedy and Russell Eberhart in 1995 [17]. The inspiration behind its development came been taken from the following concepts:

- By observing the swarming ability of animals like fish or birds
- By adopting the idea from the theory of evolutionary computation

The concept of PSO is described using the following points:

- Techniques are capable of handling and preserving a number of potential solutions every single time.
- Each solution is assessed with a reference to a function, called an objective function, to compute its fitness during each iteration.
- Each of the potential solutions in the population is regarded as a particle in the search space (fitness landscape).
- Each particle "swarm" or "fly" through the fitness landscape to find the minimum/maximum value computed by the fitness function.

During each iteration, the particles in the population (swarm) maintain the following criteria:

- Position of each particle in its search space, which include solution and fitness
- Velocity at each particle
- Best position of each individual
- Global best position in the swarm

The technique generally comprises the following steps:

1) Evaluate the fitness value of each particle in the population.
2) The individual best and the global best of the swarm are updated.
3) The velocity and its corresponding position of each particle are updated.

These mentioned steps are repeated for a predefined number of generations or until a stopping criteria is met.

The velocity of each particle is updated using the following formula:

$$v_k(t+1) = \omega v_k(t) + \iota_1 r_1(\hat{y}_k(t) - y_k(t)) + \iota_2 r_2(g(t) - y_k(t)) \tag{1.5}$$

where k represents the particle's index, ω is called the inertial coefficient, ι_1 and ι_2 are known to be the acceleration coefficients, and $0 \le \iota_1, \iota_2 \le 2$, r_1, r_2 are two random values, $0 \le r_1, r_2 \le 1$. $v_k(t)$ is represented as the particle's velocity at any time t, and $x_k(t)$ represents the position of a particle at time t. As of time t, $\hat{y}_k(t)$) and $g(t)$ are represented as the particle's individual best and the swarm's best solution.

The position of each particles is updated by using the following equation:

$$y_k(t+1) = y_k(t) + v_k(t+1) \tag{1.6}$$

where the location of the kth particle ($y_k(t)$) at the tth generation is changed to another location, $y_k(t+1)$, at the $(t+1)^{th}$ generation using velocity $v_k(t+1)$.

1.6 Ant Colony Optimization

The Ant System was the first member of a certain class of algorithms, called (ACO) [18]. This is a recent, popular metaheuristic algorithm. This algorithm was initially introduced by Colorni, Dorigo, and Maniezzo. The inspiration behind its development was the foraging behavior gathered from real ants. This foraging behavior was explored and exploited in artificial ant colonies to find the approximate solutions to several discrete/continuous optimization problems. This optimization solution is also very much applicable to various problems in telecommunications, such as load balancing and routing. Each ant in their colony randomly traverses from here to there. The indirect communication happens between the real ants with the help of chemical pheromone trails. The ants deposit this chemical in their paths from their source of the nest to the food source. This chemical enables them to search for the shortest paths to different food sources. The probability of visiting a particular path increases with the increase of pheromone deposited on that path.

The algorithm comprises the following steps:

1) A virtual trail is gathered on various path segments.
2) A path is randomly selected on the basis of the amount of "trail" available on possible paths from the initial node.
3) The ant traverses to the next available node to select the next path.
4) This process continues until the ant reaches the starting node.
5) The finished tour is recognized as a solution.
6) The whole tour is analyzed to find the optimal path.

Suppose an ant traverses from node j to node k in a graph (G, E) with a probability of p_{jk}. Then value of p_{jk} is determined by

$$p_{jk} = \frac{(\chi_{jk}^{\gamma})(\varphi_{jk}^{\delta})}{\Sigma(\chi_{jk}^{\gamma})(\varphi_{jk}^{\delta})} \tag{1.7}$$

where χ_{jk} represents the amount of pheromone deposited on the edge (j, k), γ, a parameter that is used to control the influence of χ_{jk}, φ_{jk} is defined as the desirability of edge (j, k), Like γ, δ is another parameter that is used to control the influence of φ_{jk}.

The amount of deposited pheromone is being updated with reference to the following equation:

$$\tau_{jk} = (1 - \rho)\tau_{jk} + \Delta\tau_{jk} \tag{1.8}$$

where τ_{ij} is represented as the amount of pheromone deposited on any given edge (j, k), ρ is called the evaporation rate of pheromone, and $\Delta\tau_{jk}$ is represented as the deposited amount of pheromone. The value of $\Delta\tau_{jk}$ is computed by $\frac{1}{C_k}$, if ant k traverses the edge (j, k) and C_k is the cost of that travel by that particular ant. In all other cases, the value of $\Delta\tau_{jk}$ is assumed to be zero.

1.7 Artificial Bee Colony Algorithm

Karaboga [19] introduced the artificial bee colony (ABC) algorithm is a present-day class of swarm intelligence algorithms. The inspiration behind the development of the ABC algorithm is the foraging behavior of real bee colonies. This algorithm has been applied to solve continuous optimization problems.

The ABC algorithm has three kinds of (artificial) bees as given by the following:

1) Employed bees: Each of the employed bee is connected to a nonidentical solution of the given optimization problem that is required to be solved. This class of bee explores the locality of the solution, where it was kept associated at each iteration.
2) Onlooker bees: This class of bees also explores its locality of solutions in a different manner. They probabilistically select the solution, which is explored by them in each iteration depending on the quality of the solution. Hence, the probable solutions vary for them.
3) Scout bees: For this class of bees, the locality of the solution is explored for a predefined number of times. If there is no positive outcome found, the scout bee uniformly selects a new random solution in its search space by appending an exploration property to the algorithm.

This is a population-based, efficient, local search algorithm, in which it explores the neighborhood of each solution at each iteration. The first algorithm was run to solve several standard benchmark problems, which gives inspiring results, but with respect to some state-of-the-art algorithms, its results were not so encouraging. Particularly, while considering composite and nonseparable functions, the ABC algorithm gives comparatively poor performance, and also this algorithm possesses slow convergence for high-quality solutions [20].

1.8 Local Search-Based Metaheuristic Clustering Algorithms

The local search-based algorithms have been widely used in solving several clustering problems in the literature. Some of them are presented in this section. In [21], the authors presented a simulated annealing-based clustering problem, which can be efficiently handled and solved using the metaheuristic clustering algorithms. One of the weakness that is common in is that this technique may find local minimum solutions. The proposed simulated annealing-based method solves optimization problems by taking care of such clustering weakness. The required factors have been addressed in detail in the proposed technique and it has been shown that the proposed technique converges to optimal solutions of these clustering weaknesses. Al-Sultan [22] later presented a tabu search-based clustering technique, where the author proved that the proposed technique outperforms both the k-means technique and the simulated annealing–based clustering technique. About two years later, Al-Sultan and Fedjki [23] proposed another kind of algorithm for handling the fuzzy clustering problem. In 2000, an improved version of tabu search-based clustering algorithm was presented by Sung and JinSung [24]. In their proposed work, they combined a tabu search heuristic approach with two other compatible functional approaches, known as packing and releasing. The electiveness of their proposed technique has been numerically tested and proved by comparing other works, such as the tabu search algorithm, simulated annealing technique, among others. The aforementioned local search metaheuristics, tabu search, and simulated annealing improve one candidate solution, and the problem of sucking at local minimum solutions has been rectified. Two more important points regarding the efficacy of this technique are that it is factors sensitive and also exceedingly problem-dependent in the case of tuning [25].

1.9 Population-Based Metaheuristic Clustering Algorithms

In the literature, the population-based metaheuristic clustering algorithms, designed by several authors, have been comprehensively applied in fuzzy clustering. A few efficient algorithms of this kind is presented in this section. Evolutionary algorithms (EAs) for fuzzy clustering that can adapt the current techniques. The approaches taken by EAs can be principally grouped into two categories [10]. The first one is common, which can be further divided into two of the following steps.

1) Search for apposite cluster centers via evolutionary algorithm.
2) The cluster centers attained as the outcome of the former step are used as the initial cluster center on which the FCM algorithm is applied.

The second one is another popular approach that uses the evolutionary algorithm as a clustering algorithm by itself. A few of its kind or its other variations use as a local search engine for supporting the performance of them to speed up their convergence. This approach is also appropriate to metaheuristic-based hard clustering techniques. A few of this kind of algorithms are described next.

1.9.1 GA-Based Fuzzy Clustering

Hall et al. [26], Hall and Ozyurt [27], and Hall et al. [28] presented different works, in which the authors claimed that their proposed algorithms can be used as efficient clustering tools. In their proposed algorithms, the genetic algorithm was applied to search for the near optimal cluster centers and, on the other side, was applied to accomplish the clustering. For encoding purposes, a real encoding scheme was introduced in the population of genetic algorithm. The authors proved that the proposed algorithms found an encouraging result in comparison with random initialization. The limitation of these works are that their GA method is incapable of focusing on small advancements to the cluster centers to hold up a final clustering. In comparison with the previous method, the GA-guided clustering algorithm has the higher sensitivity to the random solution generated initially, which can be applied to create an initial population. Moreover, more experiments were needed to prove the capability of the proposed algorithm for avoiding a premature convergence. Liu and Xie [29] presented a paper in which they proved that their proposed approach possesses much higher probabilities of reaching the global optimal solutions compared to the traditional techniques. In this algorithm, a binary encoding scheme and the standard operators of genetic algorithms were used to represent cluster centers in each chromosome. Experimentally, the authors proved that their proposed algorithm outperforms others. The shortcoming of this approach is that if the size of population is small, it may get stuck in a local optima problem. Van Le Van [30] presented two separate approaches, based on a genetic algorithm and evolutionary programming, to deal with fuzzy clustering problems. After conducting several experiments, the authors concluded that the success rate of this proposed algorithm is better compared to the FCM algorithm, and the author concluded that the evolutionary programming-based method produces the best results. Klawonn and Keller [31] designed an evolutionary programming model for clustering various types of cluster shapes like solid and shell clusters. For a shell shape, the proposed algorithm does not produce any encouraging results but for a solid shape, the results seems to be good. Egan et al. [32] introduced a genetic algorithm–based fuzzy clustering technique for noisy data. In this technique, an additional cluster representing noise data, known as a noise cluster, is clubbed to each chromosome. The experimental results showed that the binary representation possesses a better result compared to a real-valued representation in this particular domain. Hall et al. [28] presented another algorithm, in which the proposed algorithm showed a promising result for less noise data [33], but for noise data, the algorithm does not perform satisfactorily [28]. Maulik and Saha [34] developed a modified differential evolution-based fuzzy clustering algorithm. In this algorithm, a modified mutation process was introduced using the thoughts of local and global best vectors as in the PSO algorithm. These theories were used during this modified mutation process for pushing the trial vector speedily toward a global optima. They have successfully used their proposed algorithm in the image segmentation algorithm. They have also used the proposed algorithm in a number of synthetic, real-life datasets and standard benchmark functions to prove the applicability of this algorithm.

1.9.2 PSO-Based Fuzzy Clustering

Xiao et al. [35] used a novel and self-organizing map (SOM) method for clustering. The authors have used the gene expression data for clustering purposes. In this proposed method, a conscience factor has been added to increase the rate of convergence. In this approach, the concepts of PSO have been utilized for developing the weights and, thereafter, is used to train these weights in the first phase. Afterward, in the next phase, PSO is applied to improve them. This hybrid SOM-PSO approach gives encouraging outcome while applied on the gene expression data of Rat Hepatocytes and Yeast. Cui et al. [36] and Cui and Potok [37] introduced PSO-based hybrid methods to classify the text documents. For hybridization, two-step clustering approaches have been used. Firstly, PSO-based fuzzy clustering is used for clustering for a predefined maximum number of iterations. Thereafter, the k-means algorithm is introduced to initialize the cluster centers that were achieved from the previous step and then accomplish the last clustering process. These two steps have been used at one time to improve the performance and also speed up its convergence mainly for large datasets. The authors examined the PSO, as well as a hybrid PSO clustering algorithm on four various text document datasets. According to their observation, highly compact clustering is generally generated by the hybrid PSO clustering algorithm over a short period of time compared to the k-means algorithm.

1.9.3 Ant Colony Optimization–Based Fuzzy Clustering

The ant colony optimization (ACO) [18] algorithm is also applied to overcome the shortcomings of the fuzzy clustering methods. Yu et al. [38] proposed a hybrid based on ACO to segment the noisy images. They also proposed a possibilistic c-means (PCM) algorithm. In this approach, the clustering problem is solved by using pre-classified pixel information and furnishes the near optimal initialization of the number of clusters and their centroids [38]. Image segmentation is done using ACO-based fuzzy clustering [39]. In this approach, the ant is considered an individual pixel in the image, and the membership function is calculated on the basis of heuristic and pheromone information on each cluster center. The performance of the image segmentation algorithm improvised by including the spatial information in the membership [39]. A hybrid clustering algorithm, i.e., one that is hybridized with the PCM algorithm, is presented to segment the medical images [40]. This hybridized algorithm overcomes the drawback of the image segmentation. Niknam and Amiri [41] proposed a hybrid approach based on PSO, ACO, and k-means for cluster analysis. This approach is applied to find better cluster partition. The performance of the FCM is improved with the ant colony optimization algorithm, and the min-max ant system is induced in the ACO algorithm in this method [42]. Gajjar et al. [43] presented fuzzy and ant colony optimization based on combining MAC, routing, and the unequal clustering cross-layer protocol for wireless sensor networks (FAMACROW). This combined network consists of several nodes and is used to send the sensed data to the master station. The clustering algorithm hybridized with an improved ant colony algorithm is applied for fault identification and fault classification [44]. The fuzzy clustering numbers and initial clustering center are identified by the algorithm. Mary and Raja [45] proposed an ACO-based improved FCM to segment the medical images. The FCM and four-chain quantum bee colony optimization (QA BC) is applied for image segmentation [46]. A modified ACO-based fuzzy clustering algorithm is proposed by Supratid and Kim [47]. ACO, FCM, and GA are combined in this algorithm to overcome the problem of the frequent improvement of cluster centers.

1.9.4 Artificial Bee Colony Optimization–Based Fuzzy Clustering

Alrosan et al. [48] proposed a clustering method by coupling artificial bee colony with the fuzzy c-means (ABC-FCM) algorithm. This approach took advantage of the searching capabilities of optimum initial cluster centers and applies these clusters as the initial cluster centers. The proposed approach proved its superiority when applied on two sets of MRI images: simulated brain data and real MRI images [48]. The weakness over the control of the local optimum of the technique is also handled by Pham et al. [49]. In this regard, they exploit the search ability of the ABC algorithm. In this method, a real number is used in each bee to determine the appropriate cluster centers. The supremacy of this approach is established by comparing the proposed algorithm with FCM and the GA-based clustering algorithm on some numerical benchmark data. A modified artificial bee colony algorithm–based fuzzy C-means algorithm (MoABC-FCM) is presented by Ouadfel and Meshoul [50]. Inspired from differential evolution (DE), a new mutation method was introduced in the ABC algorithm to improve the exploitation process. Ultimately, the proposed MoABC-FCM algorithm enhanced the effectiveness of the original FCM algorithm, and it is proved that this new approach is better than optimization-based search algorithms, such as the standard ABC, modified ABC, and PSO. A novel spatial fuzzy clustering algorithm optimized by the ABC algorithm, in short, ABC-SFCM, is employed to segment the synthetic and real images [51]. This algorithm is advantageous for two reasons. First, it is able to tackle noisy image segmentation efficiently by using the spatial local information in the membership function. Second, the global performance that results from taking advantage of the global search capability of ABC is improved by the proposed method [51]. It is also noted that this method is more robust to noise than other known methods. An image segmentation procedure utilizing the ABC algorithm was presented by Hancer et al. [52] to identify brain tumors from the MRI brain images and is one of the standard valuable tools applied for diagnosing and treating medical cases. The proposed procedure includes three stages: preprocessing the input MRI image, applying the ABC-based fuzzy clustering method for segmentation, and in the last stage, i.e., in the post-processing stage, extracting the brain tumors. The proposed procedure includes examining MRI images in various areas of a patient's brain with different approaches like the k-means, FCM, and GA algorithms. Shokouhifar and Abkenar [53] applied the ABC algorithm to classify all pixels into two categories: normal and noisy. They introduced a noise probability for each pixel within the image, and based on that noise probability the pixels are grouped. In this proposed method, ABC optimization is employed before the FCM clustering algorithm to segment the real-life MRI images, and it was shown that this approach is better than the previous methods. Karaboga and Ozturk [54, 55] applied successfully the ABC algorithm to optimize fuzzy clustering to some benchmark medical data. The proposed method proved its superiority compared to the FCM algorithm. A combined approach of the FCM algorithm and the ABC algorithm is employed to segment MR images efficiently [56]. Two new parameters are introduced in that approach: the difference between neighboring pixels in the image and the relative location of the neighboring pixels. It was shown that these parameters improved the performance of FCM using the ABC algorithm [56]. Bose and Mali [57] presented a combined ABC and FCM algorithm, named FABC, for unsupervised classification. The Predefining the initial cluster centers solved by the FABC and the proposed method works better in respect of convergency, time complexity, robustness, and segmentation accuracy [57]. The property of the randomization of the ABC algorithm applied for the initialization of the cluster centers in the FABC algorithm.

1.9.5 Differential Evolution–Based Fuzzy Clustering

Das and Konar [58] presented a fuzzy clustering method in combination with modified differential evolution, named automatic fuzzy clustering differential evolution for image segmentation. In this approach, the chromosome representation in the DE algorithm was modified and applied for the determination of fuzzy clusters in the intensity space of an image automatically. The symmetry-based fuzzy clustering validity index [59] was employed with this modified DE algorithm, and the convergence property of the DE algorithm also improved. This presented approach applied on six different types of images including the natural image, MRI brain image, and satellite image. The mutation constant factor, F, played a vital role in the DE algorithm, and its value was assigned randomly ranged between 0.5 and 1 in AFDE [58]. Second, the crossover rate (Cr) is not fixed during the evolving process as its value changes accordingly during the iteration steps. The starting value of Cr is 1, and it decreases linearly to the minimum acceptable value, which is 0.5. The authors presented a real coded chromosome representation in such a way that can dynamically determine the appropriate number of clusters that the dataset may have [58]. Another version of the AFDE is found in [60] as the automatic clustering DE (ACDE) algorithm. In this approach, the authors applied different objective functions named DB index [61] and CS index [62] to evaluate the quality of the clustered data. Gong et al. [63] also proposed an automatic clustering DE techniques to solve the clustering problem. This method is described by three ways: (i) a modified point symmetry-based cluster validity index (CVI) presented to evaluate the validity of the corresponding partitioning, (ii) the Kd-tree nearest neighbor search is applied to decrease the complexity of finding the closest symmetric point, and (iii) a new chromosomal representation is induced to represent individuals. After being applied on six artificial datasets of diverse complexities, it has been proved that the proposed approach is suited for both the symmetrical intra clusters and the symmetrical inter clusters [63]. Maulik and Saha [64] presented a modified DE-based technique of fuzzy clustering (MoDEFC), and the authors applied real coded encoding technique for the cluster centers. The advantage of the global best (GBest) and local best (LBest) concepts of the PSO algorithm induced in the standard mutation process of differential evolution algorithm to push the trial vector quickly toward the global optima. In the initial stage, the LBest, i.e., the best vector in the current stage, is the more important for evolving the mutant vector than in the later stage [64]. As the generation increases, the contribution of GBest, i.e., the best vector evaluated until the current generation, increases the contribution of LBest for the mutant vector decreases.

1.9.6 Firefly Algorithm–Based Fuzzy Clustering

To overcome the shortcomings of FCM, a new fuzzy subspace clustering algorithm based on improved firefly algorithms is presented in [65]. In this approach, the global optimization capability of the firefly algorithm, strong local search features of FCM, and learning calculation for feature weights of reliability-based k-means are taken into consideration [65]. This algorithm is applied accurately and efficiently on different feature subspace-based clustering problems. Alomoush et al. [66] proposed a hybridized segmentation algorithm, firefly algorithm (FA), and fuzzy c-means algorithm (FCM) to segment magnetic resonance imaging (MRI) brain images. MRI images are not easy to segment as normal and abnormal tissues are very much similar in view. The firefly algorithm is employed to determine the optimal cluster centers for FCM, and that improves the efficiency of FCM to segment the MRI images. Sharma et al. [67] presented a k-means algorithm and firefly algorithm image segmentation approach. In this method, the firefly algorithm is used to optimize the k-means algorithm as the k-means algorithm gets trapped in the local optima. The firefly algorithm is applied to solve the multithreshold problem in respect to the image segmentation [68]. The firefly algorithm is also hybridized with the k-means algorithm to cluster different types of data [69]. In the first step, the firefly algorithm is applied to find the centroid of the user-specified number of clusters. The centroids and clusters are refined using the k-means algorithm in the next step.

1.10 Conclusion

In this chapter, clustering algorithms in the fuzzy perspective were presented. The fuzzy c-means algolrihm was discussed. The advantages and drawbacks of this algorithm were also covered. Different local-search-based and population-based metaheuristics algorithms were presented. Fuzzy clustering algorithms in combination with metaheuristic algorithms were also illustrated in this chapter.

References

1 Bezdek, J.C. (1981) Springer.
2 MacQueen, J.B. (1967) *Some methods for classification and analysis of multivariate observations*, in *Proceedings of 5th Berkeley Symposium on Mathematical Statistics and Probability*, University of California Press, pp. 281–297.
3 Ross, T.J. (2009) John Wiley & Sons.
4 Zadeh, L.A. (2008) Is there a need for fuzzy logic? *Information Sciences*, **178** (13), 2751–2779.
5 Zanaty, E.A., Aljahdali, S., and Debnath, N.C. (2008) Improving fuzzy algorithms for automatic magnetic resonance image segmentation. *SEDE*, pp. 61–67.
6 Dunn, J.C. (1973) A fuzzy relative of the isodata process and its use in detecting compact well-separated clusters. *Journal of Cybernetics*, **3** (3), 32–57.
7 Bezdek, J.C., Hathaway, R.J., Sabin, M.J., and Tucker, W.T. (1987) Convergence theory for fuzzy c-means: counterexamples and repairs. *IEEE Transactions on Systems, Man and Cybernetics*, **17** (5), 873–877.
8 Hathaway, R.J., C., J., and Bezdek (1986) Local convergence of the fuzzy c-means algorithms. *Pattern Recognition*, **19** (6), 477–480.
9 Kanade, P.M., O., L., and Hall (2007) Fuzzy ants and clustering. *IEEE Transactions on Systems, Man and Cybernetics, Part A: Systems and Humans*, **37** (5), 758–769.
10 Hruschka, E.R., Campello, R.J.G.B., Freitas, A.A., and Carvalho, A.P.L.F.D. (2009) A survey of evolutionary algorithms for clustering. *IEEE Transactions on Systems, Man, and Cybernetics, Part C: Applications and Reviews*, **39** (2), 133–155.
11 Bandyopadhyay, S. and Saha, S. (2013) *Clustering Algorithms*, Springer.
12 Kinnear, K.E. (1994) Advances in genetic programming, in *A Perspective on the Work in this Book. In K. E. Kinnear (Ed.)*, Cambridge: MIT Press, pp. 3–17.
13 Goldberg, D.E. (1989) in *Genetic Algorithms in Search, Optimization, and Machine Learning*, Addison-Wesley Longman Publishing Co., Inc. Boston, MA, USA.

14 Koza, J.R. (1994) Advances in genetic programming, in *Introduction to Genetic Programming. In K. E. Kinnear (Ed.)*, Cambridge: MIT Press, pp. 21–41.

15 Haupt, R.L. and Haupt, S.E. (1998) in *Practical Genetic Algorithms*, New York: Wiley Interscience.

16 Haupt, R.L. and Haupt, S.E. (2004) in *Practical Genetic Algorithms (2nd ed.)*, Hoboken: Wiley.

17 Kennedy, K. and Eberhart, R. (1995) Particle swarm optimization. *Proceedings of the IEEE International Conference on Neural Networks (ICNN95), Perth, Australia*, **4**, 1942–1948.

18 Dorigo, M., Caro, G.D., and Gambardella, L. (1999) Ant algorithms for discrete optimization. *Artificial Life*, **5**, 137–172.

19 Karaboga, D. (2005) in *An idea based on honey bee swarm for numerical optimization (Technical Report TR06)*, Computer Engineering Department, Erciyes University, Kayseri, Turkey.

20 Akay, B. and Karaboga, D. (2012) A modified artificial bee colony algorithm for real-parameter optimization. *Information Sciences*, **192**, 120–142.

21 Selim, S.Z. and Alsultan, K. (1991) A simulated annealing algorithm for the clustering problem. *Pattern Recognition*, **24** (10), 1003–1008.

22 Al-Sultan, K.S. (1995) A tabu search approach to the clustering problem. *Pattern Recognition*, **28** (9), 1431–1451.

23 Al-Sultan, K.S. and Fedjki, C.A. (1997) A tabu search-based algorithm for the fuzzy clustering problem. *Pattern Recognition*, **30** (12), 2023–2030.

24 Sung, C.S. and Jin, H.W. (2000) A tabu-search based heuristic for clustering. *Pattern Recognition*, **33** (5), 849–858.

25 Paterlini, S. and Krink, T. (2006) Differential evolution and particle swarm optimisation in partitional clustering. *Computational Statistics & Data Analysis*, **50** (5), 1220–1247.

26 Hall, L.O., Bezdek, J., Boggavarpu, S., and Bensaid, A. (1994) Genetic fuzzy clustering. *Fuzzy Information Processing Society Biannual Conference, 1994. Industrial Fuzzy Control and Intelligent Systems Conference, and the NASA Joint Technology Workshop on Neural Networks and Fuzzy Logic*, pp. 411–415.

27 Hall, L.O. and Ozyurt, B. (1995) Scaling genetically guided fuzzy clustering. *Proceedings of ISUMA-NAFIPS'95 The Third International Symposium on Uncertainty Modeling and Analysis and Annual Conference of the North American Fuzzy Information Processing Society*, pp. 328–332.

28 Hall, L.O., Ozyurt, B., and Bezdek, J.C. (1999) Clustering with a genetically optimized approach. *IEEE Transactions on Evolutionary Computation*, **3** (2), 103–112.

29 Liu, J. and Xie, W. (1995) A genetics-based approach to fuzzy clustering. *Proceedings of 1995 IEEE International Conference on Fuzzy Systems, 1995. International Joint Conference of the Fourth IEEE International Conference on Fuzzy Systems and The Second International Fuzzy Engineering Symposium*, pp. 2233–2240.

30 Van Le, T. (1995) Evolutionary fuzzy clustering. *Evolutionary Computation*, pp. 753–758.

31 Klawonn, F. and Keller, A. (1998) Fuzzy clustering with evolutionary algorithms. *International Journal of Intelligent Systems*, **13** (10–11), 975–991.

32 Egan, M., Krishnamoorthy, M., and Rajan, K. (1998) Evolutionary computation proceedings, in *Comparative study of a genetic fuzzy c-means algorithm and a validity guided* *fuzzy c-means algorithm for locating clusters in noisy data*, The 1998 IEEE International Conference on IEEE World Congress on Computational Intelligence., pp. 440–445.

33 Dave, R.N. (1991) Characterization and detection of noise in clustering. *Pattern Recognition Letters*, **12** (11), 657–664.

34 Maulik, U. and Saha, I. (2009) Modified differential evolution based fuzzy clustering for pixel classification in remote sensing imagery. *Pattern Recognition*, **42** (9), 2135–2149.

35 Xiao, X., Dow, E.R., Eberhart, R., Miled, Z.B., and Oppelt, R.J. (2003) Gene clustering using self-organizing maps and particle swarm optimization. *Parallel and Distributed Processing Symposium, 2003. Proceedings. International*, p. 10.

36 Cui, X., Potok, T.E., and Palathingal, P. (2005) Document clustering using particle swarm optimization. *Swarm Intelligence Symposium, 2005. SIS 2005. Proceedings 2005 IEEE*, pp. 185–191.

37 Cui, X. and Potok, T.E. (2005) Document clustering analysis based on hybrid pso+ k-means algorithm. *PaJournal of Computer Sciences (special issue)*, pp. 27–33.

38 Yu, J., Lee, S.H., and Jeon, M. (2012) An adaptive aco-based fuzzy clustering aalgorithm for noisy image segmentation. *International Journal of Innovative Computing, Information and Control*, **8** (6), 3907–3918.

39 Yu, Z., Yu, W., Zou, R., and Yu, S. (2009) On ACO-Based Fuzzy Clustering for Image Segmentation, in *Proceedings of 6th International Symposium on Neural Networks (ISNN 2009)*, vol. 2, Advances in Neural Networks, vol. 2, pp. 717–726.

40 Yu, J., Lee, S.G., and Jeon, M. (2011) Medical image segmentation by hybridizing ant colony optimization and fuzzy clustering algorithm, in *Proceedings of the 13th Annual Conference Companion on Genetic and Evolutionary Computation*, ACM, New York, NY, USA, GECCO '11, pp. 217–218, doi:10.1145/2001858.2001981.

41 Niknam, T. and Amiri, B. (2010) An efficient hybrid approach based on PSO, ACO and k-means for cluster analysis. *Applied Soft Computing*, **10** (1), 183–197, doi: https://doi.org/10.1016/j.asoc.2009.07.001.

42 Raghtate, G.S. and Salankar, S.S. (2015) Brain tumor segmentation using fuzzy c means with ant colony optimization algorithm. *Current Trends in Technology and Science*, **04** (2), 484–490.

43 Gajjar, S., Sarkar, M., and Dasgupta, K. (2016) Famacrow: Fuzzy and ant colony optimization based combined mac, routing, and unequal clustering cross-layer protocol for wireless sensor networks. *Applied Soft Computing*, **43**, 235–247, doi: https://doi.org/10.1016/j.asoc.2016.02.019.

44 Wang, G., Yin, X., Pang, Y., Zhang, M., Zhao, W., and Zhang, Z. (2010) Studies on Fuzzy C-Means Based on Ant Colony Algorithm, in *Proceedings of 2010 International Conference on Measuring Technology and Mechatronics Automation*, doi:10.1109/ICMTMA.2010.384.

45 Mary, C.I. and Raja, S.K. (2010) Improved Fuzzy C-Means Clusters With Ant Colony Optimization. *International Journal of Computer Science & Emerging Technologies*, **1** (4), 1–6.

46 Feng, Y., Yin, H., Lu, H., Cao, L., and Bai, J. (2018) Fcm-based quantum artificial bee colony algorithm for image segmentation, in *Proceedings of the 10th International Conference on Internet Multimedia Computing and Service*, ACM, New York, NY, USA, ICIMCS '18, pp. 6:1–6:7, doi:10.1145/3240876.3240907.

47 Supratid, S. and Kim, H. (2009) Modified fuzzy ants clustering approach. *Applied Intelligence*, **31** (2), 122–134.

48 Alrosan, A., Norwawi, N., Ismail, W., and Alomoush, W. (2014) Artificial bee colony based fuzzyclustering algorithms for mri image segmentation, in *Proceedings of Advances in Computer Science and Electronics Engineering (CSEE 2014)*, pp. 225–228.

49 Pham, D.T., Otri, S., Afify, A., Mahmuddin, M., and Al-Jabbouli, H. (2007) Data clustering using the bees algorithm, in *Proceedings of International Conference on Computing: Theory and Applications (ICCTA'07)*, pp. 516–522.

50 Ouadfel, S. and Meshoul, S. (2012) Handling fuzzy image clustering with a modified abc algorithm. *International Journal of Intelligent Systems and Applications*, **12**, 65–74.

51 Salima, O., Taleb-Ahmed, A., and Mohamed, B. (2012) Spatial information based image clustering with a swarm approach. *IAES International Journal on Artificial Intelligenge (IJ-AI)*, **1**, 149–160.

52 Hancer, E., Ozturk, C., and Karaboga, D. (2013) Extraction of brain tumors from mri images with artificial bee colony based segmentation methodology, in *8th International Conference on Electrical and Electronics Engineering (ELECO)*, pp. 516–520.

53 Shokouhifar, M. and Abkenar, G.S. (2011) An artificial bee colony optimization for mri fuzzy segmentation of brain tissue, in *International Conference on Management and Artificial Intelligence IPEDR*, pp. 6–10.

54 Karaboga, D. and Ozturk, C. (2011) A novel clustering approach: Artificial bee colony (abc) algorithm. *Applied Soft Computing*, **11** (1), 652–657.

55 Karaboga, D. and Ozturk, C. (2010) Fuzzy clustering with artificial bee colony algorithm. *Scientific Research and Essays*, **5** (14), 1899–1902.

56 Taherdangkoo, M., Yazdi, M., and Rezvani, M.H. (2010) Segmentation of mr brain images using fcm improved by artificial bee colony (abc) algorithm, in *10th IEEE International Conference on Information Technology and Applications in Biomedicine (ITAB)*.

57 Mali, A.B.K. (2016) Fuzzy-based artificial bee colony optimization for gray image segmentation. *Signal Image and Video Processing*, **10** (6), 1–8, doi:10.1007/s11760-016-0863-z.

58 Das, S. and Konar, A. (2009) Automatic image pixel clustering with an improved differential evolution. *Applied Soft Computing*, **9** (1), 226–236.

59 Su, M.C. and Chou, C.H. (2001) A modified version of the k-means algorithm with a distance based on cluster symmetry. *IEEE Transactions on Pattern Analysis and Machine Intelligence*, **23** (6), 674–680.

60 Das, S., Abraham, A., and Konar, A. (2008) Automatic clustering using an improved differential evolution algorithm. *IEEE Transactions on Systems, Man, and Cybernetics-Part A Syatems and Humans*, **38** (1), 218–237.

61 Davies, D.L. and Bouldin, D.W. (2008) A cluster separation measure. *IEEE Transactions on Pattern Analysis and Machine Intelligence*, **1** (2), 224–227.

62 Chou, C.H., Su, M.C., and Lai, E. (2004) A new cluster validity measure and its application to image compression. *Pattern Analysis and Applications*, **7** (2), 205–220.

63 Gong, W., Cai, Z., Ling, C.X., and Huang, B. (2009) A point symmetry-based automatic clustering approach using differential evolution, in *4th International Symposium Advances in Computation and Intelligence (ISICA)*, pp. 151–162.

64 Maulik, U. and Saha, I. (2009) Modified differential evolution based fuzzy clustering for pixel classification in remote sensing imagery. *Pattern Recognition*, **42**, 2135–2149.

65 Jia-jing, H., Heng-wei, Z., Na, W., and Kan, N. (2015) Fuzzy subspace clustering algorithm based on modified firefly algorithm, in *Third International Conference on Cyberspace Technology (CCT 2015)*, IET.

66 Alomoush, W., Abdullah, S.N.H.S., Sahran, S., and Hussain, R.I. (2014) Mri brain segmentation via hybrid firefly search algorithm. *Journal of Theoretical & Applied Information Technology*, **61** (1), 73–90.

67 Sharma, A. and Sehgal, S. (2016) Image segmentation using firefly algorithm, in *2016 International Conference on Information Technology (InCITe) - The Next Generation IT Summit*, pp. 99–102.

68 Yu, C., Jin, B., Lu, Y., Chen, X., Yi, Z., and adn S. Wang, K.Z. (2013) Multi-threshold image segmentation based on firefly algorithm, in *2013 Ninth International Conference on Intelligent Information Hiding and Multimedia Signal Processing*, pp. 415–419.

69 Hassanzadeh, T. and Meybodi, M.R. (2012) A new hybrid approach for data clustering using firefly algorithm and k-means, in *16th CSI International Symposium on Artificial Intelligence and Signal Processing (AISP 2012)*, pp. 7–11.

2

Hybrid Harmony Search Algorithm to Solve the Feature Selection for Data Mining Applications

Laith Mohammad Abualigah[1], Mofleh Al-diabat[2], Mohammad Al Shinwan[3], Khaldoon Dhou[4], Bisan Alsalibi[5], Essam Said Hanandeh[6], and Mohammad Shehab[7]

[1] Faculty of Computer Sciences and Informatics, Amman Arab University, Jordan
[2] Department of Computer Science, Al Albayt University, Jordan
[3] Faculty of Computer Sciences and Informatics, Amman Arab University, Jordan
[4] Breech School of Business, Drury University, Springfield, MO, United States
[5] School of Computer Sciences, Universiti Sains Malaysia, Malaysia
[6] Department of Computer Information System, Zarqa University, Jordan
[7] Computer Science Department, Aqaba University of Technology, Aqaba, Jordan

2.1 Introduction

Lately, the increasing size of all sorts text and data information on websites makes the method of text clustering (TC) a lot more complicated. The TC technique is employed to cluster an enormous variety of documents into a set of intelligible and connected clusters [1, 2]. Usually, TC is employed in several domains like text mining, data processing, pattern recognition, image clustering [3, 4].

The vector house model (VSM) may be a mutual arrangement pattern utilized in the text field to simplify a document's parts as an array [i.e., row of features (vectors)]. Consequently, the entire document is painted as a vector of features or terms score (weighing values), and every term weight price is painted within a row (dimension space). For this reason, a multi-dimensional house may have mutual and massive downside issues over the text clustering technique. This downside affects the TC method by reducing its performance and increasing the general system runtime [5].

Usually, any text documents containing informative and uninformative features, wherever associate degree uninformative is as extraneous, redundant, and uniformly distributed feature [6, 7]. These varieties of features cut back on the execution of the application of the clustering technique and affect the method in a very dangerous manner because every document contains several extraneous features. An unsupervised feature section (FS) may be a common downside in this domain, and it's a crucial assignment wont to realize a replacement set of feature to reinforce the accuracy of the text clustering rule. This method is enforced with no premonition of the document's category label. A feature choice downside is outlined as associate degree optimization downside with two constraints (i.e., two objective measures: minimizing the involved text feature and maximizing the performance

Recent Advances in Hybrid Metaheuristics for Data Clustering, First Edition.
Edited by Sourav De, Sandip Dey, and Siddhartha Bhattacharyya.
© 2020 John Wiley & Sons Ltd. Published 2020 by John Wiley & Sons Ltd.

value of the implied clustering algorithm) [5]. Numerous scopes within the text mining field profit from the feature choice technique like the image analysis and clustering applications [8], text clustering [9], cancer classification [10], world numerical optimization issues [11], systems management [7], image cryptography and lossless compression [12], cistron choice [13], and data retrieval [14].

Text pages have become a necessary resource within electronic sites that contain an unorganized large quantity of text documents; these sites include news sites, minutes, reports, and science info digital libraries [15]. TC is a lively information approach that partitions several documents into some clusters, each containing similar text. This method makes sites easier to access, clearer to understand, and more organized. Any TC algorithmic program tries to seek out coherent clusters by partitioning the text documents into clusters so as to assign every document to the best cluster supported by the document contents [16].

Harmony search (HS) is a kind of robust meta-heuristic algorithm propositioned by Prof. Zong Woo Geem in 2001 [17]. It follows the music discovery method and has had success tackling several laborious improvement issues such as vanishing purpose detection for self-driving automobiles [18], numerical performance improvement [19], text document clustering [2], optimum power flow [20], and timetabling issues [21, 22].

Harmony search is one of the stronger algorithms within the domain that can resolve several random issues, particularly for acquiring quality subsets of features for reconnoitering the entire benchmark datasets. A completely unique feature choice exploitation is used by the harmony search technique for extracting a replacement set of informative features, and it had been used with several feature subsets [23]. Harmony search integrity was utilized to scale back the runtime quality and enhance the accuracy of the feature choice in terms of the method performance. Experimental results exhibited that the planned feature choice technique improved the performance of the text cluster method.

The genetic algorithmic program (GA) is will settle on a singular set of informative features for developing the execution of the text clustering process. This technique uses the frequency-inverse document frequency (TF–IDF) as a coefficient score or theme to cut back every term relationship [24]. Experiment analysis was applied on text spam email. The results said that the planned genetic algorithmic program for finding the feature choice drawback improved the performance value of the clustering process.

The downside of feature choice may be an optimization problem that is employed to get a replacement set of excellent features [23]. The cat swarm optimization (CSO) formula has been introduced additionally to reinforce optimization issues. Yet, Cat swarm optimization is restricted to long runtimes. They modify the formula to extend and improve the feature choice downside within the method of the text classification [25]. Experiment results showed that the planned changed formula (cat swarm optimization) succeeds and got better results in comparison with the initial version (cat swarm optimization) and got a lot of correct results in feature choice method than victimization TF-IDF alone.

One of the distinctive feature choice techniques has been projected by exploitation the harmony search rule for selecting and obtaining a replacement set of informative knowledge feature [23]. The projected rule during this paper was to cut back the runtime of the system and to decrease the uninformative knowledge feature. Finally, their results said that the projected modification of the harmony search rule enriched the performance value of the feature choice method in regard to the correct set, owing to its fine features.

Particle swarm improvement (PSO) may be a powerful formula projected by Kennedy, Eberhart. It selects a singular set of a lot of informative features for developing the performance of the text clustering. This technique uses the term frequency-inverse document frequency (TF–IDF) as a weight theme for cutting back every term relationship [26]. Experiment analysis and discussion were made in huge Brobdingnagian text documents. The results exhibited that the projected particle swarm improvement methodology for finding the text feature choice downside got better results.

Recently, several optimization algorithms are applied with success to resolve varied straightforward and onerous optimization issues [9, 27–31]. In this paper, we tend to introduced a unique feature choice technique exploitation the harmony search algorithmic rule, namely, FSHSTC. This approach is applied to choose a definite set of fine informative features for making the text agglomeration technique making productive. The biggest objective of this paper is to replace the term or feature choice technique for supporting the performance value of the text agglomeration procedure. Experimental results and its analysis were conducted on four varied datasets to prove and check the utilized algorithmic rule. The results showed that the FSHSTC got better results in comparison with the opposite comparative ways in terms of two evaluation measures (i.e., F-measures and accuracy).

The structure of this paper is provided as follows: Section 2 describes the overall analysis framework for explaining the feature choice downside. Section 3 shows a way to prepare the text clustering victimization of the pre-processing steps. Section 4 presents, however, that the feature choice downside enforces victimizaton on the essential harmony search rule. Section 5 shows the essential steps of the projected hybrid harmony search rule for feature choice downside. Section 6 defines the best suggestions the text clustering technique. Section 7 illustrates the best suggestions for the k-means clustering rule. Experiments analysis and the results are provided in Section 8. Finally, Section 9 gives our conclusions.

2.2 Research Framework

The text preprocessing steps have been adjusted to choose an optimum solution by giving a replacement set of options (informative features) for increasing the performance of the underlying text document agglomeration algorithms and cutting back on its procedure time. Consequently, this paper projected associate economical and effective classification to pronounce a replacement optimum set of text options so as to comprehend the paper's aims. In the end, these techniques are enforced so as to alter the rule of text agglomeration in keeping with the order of many steps. Figure 2.1 shows the methodology of the projected hybrid feature section technique supported by the harmony search rule for the text agglomeration method (H-HSA).

In the beginning, the preprocessing steps are utilized to prepare the document within the kind of numerical style (data). In the second step, the harmony search rule is adjusted to resolve the feature choice drawback by reducing uninformative options and come up with a replacement set of fine options. The feature choice procedure is examined as a preprocessing step in pattern analysis and recognition, computing, machine unsupervised learning, etc. It is applied as a decision-maker to decide which set of informative text features is most

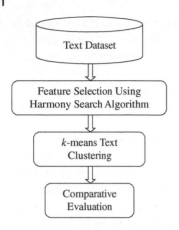

Figure 2.1 Research framework of the proposed hybrid method

efficient by excluding uninformative text features. Then, within the third step, the *k*-means text agglomeration technique is used to assign every document to the fitting cluster. The *k*-means text agglomeration rule is best as a result of it being a wise text analysis technique to assess the performance of the feature choice methodology to improve the projected harmony search rule.

2.3 Text Preprocessing

TC needs text design and representation [32]. The linguistic communication process (NLP) is a technology used in interactions linking humans and PC languages. This method is critical and could be a critical step in the text mining domain. It examines the fundamental text preprocessing to acquire document options by processing a variety of symbols like words, thereby removing stop words for a text illustration [2]. The projected technique relies on the text FS domain and TD cluster classifications domain, just like the preprocessing for the illustration of TD. The preprocessing levels are divided into four major levels or processes. The first one is tokenization, the second one is stop word removal, the third one is stemming, and finally the last one is text representation [5, 33].

2.3.1 Tokenization

Tokenization is the task of isolating words into tokens, likely losing a few assortments, like accentuation. These tokens are in some cases connected to terms or words; in any case, it's fundamental to make a type/token refinement. A token is a word illustration of an arrangement of characters in an archive that's joined to a supportive syntactic unit. A sort means the assortment of all tokens alongside the indistinguishable character arrangement. A term may be a sort that's consolidated inside the data recovery system's lexicon [34].

2.3.2 Stop Words Removal

Stop words are current common words, like *in, no, an, that, yes* and *a few*, encouraged as elective common words that are part of ordinarily utilized and minor accommodating words inside the TD. These words ought to be far away from content archives as they ordinarily have tall recurrence, which decreases the execution of the TC strategy. The list[1] of stop words contains a total of 571 words [5].

2.3.3 Stemming

Stemming is the strategy of diminishing curved terms to their term stem (root). The stem running the show isn't indistinguishable from the morphological root handle; it outlines words to the indistinguishable stem, whether or not this stem isn't in itself an immaculate root. The Porter (http://tartarus.org/martin/PorterStemmer/) stemmer is the common stemming method embraced in content mining [2, 34]. All content preprocessing steps come from Python NLTK demos for tongue content processing.[2]

2.3.4 Text Document Representation

Vector space model (VSM) is a good example of TDs in an ordinary use [15]. It comes from the early seventies. Each archive is spoken to as a vector of term weight to encourage character calculation. Each term inside the set speaks to a measurement of the weighted worth to create the standard of the content elucidation algorithm running the show and to scale back the time estimation.

The term coefficient is used by the vector show model (VSM) to point out the TDs in an exceedingly ordinary organization, as in Eq. (2.1). This show speaks to each archive as a vector, as in Eq. (2.2) [16]. Eq. (2.1) speaks to n reports and t terms, as in:

$$VSM = \begin{bmatrix} w_{1,1} & w_{1,2} & \cdots & w_{1,(t-1)} & w_{1,t} \\ \cdots & \cdots & \cdots & \cdots & \cdots \\ \vdots & \vdots & \ddots & \vdots & \vdots \\ \vdots & \vdots & \ddots & \vdots & \vdots \\ w_{(n-1),1} & w_{(n-1),2} & \cdots & \cdots & w_{(n-1),t} \\ w_{n,1} & w_{n,2} & \cdots & w_{n,(t-1)} & w_{n,t} \end{bmatrix} \tag{2.1}$$

$$d_i = (w_{i,1}, w_{i,2}, \ldots, w_{i,j}, \ldots, w_{i,t}), \tag{2.2}$$

2.3.5 Term Weight (TF-IDF)

Term weight is a critical numerical datum used to consider the weight of record words (highlights or terms) for TD agglomeration forms in line with the term reiteration [35]. A common term weighting subject in text mining is term frequency-inverse archive recurrence (TF-IDF) [3, 36].

TF-IDF may well be a conventional weight topic that's similar to gage term weight in content mining for archive outlines. Each archive is portrayed as a vector of term weight [5]. The term weight is calculated by Eq. (2.3), as shown here:

$$w_{i,j} = tf(i,j) * log(n/df(j)), \tag{2.3}$$

---

1 http://www.unine.ch/Info/clef/
2 http://text-processing.com/demo/

where emph$w_{i,j}$ speaks to the weight of term j within the report number i, $tf(i,j)$ is the occurrence of term j within the record number i, n is the number of all reports in the dataset, and $df(j)$ is the number of records that contain the term number j [36].

2.4 Text Feature Selection

This area clarifies the proposed harmony that is used in the calculation of tackling the FS problem.

2.4.1 Mathematical Model of the Feature Selection Problem

The feature selection issue can defined as an NP-Hard issue in the form of an optimization issue to create an ideal subset of more enlightened highlights. Given f_i a collection of content highlights $f_i = f_{i1}, f_{i2}, ..., f_{it}$, where t is the number of all interesting content highlights in all archives, and i is the number of a report. Let sf_i be an unused subset of instructive content features $sf_i = s_{i1}, s_{i2}, ..., s_{ij}, s_{im}$, m may be a unused special number of all highlights in all reports, in the event that $s_{ij} = 1$ suggests the j_{th} highlight is chosen as an enlightening include in archive i, in the event that $s_{ij} = 0$ suggests the j_{th} include is an informative in report i [2, 5, 37–39].

2.4.2 Solution Representation

In this paper, the include determination strategy is based on the agreement look calculation, which begins with irregular arrangements (arbitrary starting arrangements) and progresses with the populace (arrangements) by getting a universally ideal arrangement [5, 7, 39]. Each special highlight (one position) within the archive considers the measurement of the look space. Table 2.1 presents the arrangement of the include determination issue [40].

Note, X speaks to a single arrangement of the included determination issue. In the event that the esteem of position number j (j_{th}) is *1*, the j_{th} highlight is chosen in this arrangement as an instructive highlight. On the off-chance that the esteem of position number j (j_{th}) is *0*, the j_{th} include isn't chosen in this arrangements as an instructive include (uninformative/non-informative), at long last, on the off-chance that the esteem of position number j (j_{th}) −1, the j_{th} include was not included within the unique content archive at the start.

2.4.3 Fitness Function

The fitness function (FF) is a particular type of objective function that summarizes, as shown in Table 2.1, how close a given design solution is to achieving the set aims [41]. Inside

Table 2.1 Feature selection solution representation

X	0	1	1	−1	−1	1	0	−1	1	−1

the concordance look algorithmic program for finding the highlight choice drawback, the cruel supreme qualification (frantic) is utilized as a fitness perform. This fitness perform is predicated on using the coefficient subject (TF-IDF) as the relate degree objective perform for each position. Cruel outright refinement may be a common way to find the highlight choice drawback in this space to allot a significance score for alternatives by plotting the qualification between the standard steady ones and the alternatives weight scores [34]. At that point, computing the refinement between the cruel and middle of $x_{i,j}$ [36, 42] looks like the following equation:

$$MAD_{(Xi)} = \frac{1}{a_i} \sum_{j=1}^{t} |x_{i,j} - \bar{x}_i|, \tag{2.4}$$

where,

$$\bar{x}_i = \left(\frac{1}{a}\right) \sum_{j=1}^{t} x_{ij}, \tag{2.5}$$

$x_{i,j}$ is the current value of the feature in position number j in document number i, a_i is the number of selected features in document number i, t is the number of all unique features in the dataset, and $\bar{x}_i$ is the mean of vector i (document number i).

2.5 Harmony Search Algorithm

The harmony search rule produces (generates) irregular harmony memory (HM), which contains a collection of candidate solutions. The harmony search rule then reinforces the harmony memory to attain the best answer to unravel the matter (associate degree best set of a lot of informative features). Every position or musician (unique term) may be a dimension within the search area. The solutions of the harmony search that are assessed by the mentioned fitness function operate as in the equivalent weight of Eq. 2.4, it's accustomed get associate degree best harmony (global best solution) [7, 17]. The harmony search rule provides the solutions in five main steps. covered next.

2.5.1 Parameters Initialization

The feature choice drawback is delineated as associate optimization drawback by means of attempting to find the maximize worth of the fitness operation $f_{(x)}$, where x_i is the i_{th} position worth. Some parameters are employed in the harmony search algorithmic rule for feature choice drawback supported literature studies as harmony memory solutions=50 (number of solutions), concordance memory thought rate (HMCR)=0.9 is that the probability of choosing the choice variable whether or not from memory or each which way, least pitch altering rate (PARmin)=0.45 is that the least pitch altering rate, most pitch altering rate (PARmax)=0.9 is that the foremost pitch altering rate, bwmin=0.1 is that the least data measure, bwmax=1 is that the foremost data degree, and (NI) is that the assortment of all cycles [7, 21, 43].

2.5.2 Harmony Memory Initialization

The calculation incorporates a store of arrangements within the harmony memory (HM) lattice that's filled by creating HMS haphazardly, as shown here:

$$
\text{HMS} =
\begin{bmatrix}
x_1^1 & \cdots & x_{t-1}^1 & x_t^1 \\
x_1^2 & \cdots & x_{t-1}^2 & x_t^2 \\
\vdots & \ddots & \vdots & \vdots \\
x_1^{HMS-1} & \cdots & x_{t-1}^{HMS-1} & x_t^{HMS-1} \\
x_1^{HMS} & \cdots & x_{t-1}^{HMS} & x_t^{HMS}
\end{bmatrix}
\tag{2.6}
$$

$$
x_i^j = LB_i + Rand * (UB_i - LB_i), \qquad j = 1, 2, ..., HMS.
\tag{2.7}
$$

The agreement harmony memory is made as a lattice in Eqn. 2.6, where $[LB_i]$ is the lower bound and $[UB_i]$ is the upper bound.

2.5.3 Generating a New Solution

Generating a new solution follows these three rules: memory consideration, pitch adjustment, and random selection in Algorithm 1 [7, 16].

$$
X' = (x_1', x_2', ..., x_t')
\tag{2.8}
$$

Arrangements of the concordance look calculation are powerfully merged, agreeing to the *PAR(I)* esteem and *bw(I)* values [7, 16, 22]. If an arbitrary number between [0, 1] is created and decreased or increased to the likelihood of standard, then the modern choice variable for the following iteration (x) is decided ':

$$
PAR(I) = PAR_{min} + \left(\frac{PAR_{max} - PAR_{min}}{I_{max}} \right) * I,
\tag{2.9}
$$

where

$$
bw(I) = bw_{max} exp \left(\frac{In \left(\frac{bw_{min}}{bw_{max}} \right)}{I_{max}} \right) * I,
\tag{2.10}
$$

Algorithm 1 Improvise a new solution

1: **Input**: Harmony memory *HM* solutions
2: **Output**: A new solution as vector represented in 2.8
3: **for** each $j \in [1, t]$ **do**
4:      **if** Rand (0,1) $\leq$ HMCR **then**
5:          $x_j' = HM[i][j] where i \sim U(1, 2, ..., HMS)$
6:          **if** Rand(0,1) $\leq$ PAR **then**
7:              $x_j' = x_j' \pm rand \times$ bw, where r$\sim$ U(0,1) and *bw* is distance bandwidth
8:
9:          **else** $x_i' = LBj + rand \times (UBj - LBj)$
10:          **end if**
11:      **end if**
12: **end for**

$PAR(I)$ is the pitch altering rate for a modern arrangement, I is the number of the current cycle, I_{max} is the max number of cycles, bw_{min} is the least altering rate, and bw_{max} is the most extreme altering rate.

2.5.4 Update Harmony Memory

In the event that the modern arrangement has way better wellness or fitness, the work esteem will replace the most noticeably awful concordance arrangement.

2.5.5 Check the Stopping Criterion

When the agreement look calculation comes to the greatest number of iterations, it will halt, and the *HMCR* and *PAR* parameters of the concordance look that offer assistance to seek for the universal and local arrangements [7, 16, 19].

2.6 Text Clustering

In this section, we show the steps of the content cluster method after making a fresh set of choices by changing the concordance look algorithmic program to improve the content cluster procedure (FSHSTC), improve the k-mean algorithmic program, and update the cluster centers of mass and similarity.

2.6.1 Mathematical Model of the Text Clustering

The content clustering method is portrayed as follows: given D and a bunch of content archives $D = d_1, d_2, ..., d_j, ..., d_n$, D is the number of all records inside the dataset (reports), and d_1 denotes the favorite document, Cos_{di} is an objective work that is an irrelevant record based on d_i. By and large, these common features judge the execution of the content clustering strategy [16, 44].

2.6.2 Find Clusters Centroid

In arrange to segment (cluster or gather) a set of colossal records into a subset of significant clusters, within each cycle, the cluster centroids are overhauled according to the substance of the clusters. Each archive within the dataset is compared to the comparable cluster centroid (to one cluster). Here, ck is the cluster centroid $ck = (ck1, ck2, ..., ckj, ..., ckK)$, and ckj is the centroid of cluster number j [16, 45]. This is what it looks like after modifying the cluster's centroid:

$$c_{kj} = \frac{\sum_{i=1}^{n}(a_{ki})d_i}{\sum_{j=1}^{r_i} a_{kj}}, \tag{2.11}$$

where d_i is the report i that has a place to the c_j centroid of the cluster j, a_{kj} is the number of reports that have a place to cluster j, and r_i is the number of reports in cluster i [16].

2.6.3 Similarity Measure

Cosine closeness is the common closeness degree utilized within the content report clustering procedure to calculate the likeness between two vectors; here, d_1 is record number 1, and d_2 is the cluster centroid. This is the equation:

$$Cos(d_1, d_2) = \frac{\sum_{j=1}^{t} w(t_j, d_1) \times w(t_j, d_2)}{\sqrt{\sum_{j=1}^{t} w(t_j, d_1)^2} \sqrt{\sum_{j=1}^{t} w(t_j, d_2)^2}}, \tag{2.12}$$

where $w_{tj,d1}$ is the weight score of term number j within the archive number 1, $w_{tj,d2}$ is the weight score of term number j within the archive number 2 $\sum_{j=1}^{t} w(t_j, d_1)^2$ is the summation of all terms' weight within record 1 under square from term number $\{j = 1 \text{ to } t\}$, and $\sum_{j=1}^{t} w(t_j, d_2)^2$ is the summation of all terms' weight within record 2 under square from term number $\{j = 1 \text{ to } t\}$, and d_2 speak is the cluster centroid [42, 45].

2.7 *k*-means text clustering algorithm

The k-means clump was introduced in 1967 as an area search clump rule [46]. It is a clustering rule utilized in the space of the text document clump; as a result, it is thought of as the correct clustering rule to settle on the initial cluster centroids in this area. The k-means is utilized to parcel (cluster) a set of content reports with a multidimensional region and bounty of region content highlights $D = (d_1, d_2, d_3, ..., d_n)$ into comparable and associated clusters. The k-means content clump runs the show using the most extreme likeness as a likeness content for tasks in each record of the comparative cluster by proportionate weight; see Eq. 2.12. It uses X as the information lattice $n * k$, where n is the number of all reports within the given dataset, K is the number of all clusters as predefined, k is the cluster centroid number, each report within the dataset is a vector of term weight scores $d_i = (w_{i1}, w_{i2}, w_{i3}, ..., w_{it})$, t is the number of all interesting highlights within the dataset D, k-means calculation looks approximately like the ideal $n * k$ [16, 35].

The k-means clustering strategy takes place in these five primary steps:

1) Each record inside the dataset is a vector of terms weight score.
2) Initialize the centroids of the clusters randomly with the reports matrix X.
3) Work out the likeness score or worth for each record with the middle of the clusters dividing each archive into a parcel of associated centroids by the circular work closeness in Eq. 2.11.
4) Update the center of the clusters with the updated documents that relate to every cluster center of mass in line with the current state of affairs for obtaining the correct cluster centroid exploitation of two weighting schemes [47].

Algorithm 2 k-means clustering algorithm

1: **Input**: D is huge collection of documents, K is the number of all clusters.

2: **Output**: Assign D to K.

3: **Termination criteria**

4: Randomly choosing K document as clusters centroid $C = (c_1, c_2, ..., c_K)$

5: Initialize matrix X as zeros

6: **for** all d in D **do**

7:     let $j = arg_{min}$ k based on $Cos(d_i, c_k)$

8: **end for**

9: Update the centroids of the clusters using Eqn. 2.11

10: **End**

2.8 Experimental Results

We have programmed the entire system (i.e., harmony search algorithmic rule for determination the feature choice downside and k-means for text clump problem) using the Matlab software package (version seven 7.10.0). We will outline each dataset's elements and organization, make a case for the examination criteria, and show the results.

Table 2.2 presents the datasets utilized within the test of this chapter. There are seven typical benchmark datasets we will explore and compare the execution of the k-means algorithmic for the include choice strategy and the include choice procedure. The datasets are available at (http://sites.labic.icmc.usp.br/text_collections). The main dataset (DS1), known as CSTR, contains 100 irregular archives from the abstracts of specialized reports that has a place to 2 points. The second dataset (DS2), known as Twenty Newsgroups, contains 200 arbitrary records from completely distinctive newsgroups that have a place to four themes. The third dataset (DS3), known as Domz-business, contains 250 arbitrary archives from a web catalog of web assets that has a place to 6 subjects. The fourth dataset (DS4), known as Domz-computer, contains 300 arbitrary records from completely distinctive newsgroups that have a place to 10 themes. The fifth dataset (DS5), known as Reuters–21578, contains 350 arbitrary archives from the newswire from 1987 that have a place to 10 subjects. The 6th dataset (DS6), called ACM, contains 200 arbitrary archives from an affiliation for computing apparatus that has a place to 10 points. The seventh dataset (DS7), known as WebAce, contain 1,560 irregular archives from a web specialist for record categorization and investigation that has a place to 15 points.

2.8.1 Evaluation Measures

The comparative assessments were done utilizing one inner assessment measure, likeness degree, and two outside assessment measures, precision (Ac) and F-measure (F). These

Table 2.2 Text Datasets Characteristics

Datasets	Source	Number of Documents	Number of Terms	Number of Clusters
DS1	CSTR	100	1260	2
With FS			533	
DS2	20Newsgroup	200	6518	4
With FS			1051	
DS3	Domz-Businss	250	1156	6
With FS			111	
DS4	Domz-Computer	300	1247	8
With FS			214	
DS5	Reuters-21578	350	3258	10
With FS			1048	
DS6	ACM	350	24457	10
With FS			9891	
DS7	WebAce	1560	8880	20
With FS			4540	

measures are common assessment criteria utilized in the content clustering space to assess the clusters precisely [36].

2.8.1.1 F-measure Based on Clustering Evaluation

The F-measure (F) could be a common judgment utilized within the content clustering region. It controls the degree of truth clusters and depends on two judgments: exactness (P) and review (R) [47]. The F-measure controls for the cluster j and lesson (document) i is decided by the following:

$$P(i,j) = \frac{n_{i,j}}{n_j}, \quad R(i,j) = \frac{n_{i,j}}{n_i}, \tag{2.13}$$

where n_{ij} is the number of individuals of course i in cluster j, n_j is the number of individuals of cluster j, and n_i is the number of individuals of lesson i.

$$F(i,j) = \frac{2P(i,j)R(i,j)}{P(i,j)R(i,j)}, \tag{2.14}$$

where $P(i,j)$ is the accuracy of individuals of course i in cluster j, $R(i,j)$ is the review of individuals of course i in cluster j, and the F-measure for all is clusters is calculated by the following:

$$F = \sum_j \frac{n_j}{n} \max_i \{n(i,j)\}, \tag{2.15}$$

2.8.1.2 Accuracy Based on Clustering Evaluation

Precision (AC) is the common outside estimation that is utilized accurately to find out the rate of the archives of each cluster related to the following [47]:

$$Ac = \sum_{i=1}^{k} \frac{1}{n} P(i,j) \qquad (2.16)$$

where $P(i,j)$ is the exactness esteem for lesson i in cluster j, n is the number of all records in each cluster, and k is the number of all clusters.

2.8.2 Results and Discussions

This paper utilized the k-means algorithmic rule to resolve the text agglomeration downside supported by two methods. The first one was the k-means text agglomeration using the feature choice technique, namely, KMTC. In the second method, k-means is applied to resolve text agglomeration by using the feature choice ways exploitation harmony search algorithmic rule, namely, FSHSTC.

The anticipated k-means content agglomeration with the highlight choice method was better than the k-means content agglomeration strategy. It did not include the choice procedure inside DS1, DS3, DS5, DS6, and DS7 in general estimations, but it made strides with the F-measure in DS2 and DS4. We tried to misuse seven common datasets that appeared in Table 2.1. Note that applying the feature choice technique before the text agglomeration technique was beneficial to enhance the agglomeration method by handling an occasional variety of options, which makes the agglomeration procedure easier to use to partition an enormous number of text documents.

For accurate results, we performed the experiments more than 20 times, and the harmony search is an international search algorithmic rule that runs 500 iterations in every run. This extensiveness is supported by the literature that validates the projected technique (FSHSTC). When using 500 cycles, the world look algorithmic had better results for the include choice strategy. The k-means may be a better local look algorithmic. So, 100 cycles is enough for the local look algorithmic to run the show for the content archive agglomeration procedure [16].

Table 2.3 shows that the execution of different methods depends on a cluster's quality. For the most part, the arranged FS method doesn't perform well with the look equation, and but content clustering method upheld the estimations that utilized over the seven benchmark content datasets. The choice of dataset is a vital step still for the content clustering strategy to get fewer content alternatives for the best record clusters. Rationally, any system that deals with the related features will perform the text analysis with efficiency.

The arranged FSHSTC performd okay after content clustering, and it diminished the number of choices. In other words, it scaled back the number of alternatives in DS1 (1,260 to 533), scaled back the number of choices in DS2 (6,518 to 1,051), scaled back the number of choices in DS3 (1156 to 111), scaled back the number of alternatives in DS4 (1,247 to 214), scaled back the number of alternatives in DS5 (3258 to 1,048), scaled back the number of

Table 2.3 The Algorithm Efficacy Based on Clusters' Quality Results

Dataset	Method	KMTC	FSHSTC
DS1			
	Accuracy	0.5800	**0.6060**
	F-measure	0.5795	**0.5808**
	Rank	2	1
DS2			
	Accuracy	0.3630	**0.3755**
	F-measure	**0.3782**	0.3774
	Partial rank	1	1
DS3			
	Accuracy	0.3578	**0.3687**
	F-measure	0.3478	**0.3625**
	Partial rank	2	1
DS4			
	Accuracy	0.2714	**0.2854**
	F-measure	**0.2584**	0.2558
	Partial rank	1	1
DS5			
	Accuracy	0.4509	**0.4688**
	F-measure	0.3855	**0.4005**
	Partial rank	2	1
DS6			
	Accuracy	0.3857	**0.3989**
	F-measure	0.3140	**0.3362**
	Partial rank	2	1
DS7			
	Accuracy	0.4822	**0.4954**
	F-measure	0.4350	**0.4440**
	Final ranking	2	1
Mean rank		1.71	**1**
Final rank		2	**1**

choices in DS6 (24,457 to 9,891), and scaled back the number of alternatives in DS7 (8,880 to 4,540). The diminishing assortment of alternatives is influenced by the execution time to be less and increment the fundamental clustering execution. The arranged FSHSTC overcomes the k-means stand-alone in all the cases.

Figure 2.2 and Figure 2.3 shows that the execution (precision and F-measure) of the anticipated method (FSHSTC) upheld its clusters' quality using seven standard content

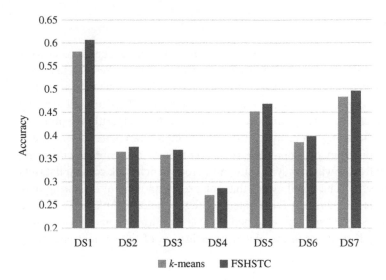

Figure 2.2 The accuracy of the *k*-means text clustering methods

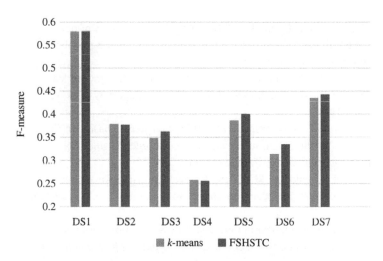

Figure 2.3 The F-measure score of the *k*-means technique

datasets. It's clear that the anticipated FSHSTC performed affirmatively and overcame the inverse comparative procedure (*k*-means clump stand-alone) bolstered by the content clump method with the clump exactness and F-measure.

The projected FSHSTC scored better on accuracy and F- as an external measure in all the datasets. All experiments produced better results once the projected system applied FSHSTC to support the two measurements expected for DS2 and DS4; however, the results virtually are identical. Also, there were no improvements even with a shorter execution time (runtime). Finally, the anticipated method (i.e., FSHSTC) was better than the inverse associated procedure and obtains the results.

2.9 Conclusion

In this chapter, the modern highlight choice strategy is utilized with the concordance look algorithmic program to look for an ideal unused subset of data to make the clustering strategy successfully by getting extra adjusted clusters. This technique was presented so as to improve the execution of the content clustering procedure. This unused strategy is called the highlight choice strategy misuse concordance look algorithmic program for the content were clustering procedure (FSHSTC), which overcomes the k-means clustering algorithmic program by improving the execution of the content clustering algorithmic program. FSHSTC was surveyed using numerous benchmark content datasets (seven benchmark datasets). The results were that the execution content clustering may be developed and make strides with the anticipated highlight choice technique. For future work, the anticipated FSHSTC may be changed as a greenhorn adaptation (adjusted, crossbreed, and improved) to upgrade the global investigation of the content clustering technique.

References

1 Abualigah, L.M., Khader, A.T., and Hanandeh, E.S. (2016) A combination of objective functions and hybrid krill herd algorithm for text document clustering analysis. *Engineering Applications of Artificial Intelligence.*

2 Bharti, K.K. and Singh, P.K. (2015) Hybrid dimension reduction by integrating feature selection with feature extraction method for text clustering. *Expert Systems with Applications*, **42** (6), 3105–3114.

3 Wang, X., Cao, J., Liu, Y., Gao, S., and Deng, X. (2012) Text clustering based on the improved tf-idf by the iterative algorithm, in *Electrical & Electronics Engineering (EEESYM), 2012 IEEE Symposium on*, IEEE, pp. 140–143.

4 Mouring, M., Dhou, K., and Hadzikadic, M. (2018) A novel algorithm for bi-level image coding and lossless compression based on virtual ant colonies., in *COMPLEXIS*, pp. 72–78.

5 Bharti, K.K. and Singh, P.K. (2016) Opposition chaotic fitness mutation based adaptive inertia weight bpso for feature selection in text clustering. *Applied Soft Computing*, **43**, 20–34.

6 Al-Sai, Z.A. and Abualigah, L.M. (2017) Big data and e-government: A review, in *Information Technology (ICIT), 2017 8th International Conference on*, IEEE, pp. 580–587.

7 Zheng, L., Diao, R., and Shen, Q. (2015) Self-adjusting harmony search-based feature selection. *Soft Computing*, **19** (6), 1567–1579.

8 Zhang, Q., Xiao, Y., Suo, J., Shi, J., Yu, J., Guo, Y., Wang, Y., and Zheng, H. (2017) Sonoelastomics for breast tumor classification: a radiomics approach with clustering-based feature selection on sonoelastography. *Ultrasound in Medicine and Biology*, **43** (5), 1058–1069.

9 Abualigah, L.M., Khader, A.T., and Hanandeh, E.S. (2017) A new feature selection method to improve the document clustering using particle swarm optimization algorithm. *Journal of Computational Science.*

10 Alomari, O.A., Khader, A.T., Al-Betar, M.A., and Abualigah, L.M. (2017) Gene selection for cancer classification by combining minimum redundancy maximum relevancy and bat-inspired algorithm. *International Journal of Data Mining and Bioinformatics*, **19** (1), 32–51.

11 Abualigah, L.M., Khader, A.T., and Hanandeh, E.S. (2019) Modified krill herd algorithm for global numerical optimization problems, in *Advances in Nature-Inspired Computing and Applications*, Springer, pp. 205–221.

12 Dhou, K. (2018) A novel agent-based modeling approach for image coding and lossless compression based on the wolf-sheep predation model, in *International Conference on Computational Science*, Springer, pp. 117–128.

13 Alomari, O.A., Khader, A.T., Mohammed, A.A.B., Abualigah, L.M., Nugroho, H., Chandra, G.R., Katyayani, A., Sandhya, N., Hossain, J., Sani, N.F.M. et al. (2017) Mrmr ba: A hybrid gene selection algorithm for cancer classification. *Journal of Theoretical and Applied Information Technology*, **95** (12).

14 Abualigah, L.M.Q. and Hanandeh, E.S. (2015) Applying genetic algorithms to information retrieval using vector space model. *International Journal of Computer Science, Engineering and Applications*, **5** (1), 19.

15 Abualigah, L.M., Khader, A.T., Al-Betar, M.A., and Alomari, O.A. (2017) Text feature selection with a robust weight scheme and dynamic dimension reduction to text document clustering. *Expert Systems with Applications*, **84**, 24–36.

16 Forsati, R., Mahdavi, M., Shamsfard, M., and Meybodi, M.R. (2013) Efficient stochastic algorithms for document clustering. *Information Sciences*, **220**, 269–291.

17 Geem, Z.W., Kim, J.H., and Loganathan, G. (2001) A new heuristic optimization algorithm: harmony search. *Simulation*, **76** (2), 60–68.

18 Moon, Y.Y., Geem, Z.W., and Han, G.T. (2018) Vanishing point detection for self-driving car using harmony search algorithm. *Swarm and Evolutionary Computation*.

19 Al-Betar, M.A., Khader, A.T., and Zaman, M. (2012) University course timetabling using a hybrid harmony search metaheuristic algorithm. *Systems, Man, and Cybernetics, Part C: Applications and Reviews, IEEE Transactions on*, **42** (5), 664–681.

20 Reddy, S.S. (2018) Optimal power flow using hybrid differential evolution and harmony search algorithm. *International Journal of Machine Learning and Cybernetics*, pp. 1–15.

21 Al-Betar,M.A. and Khader, A.T. (2012) A harmony search algorithm for university course timetabling. *Annals of Operations Research*, **194** (1), 3–31.

22 Al-Betar, M.A., Khader, A.T., and Liao, I.Y. (2010) A harmony search with multi-pitch adjusting rate for the university course timetabling, in *Recent advances in harmony search algorithm*, Springer, pp. 147–161.

23 Diao, R. (2014) *Feature selection with harmony search and its applications*, Ph.D. thesis, Aberystwyth University.

24 Shamsinejadbabki, P. and Saraee, M. (2012) A new unsupervised feature selection method for text clustering based on genetic algorithms. *Journal of Intelligent Information Systems*, **38** (3), 669–684.

25 Lin, K.C., Zhang, K.Y., Huang, Y.H., Hung, J.C., and Yen, N. (2016) Feature selection based on an improved cat swarm optimization algorithm for big data classification. *The Journal of Supercomputing*, pp. 1–12.

26 Abualigah, L.M., Khader, A.T., AlBetar, M.A., and Hanandeh, E.S. (2017) Unsupervised text feature selection technique based on particle swarm optimization algorithm for improving the text clustering. *EAI Google Scholar.*

27 Alyasseri, Z.A.A., Khader, A.T., Al-Betar, M.A., and Abualigah, L.M. (2017) Ecg signal denoising using β-hill climbing algorithm and wavelet transform, in *Information Technology (ICIT), 2017 8th International Conference on*, IEEE, pp. 96–101.

28 Bolaji, A.L., Al-Betar, M.A., Awadallah, M.A., Khader, A.T., and Abualigah, L.M. (2016) A comprehensive review: Krill herd algorithm (kh) and its applications. *Applied Soft Computing.*

29 Abualigah, L.M., Khader, A.T., Al-Betar, M.A., and Awadallah, M.A. (2016) A krill herd algorithm for efficient text documents clustering, in *Computer Applications & Industrial Electronics (ISCAIE), 2016 IEEE Symposium on*, IEEE, pp. 67–72.

30 Shehab, M., Khader, A.T., Al-Betar, M.A., and Abualigah, L.M. (2017) Hybridizing cuckoo search algorithm with hill climbing for numerical optimization problems, in *Information Technology (ICIT), 2017 8th International Conference on*, IEEE, pp. 36–43.

31 Abualigah, L.M., Khader, A.T., Hanandeh, E.S., and Gandomi, A.H. (2017) A novel hybridization strategy for krill herd algorithm applied to clustering techniques. *Applied Soft Computing*, **60**, 423–435.

32 Abualigah, L.M.Q. (2019) *Feature Selection and Enhanced Krill Herd Algorithm for Text Document Clustering*, Springer.

33 Abualigah, L.M.Q. (2019) Proposed methodology, in *Feature Selection and Enhanced Krill Herd Algorithm for Text Document Clustering*, Springer, pp. 61–103.

34 Abualigah, L.M. and Khader, A.T. (2017) Unsupervised text feature selection technique based on hybrid particle swarm optimization algorithm with genetic operators for the text clustering. *The Journal of Supercomputing*, **73** (11), 4773–4795.

35 Abualigah, L.M., Khader, A.T., and Hanandeh, E.S. (2018) A novel weighting scheme applied to improve the text document clustering techniques, in *Innovative Computing, Optimization and Its Applications*, Springer, pp. 305–320.

36 Bharti, K.K. and Singh, P.K. (2014) A three-stage unsupervised dimension reduction method for text clustering. *Journal of Computational Science*, **5** (2), 156–169.

37 Tsai, C.F., Eberle, W., and Chu, C.Y. (2013) Genetic algorithms in feature and instance selection. *Knowledge-Based Systems*, **39**, 240–247.

38 Mohamad, M.S., Deris, S., Yatim, S., and Othman, M. (2004) Feature selection method using genetic algorithm for the classification of small and high dimension data, in *Proceedings of the 1st International Symposium on Information and Communication Technology*, pp. 1–4.

39 Abualigah, L.M., Khader, A.T., and Al-Betar, M.A. (2016) Unsupervised feature selection technique based on genetic algorithm for improving the text clustering, in *2016 7th International Conference on Computer Science and Information Technology (CSIT)*, pp. 1–6, doi:10.1109/CSIT.2016.7549453.

40 Abualigah, L.M.Q. (2019) Krill herd algorithm, in *Feature Selection and Enhanced Krill Herd Algorithm for Text Document Clustering*, Springer, pp. 11–19.

41 Uğuz, H. (2011) A two-stage feature selection method for text categorization by using information gain, principal component analysis and genetic algorithm. *Knowledge-Based Systems*, **24** (7), 1024–1032.

42 Zhao, Z., Wang, L., Liu, H., and Ye, J. (2013) On similarity preserving feature selection. *Knowledge and Data Engineering, IEEE Transactions on*, **25** (3), 619–632.

43 Abualigah, L.M., Khader, A.T., and Hanandeh, E.S. A hybrid strategy for krill herd algorithm with harmony search algorithm to improve the data clusterin. *Intelligent Decision Technologies*, (Preprint), 1–12.

44 Rashaideh, H., Sawaie, A., Al-Betar, M.A., Abualigah, L.M., Al-Laham, M.M., Ra'ed, M., and Braik, M. A grey wolf optimizer for text document clustering. *Journal of Intelligent Systems*.

45 Abualigah, L.M., Khader, A.T., and Al-Betar, M.A. (2016) Multi-objectives-based text clustering technique using k-mean algorithm, in *2016 7th International Conference on Computer Science and Information Technology (CSIT)*, pp. 1–6, doi:10.1109/CSIT.2016.7549464.

46 MacQueen, J. et al. (1967) Some methods for classification and analysis of multivariate observations, in *Proceedings of the fifth Berkeley symposium on mathematical statistics and probability*, vol. 1, Oakland, CA, USA., vol. 1, pp. 281–297.

47 Forsati, R., Meybodi, M., Mahdavi, M., and Neiat, A. (2008) Hybridization of k-means and harmony search methods for web page clustering, in *Proceedings of the 2008 IEEE/WIC/ACM International Conference on Web Intelligence and Intelligent Agent Technology-Volume 01*, IEEE Computer Society, pp. 329–335.

3

Adaptive Position–Based Crossover in the Genetic Algorithm for Data Clustering

Arnab Gain and Prasenjit Dey

[1]*Department of Computer Science and Engineering, Cooch Behar Government Engineering College, India*

3.1 Introduction

In the modern era, the data has become the most important factor when analyzing the pattern/behavior of a system or an organization. Many researchers have come up with statistical and machine learning-based approaches to analyze this data. These approaches have been used to analyze the behavior of a large volume of data such as analysis of its variance, regression, correlation, discrimination, multidimensional scaling, etc. While analyzing the data, sometimes it is observed that a set of data possesses similarity in the data's feature values, and this set of data is dissimilar with respect to the other set of similar data based on these feature values. Data clustering is a technique to deal with this kind of situation, where similar types of data samples are grouped together. Data clustering is an unsupervised technique as the data is clustered using the only information available in the dataset.

In this chapter, we have tried to analyze the clustering behavior of the data samples. To do that, initially we studied many research articles [1–3] based on data clustering. While studying, we observed that the k-means clustering is one of the well-known algorithms of data clustering where the number of clusters present in the dataset is k. Thus, in this chapter, we have focused on the optimization of the k-means clustering algorithm. During the analysis, we also observed that the performance of the k-means clustering improves when the clustering problem is considered as an optimization problem, although the clustering problem is a nonpolynomial optimization problem.

In the literature, nonpolynomial optimization problems are solved by metaheuristic algorithms in polynomial time. The genetic algorithm (GA) is a well-known metaheuristic-based optimization technique. In the proposed approach, we have used a modified version of GA to optimize the k-means clustering algorithm. The modified version of GA has used a new adaptive position crossover technique to improve the convergence of the GA. We have performed a simulation-based experiment with two synthetic datasets and one real-world dataset to verify the performance improvement of the proposed approach.

The simulation results support the superiority of the proposed approach. As the proposed method is related to the data clustering concept and GA, in the preliminary section, we have provided the basic details of clustering along with the k-clustering algorithm and GA.

The organization of the rest of the chapter is as follows. The basics of clustering and the genetic algorithm are discussed in Section 3.2. In Section 3.3, the related work on the GA-based data clustering is discussed. The proposed approach is demonstrated in Section 3.4. Experimental settings along with the results are provided in Section 3.5. Finally, the proposed approach concludes in Section 3.6.

3.2 Preliminaries

In this section, we discuss the clustering problem along with k-means clustering algorithm in Section 3.2.1. Then we emphasize the significance of metaheuristic approaches in data clustering. To describe metaheuristics, we present a scenario. As in real life, there exist numerous problems where an ideal solution can be achieved only in nonpolynomial (NP) time. Thus, some metaheuristics are required to solve these NP problems in polynomial (P) time. It is a high-level procedure to find, generate, or select a heuristic that may provide a sufficiently good solution to an optimization problem, especially with limited computation capacity. The genetic algorithm (GA) is a well-known metaheuristic algorithm. In Section 3.2.2, we give a brief overview of the GA.

3.2.1 Clustering

In this section, we explain the concept of clustering data in detail. According to [4], clustering is an approach where a set of data samples is divided into a number of clusters; here the characteristics of the data within one cluster should be similar to but different from the data in another cluster. Better clustering means data samples within the same cluster are more similar, and the differences between the centers of clusters are bigger [4]. Let us consider a dataset $X_n = (x_1, x_2, \cdots, x_n)$, where n is the number of samples present in the dataset, and $X_i \in R^p$ is a feature vector describing the data sample, where p is the number of features available in the data sample. Suppose these samples will be clustered into a set of clusters, i.e., $C = C_1, \cdots, C_k$, where k is the number of clusters. The clusters are disjoint, $C_i \cap C_j = \emptyset$ for $i \neq j$. The numbers of clusters may be known *a priori* or not. x'_k is assumed as center of cluster C_k. The main goal of clustering is to minimize the intra-cluster distance as follows:

$$\sum_{k=1}^{K} \sum_{x \in C_K} ||x_i - x'_k||^2 \tag{3.1}$$

3.2.1.1 *k*-means Clustering

k-means clustering is one of the well-known clustering algorithms [2]. This algorithm has been used in many applications for clustering purposes. In [3] and [5], a method of k-means clustering has been described step-by-step as follows:

Step 1: The center $(x'_1, \cdots, x'_k)$ for each of the clusters $(C_1, \cdots, C_k)$ is to be initialized.

Step 2: A new cluster member is found by assigning each data point to the closest center.
Step 3: The cluster center are recalculated.
Step 4: If all the cluster centers remained unchanged after recalculation, then stop; the process from Step 2 is to be repeated otherwise.

Though k-means clustering is an efficient approach [3, 5], still it has a few limitations, as follows. The performance of clustering is dependent on (i) the initial cluster centers and (ii) the outliers present in the dataset. k-means clustering is also stuck in a local minimum [6–8]. Furthermore, k-means clustering is time-consuming when it is applied to a large dataset [9].

To deal with these limitations, many optimization-based approaches have been adopted in the literature to solve k-means clustering. k-means clustering can be formulated as an optimization problem, and as the metaheuristic optimization techniques have global minima, it can help the k-means algorithm not to get stuck in the local minima. In this chapter, the objective is to optimize the data clustering algorithm in polynomial time with given constraints.

3.2.2 Genetic Algorithm

The GA is one of the metaheuristic approaches. The GA is a metaheuristic inspired by the process of natural selection, which is commonly used to generate high-quality solutions to optimization and search problems by relying on bio-inspired operators such as selection, crossover, and mutation [10]. The evolution of the GA usually starts from a population of randomly generated individuals/chromosomes and is an iterative process; the population in each iteration is called generation [11]. In each generation, the fitness of every individual/chromosome in the population is evaluated by the value obtained using the fitness function, which is usually an objective function in the optimization problem being solved. Fitter individuals are stochastically selected from the current population, and the genome of each individual is modified by crossover and mutation to form a new generation [12]. The new generation of candidate solutions is then used in the next iteration of the algorithm. Commonly, the algorithm terminates when either a maximum number of generations has been produced or a satisfactory fitness level has been reached for the population [12].

Crossover is an important genetic operator in the GA [13]. It is used to combine the genes of two parents to generate better offspring [13]. In literature, there exist many types of crossovers that differ based on how they are selecting and operating on the genes from their parents. In this chapter, the proposed work focuses on the crossover operator. Here, the concept of a vital gene has been proposed. One or more genes are chosen stochastically from the chromosome and termed a vital gene. It is assumed that these genes carry the vital information of a chromosome. Here, the crossover process has been divided into two phases. In Phase I, while doing the crossover, vital genes are preserved (position of the gene) from participating in crossover, and crossover is done on the rest of the genes. In Phase II, the rest of the genes in the new offsprings are formed either by replacing the genes of one parent with the genes of another parent or by performing some arithmetic operations. One of these two operations is done stochastically. This preservation technique of the parent genes in the crossover is applied to the GA to solve the data clustering problems. In the case of GA-based k-means clustering, the simulation results demonstrate that the proposed approach improves the quality of the data clustering.

3.3 Related Works

Data clustering is a multivariate statistical approach. Here, the objective is to form a different set of groups from the given dataset based on the features/variables available in the dataset. For a given dataset, depending on the clustering algorithm, the number of clusters/groups, the number of elements in the cluster, and the centers of the cluster may vary. A clustering algorithm is said to be good if it has two properties: (i) small inter-cluster distance (compactness) and (ii) large inter-cluster distance (separability). Many clustering validity indices are there based on these two properties, e.g., Davies Bouldin (DB)-index, PBMI index, BIC index, silhouette index, etc. In literature, many researchers have tried to optimize the cluster validity indices to achieve optimal data clustering. In the early days, many traditional clustering algorithms were proposed, e.g., k-means. Later, to improve cluster validity, many hybrid data clustering approaches were also proposed. In this chapter, our prime focus is on the works related to GA-based data clustering.

As most of the data clustering algorithms such as k-means clustering suffer from local optima, the GA is needed to obtain global optima. In the literature, the GA has been used as an optimization method in various domains such as image processing [14–16], data clustering [14, 17–20], etc. There are several literature reviews that focus on the application of GAs to cluster binary data [4, 6]. All of these GA-based methods showed good performance and better results when compared to other non-GA clustering methods. However, some of these GA-based methods have drawbacks and need to be improved. Syswerda et. al., in [21], proposed a position-based crossover where they have said that the position-based crossover starts by selecting a random set of positions in the parent chromosome. Their method is found to be efficient in the case of GA-based optimization. The proposed approach is motivated by their positional crossover technique.

3.3.1 GA-Based Data Clustering by Binary Encoding

In the literature, there exist many research articles based on clustering using GAs where they have used binary data instead of numeric data. Most of this research showed that binary encoding produces better results. Binary encoding was used rather than a string representation in the studies by [18, 22–25]. The first noticeable implementation of GAs for clustering using binary data was observed in 1997 in [26]. Here, they used both the nonbinary and binary datasets. In [27], the authors extended the work done by [23] by using hybrid evolutionary clustering with self-adaptive genetic operators (ECSAGO). In their work, they observed that the real encoding was much easier to do for the special genetic operators compared to the binary representation if Euclidean distance was used as the distance metric. Research by [22] and [25] used binary encoding with two crossover points and one crossover point, respectively. In [25], the encoding was done based on the number of clusters that were predetermined, whereas in [22] the encoding was done on the building blocks for the crossover operator.

In [24], the authors also used a one-point crossover and adopted the binary encoding. They used binary vectors with $N - 1$ elements to encode a minimum spanning tree (MST). An MST is a spanning tree of a connected, undirected graph. It connects all the edges with the shortest distance to its edges. There are two conditions to eliminate the edges by looking at the vector elements. They defined that if the vector elements have a value of 0, then the edges will be retained, whereas if the vector elements showed 1, the edges will be eliminated. Their algorithm is time-consuming due to the MST formation.

There is another GA-based data clustering technique that uses binary encoding called the binary small world optimization algorithm (BSWOA) in [28] and GA for the k-means initialization (GAKMI) in [29]. BSWOA is an optimization technique where local search is used to find the solutions for optimization problems by using binary encoding. In [29], the GAKMI is focused on the initialization of the centers of the k-means clustering. In most of the scenarios, their method outperformed the k-means and GKA.

3.3.2 GA-Based Data Clustering by Real Encoding

Because of a global optimization technique, the GA has been used in k-means clustering. In [10, 20], the authors used the GA for k-means clustering called genetic k-means clustering (GKA). The main objective of the GKA is to find the global optima of the given dataset and partition the data into a specified number of clusters. They used means as a search operator. They minimized the total within-cluster variation (TWCV). A fast genetic k-means algorithm (FGKA) was been proposed by the authors in [30] that was inspired by the GKA, i.e., by incorporating several improvements over the GKA. They demonstrated that the FGKA runs faster than the GKA. Both of these approaches achieved the objective to converge to the global optima. In [30], the authors defined the number of nonempty clusters $e(Sz)$ in any solution Sz as legal if $e(Sz) = 1$, and illegal otherwise. These strings are permitted but are considered to be the most undesirable solution, and the lowest fitness value was defined as $+$. These illegal strings were not permitted and were eliminated from the GKC, which showed that the FGKA was better. This process improves the performance of the time convergence. The incremental k-means algorithm (IGKA) is another variant of the GKA, proposed by Lu et al. [4, 8]. This algorithm outperforms the FGKA when the probability of mutation is small. They updated the centers of the clusters incrementally whenever the mutation probability was small. The IGKA always performs well and converges to the global optima.

In [17], the authors used real number encoding to represent the chromosome for GA-based clustering. Here, the number of clusters is always fixed. Later, this algorithm was extended by [14] and called genetic clustering for unknown K (GCUK). Here, the number of clusters is not fixed, and the number of clusters increments with the updating of the algorithm. They proposed using the symbol # or "do not care" symbol to represent any empty cluster in the strings. Both algorithms implement the elitism strategy whereby the best chromosomes are preserved at each generation outside of the population to prevent them from being eliminated during the iteration process. Simulation results demonstrate that their algorithm outperforms the k-means. In the GCUK [14], the authors used the DB index to measure the validity of the clusters. These two algorithms used the Euclidean distance to calculate the distance from a point to a cluster center. The GCUK became the most effective GA clustering method, but due to the real number representation, it took a long time to converge [18]. Thus, in [18], the authors constructed a lookup table to store the distance between each pair of data points, which improved the evaluation of the fitness value in their algorithm. In GCUK [14] and GAs clustering by [17], the string representation was used to encode the variable number of cluster centers, while [18] used the binary representation. The algorithm in [18] performed better than the GCUK in terms of validity and time efficiency. Here they used the Euclidean distance as the distance matrix and the DB index as the clustering validity metric.

3.3.3 GA-Based Data Clustering for Imbalanced Datasets

In a few studies, GA-based data clustering has also been used in the case of imbalanced datasets [31, 32]. Imbalanced datasets usually have two classes. A dataset is called imbalanced if the number of the representative of a class is much less than the number of the representative of the other class. Thus, there exist two classes; one is the majority class, and the other one is the minority class. Standard classification algorithms usually consider a balanced training set, and this problem affects the bias toward the majority class. The minority instances may be ignored by the standard clustering algorithm and may not be counted during the iteration process. Usually, the interest of the researchers is to find the relationships or the effect from the minority instances to the whole dataset. Therefore, this study will use the advantages of GAs to help with the imbalance scenario.

Both [31] and [32] have used fuzzy rules along with the GA to solve the imbalanced dataset problem. They both have used real-valued variables that were taken from a Down's syndrome problem dataset and imbalanced datasets from the database. Their simulation results showed that the implementation or the combination with GAs produced better results as compared to other classical imbalanced classification methods.

3.4 Proposed Model

In the GA, we have observed that every gene of an individual/chromosome may or may not play an important role in the fitness of it. In some cases for binary-encoded chromosomes, the genes having value 0 have no importance with respect to their fitness. Considering this fact in the proposed approach, we have introduced a concept of vital genes. The motive of the proposed work is not to update the value of one or more genes of a particular parent chromosome during a crossover operation.

Let us explain the proposed work in detail with all the GA operators in it. First, we have used the roulette wheel selection method for the selection of the parent chromosomes in the population. For the crossover operation, we have performed a position-based crossover technique along with some adaptiveness. Here, in the proposed work, we called this modified crossover technique adaptive position-based crossover (APBC). In APBC, initially, we have selected one gene at random from each parent chromosome and marked it as a vital gene. The selection of a vital gene for a particular parent chromosome is done as follows.

Locate the index of a vital gene of the selected parent chromosome $= m\%c$ where m is a random number and c is the number of genes in a particular chromosome. During crossover, we have introduced two terms: (i) apparent fitness and (ii) vital gene. They are defined as follows:

1) While exchanging the genes between two parent chromosomes following left to right associativity, at each cross-site (crossover location) the value of fitness is changed from its previous value. We termed this change in fitness value apparent fitness.
2) Sometimes the value of one or more genes of a particular chromosome is not to be updated. We termed this type of gene the vital gene.

During crossover, to form offspring, the location of the vital gene is kept unchanged, whereas for the cross-site the remaining positions are considered one by one. One of the two approaches is considered stochastically in the proposed work. These two approaches are as follows:

1) One gene from parent 2 is selected at random and is used to replace the gene under consideration in the cross-site in parent 1 and vice versa.
2) For the creation of offspring 1 from parent 1, one gene from parent 2 is selected at random. Then, some arithmetic operations are performed on it using the gene under consideration in the cross-site in parent 1. Finally, the updated gene is used to replace the gene under consideration in the cross-site in parent 1. The same process is followed for the creation of offspring 2 from parent 2.

In the proposed approach, the apparent fitness is computed to check whether it is greater than the previous fitness or not. The crossover operation is stopped if the apparent fitness is greater than the previous fitness. Otherwise, the crossover operation continues for all the genes under the cross-site. Here, one gene is selected at random from the genes of another parent and placed in the cross-site of the parent under consideration.

While generating the offspring chromosomes from the parent's chromosomes, we need to take care of the duplicate offspring generation. Hamming distance (HD), a distance metric, is used to check whether there are any duplicate entries in the offspring generation or not [33]. In [33], they have used HD between two chromosomes C_i and C_j as in Eqn. (3.2).

$$HD(C_i, C_j) = \sum_{k=1}^{m} d(C_{ik}, C_{jk}), \tag{3.2}$$

where $C_i = C_{i_1}, C_{i_2}, \cdots, C_{i_m}$ and $C_j = C_{j_1}, C_{j_2}, \cdots, C_{j_m}$ are two chromosomes within a population with length m, and where $d(C_{i_k}, C_{j_k}) = 1$ if $C_{i_k} = C_{j_k}$ and 0 otherwise. In the proposed work, HD between newly formed offspring and each existing offspring chromosomes already in the population set for the next generation is computed to check if there is a duplicate entry in offspring set or not. If there is a duplicate entry in the offspring set, then one of the vital genes of the new offspring is swapped with the nonvital gene by keeping change in the fitness function to as minimum as possible. Finally, for the mutation operation, we have used the swap mutation technique.

In the proposed work, a set of centroids is represented as a chromosome where the number of clusters is equal to the number of genes for a chromosome. Here, the initial centroids are selected from a set of data points given. The distance is calculated by using the Euclidean distance. This experiment has been done with 2, 4 and 20 clusters, and all the data points are two dimensional. The proposed algorithm is given in Algorithm 1, and the flowcharts of the proposed algorithm are given in Figures 3.1, 3.2, and 3.3, respectively.

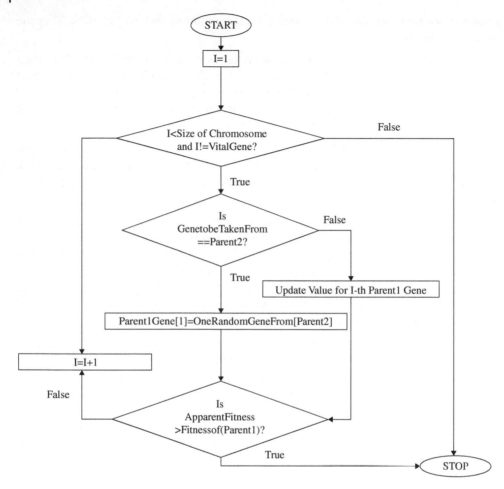

Figure 3.1 Flowchart for performing crossover for parent 1.

3.5 Experimentation

3.5.1 Experimental Settings

In this proposed work, we have performed experimentation on two synthetic datasets named as data1 and data2 and one real-life perfume dataset. Each data sample of these three datasets is two-dimensional. Here, the number of clusters is considered as two for data1 and four for data2 and twenty for the perfume dataset. Data1 has 38 data samples, which are represented in Table 3.1. For the generation of data2, we have taken 150 samples from each of the four clusters. For class 1, we have randomly generated 150 samples considering center $= (1, 2)$ and radius $= 3$. Similarly, for class 2, we have considered center $= (7, 3)$ and radius $= 2$. For class 3, we have considered center $= (15, 5)$ and radius $= 4$. For class 4, we have considered center $= (22, 4)$ and radius $= 5$. Because of the limitation of the page, we have not provided actual values for data 2. We have used the real-life

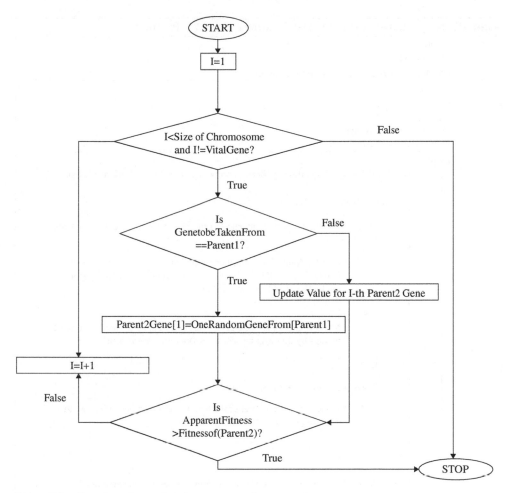

Figure 3.2 Flowchart for performing crossover for parent 2.

perfume dataset from the UCI repository [34]. The proposed algorithm is implemented with the help of the Java NetBeans software package. The experiment has been performed on a standard desktop environment of Intel Core-i3 chip that is running at 2.00 GHz. For evaluation purposes, the crossover probability (pc) is considered as 0.9, and the mutation probability (mc) is considered as 0.1.

3.5.2 DB Index

One of the well-known metrics for evaluating clustering algorithms is the Davies-Bouldin index, or DBI [35]. It is defined as a ratio of intra-cluster distance and inter-cluster distance. A detailed definition of the DB index as follows.

If the number of clusters is N, then

$$DB\ index = 1/N \sum_{i=1}^{N} D_i \qquad (3.3)$$

Algorithm 1 Adaptive Position Based Crossover (Parent 1, Parent 2)

Input: SD=Set of Data Points CS=Total Number of Gene in a chromosome
Output: OF1=Offspring 1 OF2=Offspring 2 OFit1=Fitness of Offspring 1 OFit2=Fitness of Offspring2

Begin
  MarkVitalGene()/*Any arbitrary location on both parents has to mark as vital gene */
  For i=0 to CS and i!=vitalgene
 	
    IfReplaceWithAnotherParentGene /* gene from another parent has to take to replace*/
 	
      R1=RandomlyTakenAnotherParentGene
      Parent_i_gene=R1 /*i-th gene of this parent is replaced by gene randomly taken from another parent*/
 	
    Else
      ModifyGenValPar/* the gene value of i-th gene of this parent has to modify by doing some arithmetic operation at random*/
    End
 	
    If ApparentFitness>Fitness(Parent)
      StopCrossoverForParent/*the loop has to break because more fit offspring has been found*/
    End
  End
  Return_Better_Offspring /* fitness of two offspring formed is compared and better offspring is returned*/
End

where

$$D_i = \max_{j \neq i} \frac{S_i + S_j}{M_{i,j}}$$

Here, $M_{i,j} = ||A_i - A_j||_p = (\sum_{k=1}^{n} |a_{k,i} - a_{k,j}|^p)^{(1/p)}$

And, $S_i = (1/T_i \sum_{j=1}^{T_j} |X_j - A_i|^p)^{(1/p)}$

The parameters are defined as follows:

1) $M_{i,j}$ is a measure of separation between cluster C_i and cluster C_j
2) S_i is a measure of scatter within a cluster
3) A_i is the centroid of C_i, and A_j is the centroid of C_j

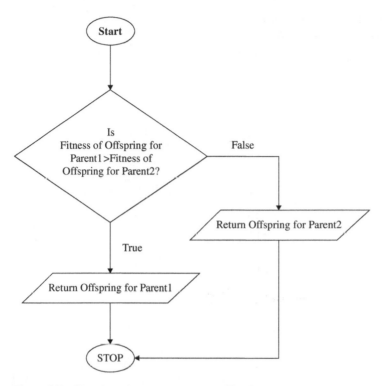

Figure 3.3 Flowchart for selecting better offspring.

4) T_j is the size of cluster j, and X_j is an n-dimensional feature vector assigned to cluster C_j
5) $a_{k,i}$ is the kth element of A_i

The performance of the genetic algorithm is measured by its fitness value. In this proposed work, the DB index has been used as the fitness function.

3.5.3 Experimental Results

In this proposed work, a new crossover technique called the adaptive position–based crossover has been proposed, and its performance has been compared with two traditional crossover techniques: one-point crossover [36] and arithmetic crossover [37]. The fitness value of all the algorithms is calculated by measuring the DB index. The experimental results of all the algorithms corresponding to the data1, data2, and perfume datasets are shown in Table 3.2, Table 3.3, and Table 3.4, respectively. The bold entries in Table 3.2, Table 3.3, and Table 3.4 are the best-performing results in the corresponding tables. The bar charts for the results given in Table 3.2 are shown in Figures 3.4 to 3.6. The bar charts for results given in Table 3.3 are shown from Figures 3.7 to 3.9. The bar charts for results given in Table 3.4 are shown from Figures 3.10 to 3.12. From the experimental results it has been observed that the overall clustering technique has been improved by applying the proposed crossover in the genetic algorithm.

Table 3.1 Tabular representation for values of data1

X Coordinate	Y Coordinate
1	1
1.1	1.2
1.5	2.1
2	1.7
1.4	1.7
1.8	2.4
1.7	2.1
2.1	2.6
−1	−1.5
−1.2	−2.1
−2	−1.7
−2.2	−2.2
−3.5	−2.7
−1.7	−2.5
−2.2	−1.1
−2.3	−2.1
−1.6	−1.2
−3.5	−2.7
−1	1.5
−1.2	2.1
−2	1.7
−2.2	2.2
−3.5	2.7
−1.7	2.5
−2.2	1.1
−2.3	2.1
−1.6	1.2
−3.5	2.7
1	−1.5
1.2	−2.1
2	−1.7
2.2	−2.2
3.5	−2.7
1.7	−2.5
2.2	−1.1
2.3	−2.1
1.6	−1.2
3.5	−2.7

Table 3.2 Comparison of one-point and arithmetic crossover with proposed work for data1 with two clusters

Datasets	# Clusters	# Populations	# Iterations	Type of Crossover	Intra-Cluster Distance	Inter-Cluster Distance	Fitness (DB Index)
Data1	2	50	60	One Point	2.621	3.529	0.743
				Arithmetic	2.789	3.525	0.791
				Proposed	2.314	3.187	**0.726**
		50	80	One Point	2.438	3.340	0.730
				Arithmetic	2.347	3.171	0.740
				Proposed	2.494	3.470	**0.719**
		50	150	One Point	2.569	3.566	0.720
				Arithmetic	2.280	2.943	0.775
				Proposed	2.449	3.445	**0.711**

Table 3.3 Comparison of one-point and arithmetic crossover with proposed work for data2 with four clusters

Datasets	# Clusters	# Populations	# Iterations	Type of Crossover	Intra-Cluster Distance	Inter-Cluster Distance	Fitness (DB Index)
Data2	4	50	60	One Point	3.124	11.398	0.274
				Arithmetic	3.416	10.999	0.311
				Proposed	2.869	10.734	**0.267**
		50	80	One Point	3.299	11.741	0.281
				Arithmetic	3.181	10.201	0.312
				Proposed	3.0401	11.451	**0.265**
		50	150	One Point	3.273	12.112	0.270
				Arithmetic	3.278	12.049	0.272
				Proposed	2.819	11.110	**0.254**

3.6 Conclusion

In this chapter, a new crossover was proposed that is adaptive and position-based crossover. From the simulation results, it was observed that it improves the convergence rate of the GA, which in consequence improves the time efficiency of the data clustering of the GA-based algorithms. According to [3], k-means clustering is a well-known data clustering algorithm that is used in this literature. Here, this proposed algorithm has been used to solve the data clustering problem based on k-means algorithm. The simulation results also demonstrate that the proposed algorithm outperforms the other two GA-based data clustering algorithms.

Table 3.4 Comparison of one-point and arithmetic crossover with proposed work for perfume dataset with 20 clusters

Datasets	# Clusters	# Populations	# Iterations	Type of Crossover	Intra-Cluster Distance	Inter-Cluster Distance	Fitness (DB Index)
Perfume	20	50	60	One Point	5.971	387.811	0.0154
				Arithmetic	8.765	338.253	0.026
				Proposed	5.185	408.502	**0.013**
		50	80	One Point	4.299	341.525	0.013
				Arithmetic	7.376	316.087	0.023
				Proposed	3.849	392.966	**0.010**
		50	150	One Point	4.014	333.356	0.012
				Arithmetic	9.042	314.802	0.029
				Proposed	4.278	397.247	**0.011**

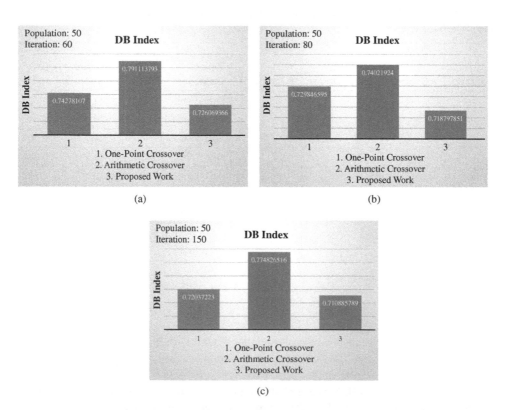

(a)   (b)

(c)

Figure 3.4 Bar chart for DB Index for Table 3.2, where the number of clusters=2 and (a) population=50 and number of iterations=60, (b) population=50 and number of iterations=80, (c) population=50 and number of iterations=150 respectively.

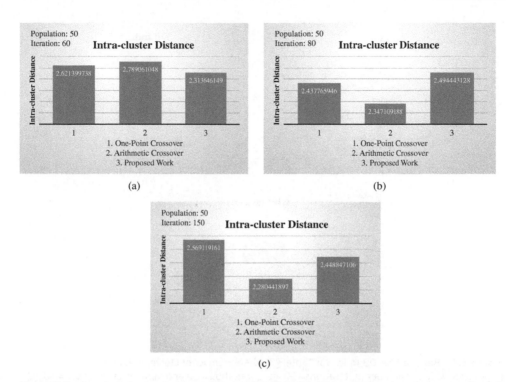

Figure 3.5 Bar chart for intra-cluster distance for Table 3.2, where the number of clusters=2, and (a) population=50 and number of iterations=60, (b) population=50 and number of iterations=80, (c) population=50 and number of iterations=150 respectively.

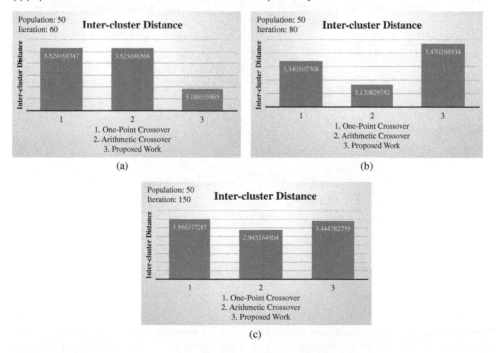

Figure 3.6 Bar chart for inter-cluster distance for Table 3.2, where the number of clusters=2, and (a) population=50 and number of iterations=60, (b) population= 50 and number of iterations=80, (c) population= 50 and number of iterations=150 respectively.

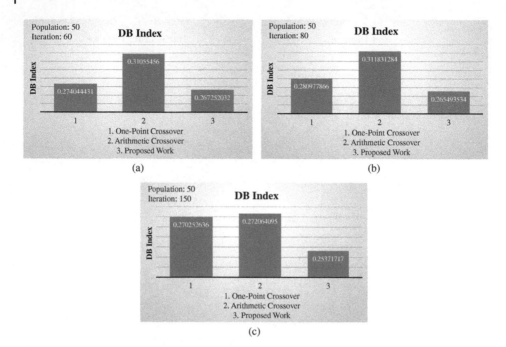

Figure 3.7 Bar chart for DB Index for Table 3.3 where number of clusters=4, and (a) population=50 and number of iterations=60, (b) population= 50 and number of iterations=80, (c) population=50 and number of iterations=150 respectively.

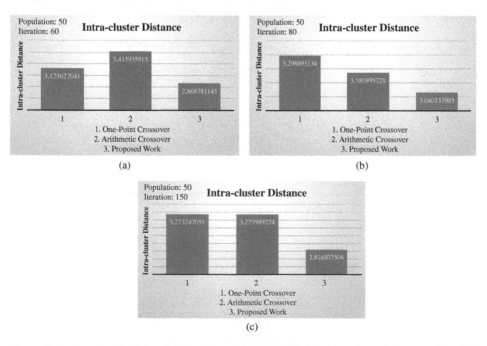

Figure 3.8 Bar chart for intra-cluster distance for Table 3.3 where number of clusters=4, and (a) population=50 and number of iterations=60, (b) population=50 and number of iterations=80, (c) population=50 and number of iterations=150 respectively.

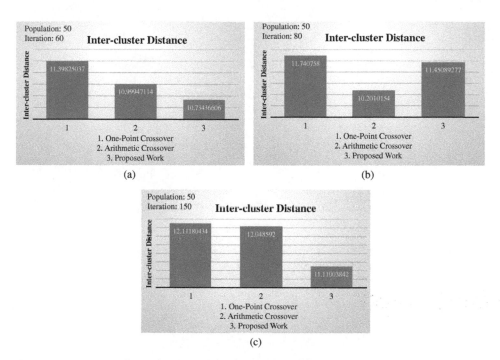

Figure 3.9 Bar chart for inter-cluster distance for Table 3.3 where number of clusters=4, and (a) population=50 and number of iterations=60, (b) population=50 and number of iterations=80, (c) population=50 and number of iterations=150 respectively.

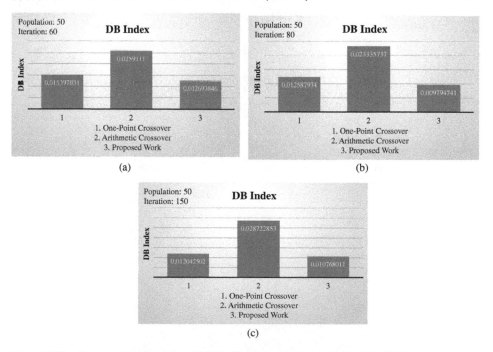

Figure 3.10 Bar chart for DB Index for Table 3.4 where number of clusters=20, and (a) population=50 and number of iterations=60, (b) population=50 and number of iterations=80, (c) population=50 and number of iterations=150 respectively.

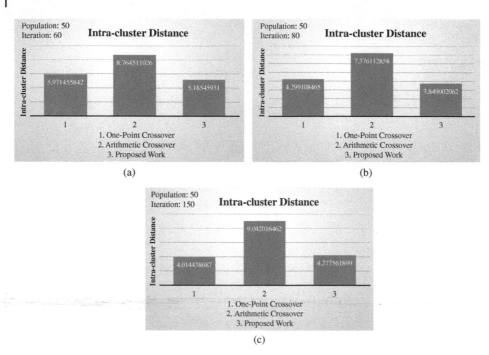

Figure 3.11 Bar chart for intra-cluster distance for Table 3.4 where number of clusters=20, and (a) population=50 and number of iterations=60, (b) population=50 and number of iterations=80, (c) population=50 and number of iterations=150 respectively.

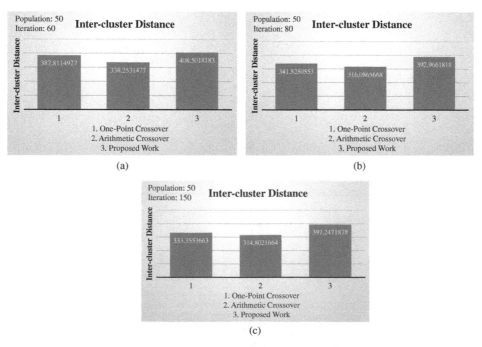

Figure 3.12 Bar chart for inter-cluster distance for Table 3.4 where number of clusters=20, and (a) population=50 and number of iterations=60, (b) population=50 and number of iterations=80, (c) population=50 and number of iterations=150 respectively.

In the future, the implementation of the data clustering algorithm using fuzzy *c*-means (FCM) clustering will be tried, and thus the fuzzy concepts in this proposed algorithm will be incorporated.

References

1 Hruschka, E.R., Campello, R.J., Freitas, A.A. et al. (2009) A survey of evolutionary algorithms for clustering. *IEEE Transactions on Systems, Man, and Cybernetics, Part C (Applications and Reviews)*, **39** (2), 133–155.

2 MacQueen, J. et al. (1967) Some methods for classification and analysis of multivariate observations, in *Proceedings of the fifth Berkeley symposium on mathematical statistics and probability*, vol. 1, Oakland, CA, USA, vol. 1, pp. 281–297.

3 Jain, A.K. (2010) Data clustering: 50 years beyond k-means. *Pattern recognition letters*, **31** (8), 651–666.

4 Saharan, S. and Baragona, R. (2013) A new genetic algorithm for clustering binary data with application to traffic road accidents in christchurch. *Far East J Theor Stat*, **45**, 67–89.

5 Jain, A.K., Murty, M.N., and Flynn, P.J. (1999) Data clustering: a review. *ACM computing surveys (CSUR)*, **31** (3), 264–323.

6 Ordonez, C. (2003) Clustering binary data streams with k-means, in *Proceedings of the 8th ACM SIGMOD workshop on Research issues in data mining and knowledge discovery*, ACM, pp. 12–19.

7 Pham, D.T., Dimov, S.S., and Nguyen, C. (2004) An incremental k-means algorithm. *Proceedings of the Institution of Mechanical Engineers, Part C: Journal of Mechanical Engineering Science*, **218** (7), 783–795.

8 Lu, Y., Lu, S., Fotouhi, F., Deng, Y., and Brown, S.J. (2004) Incremental genetic k-means algorithm and its application in gene expression data analysis. *BMC bioinformatics*, **5** (1), 172.

9 Chakraborty, S. and Nagwani, N. (2011) Analysis and study of incremental k-means clustering algorithm, in *International Conference on High Performance Architecture and Grid Computing*, Springer, pp. 338–341.

10 Mitchell, M. (1998) *An introduction to genetic algorithms*, MIT press.

11 Carr, J. (2014) An introduction to genetic algorithms. *Senior Project*, **1** (40), 7.

12 Godberg, D.E. (1989) Genetic algorithms in search. *Optimization, and Machine Learning*.

13 Mitchell, M. (1995) Genetic algorithms: An overview. *Complexity*, **1** (1), 31–39.

14 Bandyopadhyay, S. and Maulik, U. (2002) Genetic clustering for automatic evolution of clusters and application to image classification. *Pattern recognition*, **35** (6), 1197–1208.

15 Arunprasath, S., Chandrasekar, S., Venkatalakshmi, K., and Shalinie, S.M. (2010) Classification of remote sensed image using rapid genetic k-means algorithm, in *2010 International Conference on Communication Control and Computing Technologies*, IEEE, pp. 677–682.

16 Belahbib, F.Z.B. and Souami, F. (2011) Genetic algorithm clustering for color image quantization, in *3rd European Workshop on Visual Information Processing*, IEEE, pp. 83–87.

17 Maulik, U. and Bandyopadhyay, S. (2000) Genetic algorithm-based clustering technique. *Pattern recognition*, **33** (9), 1455–1465.

18 Lin, H.J., Yang, F.W., and Kao, Y.T. (2005) An efficient ga-based clustering technique. *Tamkang Journal of science and Engineering*, **8** (2), 113.

19 Cole, R.M. (1998) *Clustering with genetic algorithms*, University of Western Australia.

20 Krishna, K. and Murty, N.M. (1999) Genetic k-means algorithm. *IEEE Transactions on Systems Man And Cybernetics-Part B: Cybernetics*, **29** (3), 433–439.

21 Syswerda, G. (1991) Scheduling optimization using genetic algorithms. *Handbook of genetic algorithms*.

22 Tseng, L.Y. and Yang, S.B. (1997) Genetic algorithms for clustering, feature selection and classification, in *Proceedings of International Conference on Neural Networks (ICNN'97)*, vol. 3, IEEE, vol. 3, pp. 1612–1616.

23 Nasraoui, O. and Krishnapuram, R. (2000) A novel approach to unsupervised robust clustering using genetic niching, in *Ninth IEEE International Conference on Fuzzy Systems. FUZZ-IEEE 2000 (Cat. No. 00CH37063)*, vol. 1, IEEE, vol. 1, pp. 170–175.

24 Casillas, A., De Lena, M.G., and Martínez, R. (2003) Document clustering into an unknown number of clusters using a genetic algorithm, in *International Conference on Text, Speech and Dialogue*, Springer, pp. 43–49.

25 Pan, S.M. and Cheng, K.S. (2007) Evolution-based tabu search approach to automatic clustering. *IEEE Transactions on Systems, Man, and Cybernetics, Part C (Applications and Reviews)*, **37** (5), 827–838.

26 Fränti, P., Kivijärvi, J., Kaukoranta, T., and Nevalainen, O. (1997) Genetic algorithms for large-scale clustering problems. *The Computer Journal*, **40** (9), 547–554.

27 Leon, E., Nasraoui, O., and Gomez, J. (2006) Ecsago: evolutionary clustering with self adaptive genetic operators, in *2006 IEEE International Conference on Evolutionary Computation*, IEEE, pp. 1768–1775.

28 Wu, S., Yin, S., and Li, M. (2012) A new approach for clustering problem based on binary small world optimization algorithms, in *2012 IEEE International Conference on Computer Science and Automation Engineering (CSAE)*, vol. 3, IEEE, vol. 3, pp. 412–416.

29 Kwedlo, W. and Iwanowicz, P. (2010) Using genetic algorithm for selection of initial cluster centers for the k-means method, in *International Conference on Artificial Intelligence and Soft Computing*, Springer, pp. 165–172.

30 Lu, Y., Lu, S., Fotouhi, F., Deng, Y., and Brown, S.J. (2004) Fgka: A fast genetic k-means clustering algorithm, in *Proceedings of the 2004 ACM symposium on Applied computing*, ACM, pp. 622–623.

31 Soler, V. and Prim, M. (2009) Extracting a fuzzy system by using genetic algorithms for imbalanced datasets classification: application on downs syndrome detection, in *Mining Complex Data*, Springer, pp. 23–39.

32 Villar, P., Fernandez, A., Carrasco, R.A., and Herrera, F. (2012) Feature selection and granularity learning in genetic fuzzy rule-based classification systems for highly imbalanced data-sets. *International Journal of Uncertainty, Fuzziness and Knowledge-Based Systems*, **20** (03), 369–397.

33 Jalali Varnamkhasti, M., Lee, L.S., Abu Bakar, M.R., and Leong, W.J. (2012) A genetic algorithm with fuzzy crossover operator and probability. *Advances in Operations Research*, **2012**.

34 Lichman, M. (2013), UCI machine learning repository. URL http://archive.ics.uci.edu/ml.

35 Davies, D.L. and Bouldin, D.W. (1979) A cluster separation measure. *IEEE transactions on pattern analysis and machine intelligence*, (2), 224–227.

36 Nomura, T. (1997) An analysis on crossovers for real number chromosomes in an infinite population size, in *IJCAI (2)*, pp. 936–941.

37 Tomasz, D.G. (2006) *Genetic algorithms reference*, Tomasz Gwiazda.

4

Application of Machine Learning in the Social Network

Belfin R. V.[1], E. Grace Mary Kanaga[1], and Suman Kundu[2,3]

[1]*Department of Computer Science and Engineering, Karunya Institute of Technology and Sciences, Coimbatore, India*
[2]*Department of Computer Science and Engineering, Indian Institute of Technology, Jodhpur, India*
[3]*Department of Computational Intelligence, Wroclaw University of Science and Technology, Wroclaw, Poland*

4.1 Introduction

Social media platforms have become an integral part of day-to-day life for a majority of the world's internet users. People tend to get more erudition from social media. Apart from information, people can create content for social media to showcase their skills. An example is the video resume, which professionals create and publish on social media to show their presence. Content can take different forms such as images, text, emoticons, and videos. Since there are not many limits on content creation on social media, users generate a massive amount of data that shows all the characteristics of big data. This data can be used for different analytical and predictive applications for business. Selling data through APIs for business and educational purposes is also a business for many data giants. Structural Query Language is not sufficient to mine information from big data. It needs complex statistical and machine learning (ML) approaches to glean information from this massive data. The chapter provides a survey of different metaheuristic machine learning algorithms used for various interesting research problems in the domain of social networks and big data.

4.1.1 Social Media

A critical entity of the World Wide Web is social media, which comes in different forms including social blogs, forums, professional networks, picture sharing applications, social gaming sites, chatting applications, and most importantly social networks. Social media is mighty in the sense that estimates predict we will reach 3.02 billion monthly active social media users by 2021. A forecast by Statista.com (2018) shows that China alone will have 750 million users by 2022 and India will have one-third of a billion users. On average, internet users worldwide spend 135 minutes surfing social media. This user density has resulting in marketers promoting their products on social media in a new field named social media marketing or social digital media advertising. Recently, there has been a complete transformation in the usage of social networking sites, switching from being used on personal

Recent Advances in Hybrid Metaheuristics for Data Clustering, First Edition.
Edited by Sourav De, Sandip Dey, and Siddhartha Bhattacharyya.
© 2020 John Wiley & Sons Ltd. Published 2020 by John Wiley & Sons Ltd.

computers to now being used more often on mobile devices. The social networking giants like Facebook, Twitter, and many others give away their mobile applications to customers. There are even location-based microblogging and many other services offered to their customers through mobile applications.

4.1.2 Big Data

The amount of data generated by social networks and social media is unimaginable. It covers all four significant features of big data, the so-called 4V's. The 4V's are volume, velocity, variety, and veracity, and when present in generated social media data, the analysis on the data becomes complex. Leaving the complex data unused is not a wise decision for the technology giants. These social media organizations have started analyzing this generated data to give better prospects to their users. The users using these features are happy and excited to see applications built on their data. The application users can personalize it and share the personalized content with their friends on social media. To leverage the content generated on social media, branding and advertising departments of the top companies create marketing plans and budgets accordingly. These companies also need to understand the outcome of their advertisements, the preference of their customers, and even the negative reviews. Since the amount of data is enormous, it is impossible to do the analysis manually. Information from the historical transactions and social media data is not enough for the top officials to decide on their future goals. The organizations have to stay ahead of the competitors. Machine learning models come to the rescue to help top management make decisions.

4.1.3 Machine Learning

Machine learning and AI are the important concepts in the current scenario. Much of the human work will be replaced by machines. For example, in the future, bots will replace most of the humans in the armed forces of a country. Restaurants can replace the waiters with AI bots. Bots in restaurants are available in a few restaurants in now. There are machine learning approaches that can teach the bots to understand the environment and act accordingly. Classification, clustering, regression, and deep learning are some of the models in machine learning.

As shown in Figure 4.1 the machine learning algorithms can be divided into four types, namely, supervised learning, unsupervised learning, semisupervised learning, and

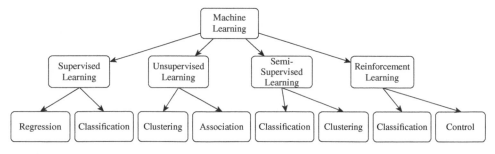

Figure 4.1 Classification of machine learning algorithms

reinforcement learning. Supervised learning algorithms are used when the target variable is continuous and categorical. Some use cases for supervised learning are regression analysis for housing price prediction and the classification of medical images. Unsupervised learning algorithms are used when there is no target variable. Clustering in marketing data for customer segmentation and market basket analysis or association rule mining of a supermarket transaction data are the use cases of unsupervised learning algorithms. Semisupervised algorithms can be used when the target variable in the data is categorical. The text classification of news data and lane finding in GPS data using clustering are some of the use cases of semisupervised learning algorithms. Reinforcement learning is an advanced level of learning algorithm that learns the environment and acts accordingly. Reinforcement learning can be implemented in the data when the target variable in the data is categorical or there is no target variable. The use cases for reinforcement learning are driver-less cars and optimizing the marketing cost of a business.

4.1.4 Natural Language Processing (NLP)

The amount of content generated by the users of social media is exponentially increasing. The text data cannot be processed by a machine efficiently like with other formats of data. A machine needs to understand human slang and language to analyze the text content. Natural language processing (NLP) helps machines understand human slang and language in the text content generated on social media. The flow of content from social media to a big data storage system and the analysis by ML and NLP are illustrated in Figure 4.2.

In recent times, machine learning and artificial intelligence play a vital role in engaging millions of social media users. Recent studies show that customers are more loyal to the companies that respond to them promptly. Bots or machine learning programs automatically understand the customers' queries using NLP and respond to them then and there. This advancement helps companies retain their customers and build stronger relationships with them. The basic model of a social media chatbot is illustrated in Figure 4.3.

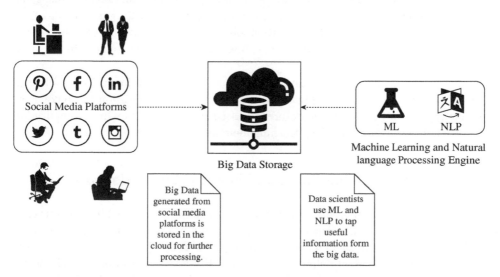

Figure 4.2 Workflow of big data, machine learning, and social media

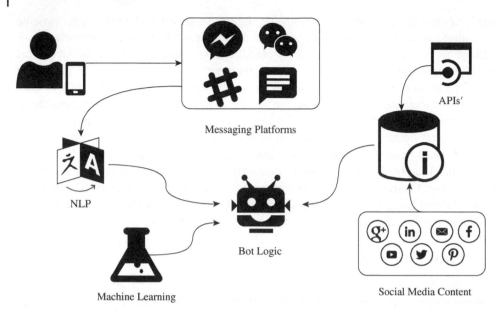

Figure 4.3 Chatbot schematic diagram

4.1.5 Social Network Analysis

Social network analysis (SNA) is a method of analyzing social relationships usually with the concepts of networks and graph theory. In SNA the social actors are usually denoted with nodes, and the relationships are denoted with edges of the graph. There are different variants in these networks like directed, undirected, and weighted networks. In recent times there have been multilayer representations to represent complex social structures. Although graph theories were at the forefront of social network analysis (Belfin et al., 2018; Belfin and Grace Mary Kanaga, 2018), there were attempts to use other theories like game theory (Narayanam and Narahari, 2011) and granular computing (Kundu and Pal, 2015a; Pal and Kundu, 2017; Kundu and Pal, 2018) to solve social network issues. This chapter is a summary of the various applications and machine learning methods available in the social network and big data literature.

This chapter has compiled classification methods and applications in section 4.2 followed by the clustering methods and applications in Section 4.3. The regression-based concepts and their application in social networks are discussed in Section 4.4. Finally, the application of evolutionary algorithms and deep learning methods are discussed in the section 4.5.

4.2 Application of Classification Models in Social Networks

Classification divides whole content in to chunks of related content. Machine learning classification is done on date that has labels associated with it. For instance, say a user has a massive number of emails in an inbox. Classifying those emails based on topics like work, promotions, and social might help the user to prioritize his work. In this example, work, social, and promotions are the labels. This process is similar to placing colored balls in the right baskets with similarly colored balls. In social networks, there are several applications where classification concepts are instrumental. This following section gives several applications, such as spam content classification, labeling data available in an online social network, medical data classification, human behavior analysis, and sentiment analysis given in the literature. The summary of the application of classification algorithm in social media has been given in the Table 4.1.

4.2.1 Spam Content Detection

The digital age has resulted in lots of strategies for businesses to market their products and pump lots of money into their digital marketing. These marketing strategies have generated lots of promotional content dispersed across social media. Most of the content that reaches users is irrelevant to them. Separating relevant user information from the irrelevant information is called spam content classification. Benevenuto et al. (2009) identifies spam users who spread impure information on YouTube using real YouTube users and content. Zhu et al. (2012) proposed a method for spam content classification to solve the problems in content and topology-based classification models. The data for the experiment was taken from China's largest social network, Renren.com. A work by Ahmed and Abulaish (2013) proposed a statistical method to analyze and filter spam content in Facebook and Twitter data. The algorithm proposed generates 14 generic statistical features to detect a user who spreads spam content.

Gender classification in social media data is an important aspect for law enforcement, target advertising, and other social-related problems. Alowibdi et al. (2013) proposed an algorithm for classifying profiles as male and female profiles. The algorithm used five features to classify the gender. The features may be the color of the profile background picture or the set of text used to post the content on social media. Li and Xu (2014) introduced a rule-based classification system based on sociology concepts to identify and label emotions in microblog posts. They used Chinese microblog post data for the experiment. SPADE Wang et al. (2014) is a social media classifier that classifies spam and useful messages across a social network. The proposed method is a generic solution for multiple social networks using cross-domain and associative classification. Bots in a social network create unrealistic text and spread false information. The classification of human accounts and bot accounts has been designed by Igawa et al. (2016). They use random forests and multi-layer perceptron classifiers to test their model in a set of scraped data related to the 2014 FIFA world cup. Tacchini et al. (2017) proposed a work that focuses on misinformation detection in social networks. They used Facebook posts as the data for their experiment. This method uses logistic regression and a Boolean crowd sourcing algorithm to build the classifier model.

4.2.2 Topic Modeling and Labeling

Topic modeling (TM) is one of the crucial areas of research in big data analytics. TM is a process where the text content in the extensive data is summarized into specific groups. An example of this method is the grouping of news content into sports, economics, and politics. This section contains a brief discussion of the literature available in topic modeling

Table 4.1 Summary Classification Applications

Reference	Problem	Dataset	Data Type	Classification Type
Ye et al. (2011)	Text annotation	Facebook check-in data	Human/Social	Binary support vector machine (SVM) classifier
Song et al. (2013)	Personalized recommendation	Sina Weibo	Human/Social	Gradient descent learning
Batool et al. (2013)	Synonym and knowledge enhancement	Twitter data	Human/Social	Domain-specific learning
Ahmed and Abulaish (2013)	Spam filtering	Facebook and Twitter data	Human/Social	Nave Bayes, Jrip, and J48
Akaichi (2013)	Complexities in conveyed texts	Facebook status data	Human/Social	Support vector machine (SVM) and naive Bayes
Li et al. (2014)	All traditional models use statistical methods	Chinese micro-blog posts	Human/Social	Rule based
Vázquez et al. (2014)	Costly sentiment analysis	English and Spanish social media data	Human/Social	Rule based
Lima and de Castro (2014)	Omission of social media metadata	Twitter data	Human/Social	Nave Bayes, SVM, multilayer perceptron neural network
(Yang, Kiang, and Shang 2015)	Adverse drug reactions (ADRs)	Medhelp website	Web text data	Latent Dirichlet allocation modeling
Igawa et al. (2016)	Text bots	2014 FIFA World Cup data	Web text data	Random forests and multilayer perceptrons
Tacchini et al. (2017)	Misinformation classifier	Facebook data	Human/social	Logistic regression
Bayot and Gonçalves (2018)	Gender classification	Adience for age and gender	Human/social	Deep CNN

and labeling in social network data. Tuulos and Tirri (2004) used social network chat room data. They tried to break up the dynamic nature of the chat data and model it into topics. Location annotation is a critical method to group locations. Ye et al. (2011) uses a support vector machine (SVM) classifier method to annotate and tag locations. Finally, it categorizes the location as various categories. SocioDim by Tang and Liu (2011) works on the classification model for social media by considering the heterogeneity of the social network. Wanichayapong et al. (2011) worked on topic modeling with traffic congestion data from social media and broke it into two categories such as point and link. McAuley and Leskovec (2012) tried to find the inter-dependencies between the images considering the metadata of the images on social media. They also considered the social community of the user who created the content below the image: the data for the work generated from the comments section below the image and the person who uploaded the image and his friends' networks. In addition, social media users add their dining, shopping, and other preferences on social media. This generated content can help marketing experts recommend products to the users. The approach in Song et al. (2013) is an iterative learning-based classifier that learns each user's content and classifies them in different user buckets. The algorithm also understands the user's friends content and provides a personalized recommendation. Customer churn prediction is another important aspect in business. Churn analysis will forecast the loyalty of customers. Verbeke et al. (2014) used real telecommunication datasets to predict customer churn. The algorithm uses a combination of relational and nonrelational classification models to predict the churn. Emails are an important part of everyone's professional life. Classification in emails can be done to separate spam emails from the critical emails and to classify the subject of the mail content. Alsmadi and Alhami (2015) proposed a method using n-grams to classify spam emails in English and Arabic. Nowadays many users of the internet have accounts on multiple online social network sites. The work in Peled et al. (2016) developed a classifier to match the entities between online social network accounts. They used the data collected from Facebook and Xing to experiment with their classifier. Himelboim et al. (2017) classifies Twitter tweets by using the information in the text and the patterns visible in the network. The authors used the density, modularity, centrality, and the faction of independent users in the network to build the classification model. The previous works are centered around the users and not on the entire network structure. Adverse drug reactions are considered to be one of the determinants of mortality in the medical field. The work in Yang et al. (2015) classifies the experiences shared by doctors and the victims on social media, micro-blogging sites, and forums. Finally, the data will be classified to form a drug reaction database.

4.2.3 Human Behavior Analysis

This type of classification methods analyzes the data and groups the users according to the user's behavior in online social networks. An example of this human behavior analysis is grouping the user's gender using their behavior in online social networks. This section will summarize state-of-the-art literature that classifies human behavior in social networks. Eleta and Golbeck (2014) classify patterns of communication on Twitter while considering its multilinguistic nature. The work resulted in understanding the global reach of social media and the flow of multilingual communication in social networks. This work also studied how multilinguistic users of Twitter mediate information sharing from a different language. User personality classification is an essential aspect for a criminology department and also for business. The work on user personality classification done by Lima and de Castro (2014) takes the group of text shared by the user and learns it using different machine learning approaches like naïve Bayes, support vector machine, and multilayer perception neural network. Bayot and Gonçalves (2018) classify the age and gender of the users in a social network using deep-convolutional neural networks (CNNs). Epilepsy is a brain disorder commonly correlated with abnormal cortical and subcortical functional networks. Zhang et al. (2011) use functional MRI data that is classified with the help of social network analysis theories to find this epilepsy.

4.2.4 Sentiment Analysis

Sentiment analysis classifies the users' emotions from the text they share on social media and microblogging sites. An example of this might be classifying the happy, neutral, and unhappy customers from the feedback data. This method aims to understand the content generated by the user and decide its emotion with computation or statistical methods. Web technology is the most significant technological advancement from the past decade. It changed the way people think and the way they purchase items. Lo and Potdar (2009) discussed opinion mining and sentiment analysis from the feedback data generated by users for e-commerce products. Batool et al. (2013) analyzed the Twitter data to understand the emotion of each tweet. The algorithm proposed includes a synonym binder module and a knowledge enhancement module to classify and summarize the tweets. Sentiment analysis and classification on Facebook status data was done by Akaichi (2013). This algorithm builds sentiment lexicons based on the emoticons, interjections, and acronyms to classify the sentiments in the status text. Vázquez et al. (2014) explains the recent trend among e-commerce customers to look at the feedback of other people to help them decide whether to buy the product. This work classifies the microblog posts based on the reviews posted by users. (Burnap et al., 2015) experimented with suicide-related communication using machine learning classification methods from the Twitter data. This proposed work classifies the text that refers to suicidal contents using the lexical, structural, emotive, and psychological features extracted from Twitter posts.

4.3 Application of Clustering Models in Social Networks

Clustering is the concept of automatically finding subgroups from massive data. In a social network the same idea can be called community detection. There are many related works that talk about community detection (Belfin et al., 2018), (Belfin and Grace Mary Kanaga, 2018) in social networks. Grouping methods can be utilized for many applications. One example of clustering a real graph data word's adjacency (Fortunato, 2010) is depicted in Figure 4.4. The dataset is the adjacency network of popular adjectives and nouns in the book *David Copperfield* by Charles Dickens. Some of the other applications of clustering mentioned in the literature are discussed next.

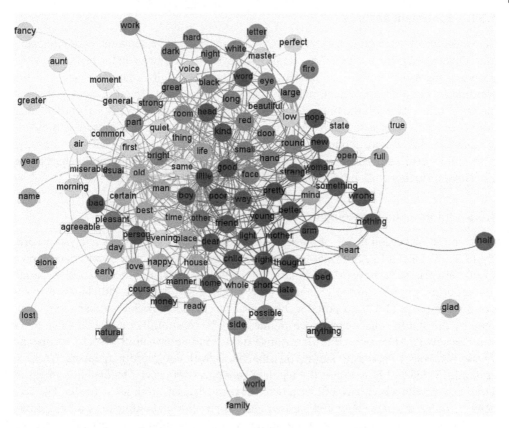

Figure 4.4 Clustering in the network data using a word adjacency dataset

4.3.1 Recommender Systems

More people are traveling today than ever before, and they often use recommendations from blogs and forums. Since one person generates the content on a microblogging site, the recommendations might not be the best for each traveler. The recommender system needs a learning engine that provides the best recommendation aggregated from the content of multiple travelers. Cenamor et al. (2017) designed a system that takes previous data, clusters it into a daily travel plan, and makes personalized recommendations to the user. Chen et al. (2017) proposed a new recommender system that suggests clustered urban functional areas with the help of collected building-level social media data. The proposed work was implemented in the Yuexiu District, Guangzhou, China with the K-values 2 and 4. These recommender systems can be used for urban planning for smart city projects. Feng et al. (2015) proposed a personalized movie recommender system that uses the community to recommend a movie. The community detection in the proposed work is done based on association rule mining. This recommender system was tested with the MovieLens and Netflix datasets.

4.3.2 Sentiment Analysis

Community detection plays a vital role in analyzing the effect of some real-world happenings. Ou et al. (2017) examined the emotion of an event that occurred in the real world—the proposed algorithm finds a community, detects the community emotion, aggregates the community emotion, and detects any community emotion burst. In other cases, most people are comfortable with the brand they use for a given product. Companies promote their brands on social media to build their customer base. The brand community will enable customers to know more about products and create a strong relationship with the customer base. Habibi et al. (2014) proposed a model for an overlapping brand community that creates a positive influence and brand trust among the customers.

4.3.3 Information Spreading or Promotion

Information dispersion is one of the significant areas in a social network analysis according to Shaji et al. (2018). Information dispersion learns about the flow of information on a social network. Social network information spreading is used in product promotion. Target marketing is an area where the marketing is targeted to a group of individuals or community. Johnston (2017) proposed a theoretical model where social media can be leveraged by the statutory agencies to communicate to the community on social media. Sitter and Curnew (2016) proposed an innovative model and described how social media can be used by social workers to share YouTube videos with community members. Croitoru et al. (2015) learned how to use the big data generated from social media after an event. Their experiment was carried out with two real-world datasets from social media. The data used includes the user-generated content and propagation data after the events Occupy Wall Street in November 2011 and the Boston Marathon bombing in April 2013. Alsmadi and Alhami (2015) proposed a method that clusters events on Twitter. The clustered events will be spread across communities. Schirr (2013) proposed a method for community-based learning and sharing educational information and curriculum development for classroom training. Zhou et al. (2012) claimed that social network communication is community specific and not individual specific. Zhou et al. proposed a method named COCOMP that shares a message with a community that is similar. Lakkaraju and Ajmera (2011) introduced a community-based application that predicts the reach of a brand or content in the future. Conover et al. (2011) experimented with the political affiliation of Twitter users using a hidden community structure. Ang (2011) proposed a model of a community with customer relationship management (CRM) data to use customers to build products. The model suggests the CRM phases as connect, converse, create, and collaborate. Ebner and Reinhardt (2009) proposed a method to build a scientific community using the Twitter community.

4.3.4 Geolocation-Specific Applications

Epidemiology is the area of learning about disease outbreaks and the spreading process. Community studies can help the health department to quickly find the epidemic and the path of a disease. Hossain et al. (2016) studied the 2014 Ebola outbreak in Africa and experimented with how a social media community study can help to defend the spreading proactively. Social media is an essential tool nowadays to report disasters, and social networks also support rescue teams in locating affected people and areas. Bakillah et al. (2015) proposed a method for geospatial clustering to spread information during a disastrous situation. The case study used for the work was Typhoon Haiyan in the Philippines, with data from Twitter. Geolocation applications are good to work on because they are location specific. Atzmanstorfer et al. (2014) proposed a citizen-oriented and location-aware spatial planning system. The social media users from the location-aware community can participate in the discussion and brainstorm and implement various planning and functional activities in and around their location. The case study used for this experiment was the participatory land-zoning process in the Capital District of Quito, Ecuador.

4.4 Application of Regression Models in Social Networks

Regression is a well-known machine learning technique used for finding relationships between independent and dependent variables in data. With people's lives intertwined with social networks, it is obvious that human emotions, behaviors, and sentiments will depend their personal and organizational social networks. Over the past few years scientists have been trying to figure out how one's social network affects their personal behaviors, emotions, performance, and other humanly attributes in relation to different life activities. Regression analysis has been at the forefront of these scientific explorations. Positional analysis of social networks started in the late 20th century and intensified in the last decades due to the availability of technology that made data collection an easy task for the researchers. Different interesting problems have been investigated by scholars with regression analysis being used as the major instrument for studying social network data. In this section, we provide a few examples of studies and show how regression analysis facilitated the understanding of correlations between different aspects of human nature and social network properties.

4.4.1 Social Network and Human Behavior

Human behavior is a complex output of their psychological and physiological states within the individual and social contexts. Sometime one's social network can affect their performance in jobs whether individual performance or a group performance. A field study was conducted in 2001 by Sparrowe et al. (2001) with 190 employee in 38 different groups. These 190 employees are from 5 different organizations. The study was conducted over two social networks between these members on an organization basis. One is an advice network, and the other is a hindrance network. Using regression analysis, they showed that the individual performance is positively and negatively related to the in-degree centrality score of an individual in the advice network and hindrance network, respectively. Group performance was also studied, and they found that the influence of hindrance network density is highly negatively significant for group performance. Both of these networks were constructed from the informal relationships between two individuals in a group, and the data was collected by interviewing all 190 participants. While the advice network was comprised of the relationships through which employees share resources and information, the hindrance network was formed from the negative relationships such as interference, threat, sabotage, and rejections. In a similar way, Collins and Clark (2003) worked with a top management network of technological firms to study the effect on the performance of their firms in terms of sales growth and stock returns. In this case, the social network was formed with the top management and their internal and external contacts. Instead of a person-to-person network, this network used the weighted links between the members of the top management team with different internal departments such as sales and marketing, research and development, etc., and external providers such as suppliers, finance institutions, customers, etc. The weight of the links in these person-to-department networks was based on the number of contacts, time span of interactions, and intensity of their relations as reported by the management team members through a survey. Hierarchical regression was performed to find the relationship between these networks and the firm's growth.

Network measures used as the independent variables have included network size, network range (Powell and Brantley, 1992; Scott, 2000), and the strength of ties (Granovetter, 1973). The regression results showed that the range and strength of an external network was significantly related to a firm's sales growth and stock returns, but the size of the external network had no significant effect. On the contrary, the network size of an internal network was significant for the sales growth but not for the stock returns, while the range of an internal network was significantly related to the stock return but not with the sales growth. In an interesting research work, Cimenler et al. (2014) tried to find a correlation between researchers' social network matrices with the researchers' citation performance. In this work, they collected four different social networks of 100 researchers from the College of Engineering at the University of South Florida. These networks included a personal communication network, a joint grant network, a co-authorship network, and a joint patent network. The H-index was taken as a dependent variable characterizing the citation performance and seven different network measures. Specifically, degree centrality, closeness centrality, betweenness centrality, eigenvector centrality, average tie strength, Burt's efficiency coefficient, and local clustering coefficient were taken as independent variables. In addition to this, researchers' demographic attributes such as gender, race, and department were taken as input variables. With this massive attribute set, they ran a separate Poison regression bi-variate model for each attribute obtained from four different social networks. They found that degree, closeness, eigenvector, betweeneness centrality, average tie strength, and local clustering coefficient of co-authorship network have a statistically significant effect on citation performance. Degree, closeness, betweenness centrality, average tie strength, and efficiency coefficient of pettent network and only degree, closeness, eigenvector and local clustering coefficient of grant proposal network have a positive significance in citation performance. Interestingly for a communication network, only closeness and eigenvector centrality had a statistically significant effect on citation performance.

In the aforesaid paragraph we show how one person's performance can be enhanced/ deducted due to their social position (centrality) in their personal and work social network. Now we will see how perception within the social network can change their attitude toward different events. Tucker (2014) studied an interesting phenomenon of human behavior using regression. Tucker reported that when a person thinks that the social network platform is honoring privacy by facilitating some software configuration, then they are more prone to accept the personalized content even though every other parameter of the personalized content remains the same. The study was conducted over the social network platform

Facebook to see the user's response to personalized advertisements and media from a few NGOs. Fortunately, in the middle of the campaign, Facebook introduced a privacy control on the platform. Regression analysis with the ad click-through before and after the introduction of the privacy control showed a different pattern. It showed that people are more responsive to the personalized content after the introduction of a privacy control. Hence, it provides evidence of the idea that perception can really affect our responses in a network.

In another experiment, Paluck et al. (2016) experimented with 24,191 students of 56 schools to support the theory of human behavior that states that one's behavior is adjusted toward the societal normative. In this experiment, the students' social network was formed by surveying in the mentioned 56 schools. Then they selected a few students from randomly chosen schools and trained them as an anti-conflict squad. Linear regression was performed over the data collected during one year of studies. The result of the regression analysis shows a more than 30% reduction in per-student conflicts in the schools where seed students played the role of anti-conflict agents. But what is more interesting is that where the seed sets were chosen based on the socially referent, more reduction in conflict was visible. Another interesting problem of peer influence on human behavior was studied by Bapna and Umyarov (2015). This experiment was conducted over the large-scale online music social network Last.fm. The network contains more than 23 million friendship links and 3.8 million users. They scanned several snapshot and extracted the user subscription data. In addition to this, several demographic information and social activity reports were collected from the website. Logistic regression was performed with this massive data. It prevails that once a person subscribes for a premium service, the chances of subscription increase in the neighborhood. Thus, the peer influence has a statistically and economically significant causal effect. In addition, the regression revealed that the strength of the peer influence is inversely proportional to the size of the friendship circle.

4.4.2 Emotion Contagion through Social Networks

Emotion contagion is an interesting research problem that states that human emotions such as happiness, loneliness, and depression can be transferred from person to person. Evidence has been found that two socially connected individuals have similar emotions. However, the casual effect of this may be attributed to either contagion or homophily. Coviello et al. (2014) conducted experiments with a massive amount of Facebook data to see whether emotions diffused through the friendship links in online social networks. Regression with instrumental variable was used to determine the emotional contagions in the network. They chose rainfall as the instrument and two different regressions were used to establish the hypothesis that (i) rainfall is correlated to negative emotions in human beings and (ii) these negative emotions diffuse to other geographically distant friends through online social networks. Although they found proof of social contagions of emotions, the ratio of an indirect to direct effect of rainfall was quite low compared to economical or political contagions.

A similar experiment with a massive amount of Facebook data was conducted by Kramer et al. (2014). This experiment was conducted with 689,003 Facebook users. The control experiments were done by reducing friends' positive and negative emotional posts from the users' news feeds. Poisson regression was performed with the percentage of reduction as a regression weight. An interesting finding with this regression analysis was that omitting emotional content reduced the number of words the person subsequently produced irrespective of the type of emotions. Later they performed weighted linear regression to show that when positive content was omitted, then the negative emotional posts increased whereas the positive decreased. The reverse was found to be true when negative contents were omitted. Thus, they found that human emotion is contagious over the online platform Facebook.

4.4.3 Recommender Systems in Social Networks

Recommender systems try to predict a user's affinity to a product or service based on either the user's or similar users' past experiences (collaborative filtering) or the attributes of similar products (content-based filtering) in a social network. With the increase of social media, network recommender systems have become more relevant in recent times.

Collaborative topic regression (CTR) (Wang and Blei, 2011) combines both of the techniques to better recommend the topic more relevant to a user. Purushotham et al. (2012) went a bit further and integrated CTR with the social matrix factorization model. This takes advantages of the social relations of users into account. The main motivation for the idea came from the fact that the social relations form between two users because they have similarities. Thus, incorporating social correlations can improve the accuracy of the recommendations. They experimented with two real-world online social networks: the online music station Last.fm and the online bookmark sharing platform Delicious. One of the challenges for correct recommeder systems was to identify the geographical location of the user. McGee et al. (2013) worked in this direction to predict a user's location based on the tie strength.

A study was conducted on Twitter, and decision tree regression was used to improve prediction. Very recently, Tacchini et al. (2017) worked on an interesting project where they tried to answer the question "Can a hoax be identified based on the users who liked it?". The authors proposed a logistic regression-based technique to classify a post as a hoax from user activities (likes) on that post. The experiment was conducted on a large amount of Facebook data that was collected during 2016. A very interesting fact about the user activities is that on average hoax posts have more likes than nonhoax posts.

4.5 Application of Evolutionary Computing and Deep Learning in Social Networks

Deep learning is a growing machine learning technique. It's a hierarchical learning technique that learns the structures inside the data. At its core, deep learning is a feed-forward artificial neural network with many hidden layers. On the other hand, evolutionary computing is a family of global optimization techniques inspired by biological evolution. Both of these tools have been used to learn and optimize social network data. In this section, we provide a few such examples where deep learning and evolutionary computing have been used to solve research issues in social networks.

4.5.1 Evolutionary Computing and Social Network

One of the first attempts to use genetic algorithms with social network analysis was by Wilson and Banzhaf (2009). The research was conducted over the huge amount of email communication data of Enron Corporation. The main objective of their study was to find the key players among the 151 employees of the organization. The social network was integrated into the genetic algorithm through the fitness function of the genetic algorithm. The fitness function used was derived from social network measures such as degree, density, and proximity prestige.

Community detection (Kundu and Pal, 2015b) is one of the most important problems of social networks where evolutionary algorithms have been effectively used. One such study was conducted by Gong et al. (2012). In this work, a multi-objective evolutionary algorithm was used to optimize two important properties of the communities. They simultaneously maximized the internal link density and minimized the density of links between communities. They used a modified version of the multi-objective evolutionary algorithm based on decomposition proposed by Qingfu Zhang and Hui Li (2007). Liu et al. (2014) used a multi-objective evolutionary algorithm to detect communities in a signed network. A signed social network is the network where both friend and foe relationships are present. This algorithm tried to optimize two contradictory objectives of a community. The algorithm maximizes positive links within a community while minimizing the negative links from it. Very recently, Rizman žalik (2019) used a multi-objective genetic algorithm to detect communities. Here, both the objective functions were minimized to get the end results. These objective functions were based on the node's centrality measure and ratio of edges. To use the genetic algorithm in community detection, they modified different steps such as initialization, mutation, and crossover of the genetic algorithm.

4.5.2 Deep Learning and Social Networks

Deep learning was first used in social networks by Perozzi et al. (2014). In this work, the authors used deep learning to represent social graphs with a latent representation in continuous vector space. This allows other well-known statistical and machine learning models to be used with social network data easily. To learn the social representation, they used a stream of short random walks. In 2015, Nikfarjam et al. (2015) used deep learning techniques to analyze user posts in social networks. Their objective was to learn about adverse drug reactions. Deep learning tools were mainly used to interpret natural languages that automatically classify unlabeled user posts. Li et al. (2014) uses the conditional temporal restricted Boltzmann machine to predict future links in dynamic social networks. A conditional temporal restricted Boltzmann machine was inherited from the original restricted Boltzmann machine (Hinton and Salakhutdinov, 2006). Multiple snapshots of the network at different timestamps were used as the input to the model and nodes' transitional pattern, and influence of local neighbors are used as the conditional and temporal properties for the model.

Hate speech classification is one field of deep learning known to perform well. However, a study conducted by Aroyehun and Gelbukh (2018) concluded the opposite. The study

Table 4.2 Summary of Clustering Applications

Reference	Problem	Dataset	Data Type	Clustering Type
(Chen et al. 2017)	Clustering urban functional areas	Building-level social media data, Yuexiu District, Guangzhou, China	Human/ social	K-Medoids
(Feng et al. 2015)	dynamic user interests	MovieLens and Netflix datasets	Movie data	Time-weighted association rule mining
(Alsaedi and Burnap 2015)	Events clustering	Twitter	Social	Online clustering method
(Bakillah, Li, and Liang 2015)	Geolocated communities	Twitter: typhoon Haiyan in the Philippines	Social	Spatial clustering
(Habibi, Laroche, and Richard 2014)	Influence brand trust	Ecommerce social media data	Social	Overlapping community
(Atzmanstorfer et al. 2014)	GeoCitizen platform	Case study: Capital District of Quito, Ecuador	Geo Social	Spatial clustering
(Conover et al. 2011)	Cluster political affiliation	Twitter	Human/ social	Latent semantic analysis
(Ebner and Reinhardt 2009)	Scientific community	Twitter	Human/ social	Online communities

objective was to compare different deep learning techniques to identify aggression or hate speech against the baseline support vector machine with naive Bayes (Wang and Manning, 2012). The other goal of the study was to see the performance of different deep neural networks in the presence of varying sizes of data. They found that on average the deep learning technique needed more data points to perform better than the baseline SVM algorithm. In another study, an interesting problem related to influence maximization (Pal et al., 2014) was attempted by Qiu et al. (2018). Here the deep learning technique was used to predict user actions for neighbors in the network, which in turn provided a way to predict a user's influence in the network. The experiment was conducted over a large-scale online social network and demonstrated its applicability in profiling the influence of a node in a social network.

4.6 Summary

In the recent times, social networks are changing the way people operate. As discussed in the chapter, social network usage happens in almost all areas of life. Some of the applications discussed will be an eye-opener for many researchers and bring in many

Table 4.3 Summary Regression Application

Reference	Problem	Dataset	Data Type	Regression Type
Sparrowe et al. (2001)	Individual performance and group performance in an employee advice and hindrance network	190 employees 38 groups 5 organizations	Human/ Social	Simple
Collins and Clark (2003)	Firms performance based on top management social network	73 companies avg. empl. 1,742	Human/ Social	Hierarchical
Tucker (2014)	Personalized advertising and privacy controls	1.2 million Facebook user	Online	Logistic
Purushotham et al. (2012)	Recommendation systems	Lastfm: 1,892 users Delicious: 1,867 users	Online	Collaborative topic regression
Cimenler et al. (2014)	Researchers' citation performance based on their social network	100 researchers 4 different social networks	Human/ Social	Poisson
Coviello et al. (2014)	Emotion contagion	Massive Facebook data	Online	With instrumental variables
Kramer et al. (2014)	Emotion contagion	Facebook with 689,003 users	Online	Poisson
Bapna and Umyarov (2015)	Peer influence in a music website	Last.fm 3.8m users 23m edges	Online	Logistic
Paluck et al. (2016)	Reducing the conflict between students using SNA	24,191 students 56 schools	Human/ Social	Linear & least-square
Tacchini et al. (2017)	Hoax post identification	Facebook	Online	Logistic

interdisciplinary applications in the future. The literature discussed was summarized in tables. The application classification in the social network has been summarized in Table 4.1, the clustering application in social media was summarized in Table 4.2 and finally, the application of regression in social network has been summarized in Table 4.3.

Acknowledgments

Suman Kundu acknowledges the National Science Center, Poland, for the grant 2016/23/B/ST6/01735.

References

Ahmed, F. and Abulaish, M. (2013) A generic statistical approach for spam detection in Online Social Networks. *Computer Communications*, **36** (10-11), 1120–1129, doi:10.1016/j.comcom.2013.04.004.

Akaichi, J. (2013) Social networks' Facebook' statutes updates mining for sentiment classification, in *Proceedings - SocialCom/PASSAT/BigData/EconCom/BioMedCom 2013*, pp. 886–891, doi:10.1109/SocialCom.2013.135.

Alowibdi, J.S., Buy, U.A., and Yu, P. (2013) Language independent gender classification on Twitter, in *Proceedings of the 2013 IEEE/ACM International Conference on Advances in Social Networks Analysis and Mining - ASONAM '13*, pp. 739–743, doi:10.1145/2492517.2492632.

Alsmadi, I. and Alhami, I. (2015) Clustering and classification of email contents. *Journal of King Saud University - Computer and Information Sciences*, **27** (1), 46–57, doi:10.1016/j.jksuci.2014.03.014.

Ang, L. (2011) Community relationship management and social media. *Journal of Database Marketing and Customer Strategy Management*, **18** (1), 31–38, doi:10.1057/dbm.2011.3.

Aroyehun, S.T. and Gelbukh, A. (2018) Aggression Detection in Social Media: Using Deep Neural Networks, Data Augmentation, and Pseudo Labeling, in *Proceedings of the First Workshop on Trolling, Aggression and Cyberbullying*, pp. 90–97.

Atzmanstorfer, K., Resl, R., Eitzinger, A., and Izurieta, X. (2014) The GeoCitizen-approach: Community-based spatial planning - An Ecuadorian case study. *Cartography and Geographic Information Science*, **41** (3), 248–259, doi:10.1080/15230406.2014.890546.

Bakillah, M., Li, R.Y., and Liang, S.H. (2015) Geo-located community detection in Twitter with enhanced fast-greedy optimization of modularity: the case study of typhoon Haiyan. *International Journal of Geographical Information Science*, **29** (2), 258–279, doi:10.1080/13658816.2014.964247.

Bapna, R. and Umyarov, A. (2015) Do Your Online Friends Make You Pay? A Randomized Field Experiment on Peer Influence in Online Social Networks. *Management Science*, **61** (8), 1902–1920, doi:10.1287/mnsc.2014.2081.

Batool, R., Khattak, A.M., Maqbool, J., and Lee, S. (2013) Precise tweet classification and sentiment analysis, in *2013 IEEE/ACIS 12th International Conference on Computer and Information Science, ICIS 2013 - Proceedings*, pp. 461–466, doi:10.1109/ICIS.2013.6607883.

Bayot, R.K. and Gonçalves, T. (2018) Age and gender classification of tweets using convolutional neural networks, in *Lecture Notes in Computer Science (including subseries Lecture Notes in Artificial Intelligence and Lecture Notes in Bioinformatics)*, vol. 10710 LNCS, vol. 10710 LNCS, pp. 337–348, doi:10.1007/978-3-319-72926-8_28.

Belfin, R.V., E., G.M.K., and Bródka, P. (2018) Overlapping community detection using superior seed set selection in social networks. *Computers and Electrical Engineering*, doi:10.1016/j.compeleceng.2018.03.012.

Belfin, R.V. and Grace Mary Kanaga, E. (2018) Parallel seed selection method for overlapping community detection in social network. *Scalable Computing*, doi:10.12694/scpe.v19i4.1429.

Benevenuto, F., Rodrigues, T., Almeida, J., Gonçalves, M., and Almeida, V. (2009) Detecting spammers and content promoters in online video social networks, in *Proceedings - IEEE INFOCOM*, doi:10.1109/INFCOMW.2009.5072127.

Burnap, P., Colombo, W., and Scourfield, J. (2015) Machine Classification and Analysis of Suicide-Related Communication on Twitter, in *Proceedings of the 26th ACM Conference on Hypertext & Social Media - HT '15*, pp. 75–84, doi:10.1145/2700171.2791023. 0305058.

Cenamor, I., de la Rosa, T., Núñez, S., and Borrajo, D. (2017) Planning for tourism routes using social networks. *Expert Systems with Applications*, **69**, 1–9, doi:10.1016/j.eswa.2016.10.030.

Chen, Y., Liu, X., Li, X., Liu, X., Yao, Y., Hu, G., Xu, X., and Pei, F. (2017) Delineating urban functional areas with building-level social media data: A dynamic time warping (DTW) distance based k-medoids method. *Landscape and Urban Planning*, **160**, 48–60.

Cimenler, O., Reeves, K.A., and Skvoretz, J. (2014) A regression analysis of researchers' social network metrics on their citation performance in a college of engineering. *Journal of Informetrics*, **8** (3), 667–682, doi:10.1016/j.joi.2014.06.004.

Collins, C.J. and Clark, K.D. (2003) Strategic human resource practices, top management team social networks, and firm performance: The role of human resource practices in creating organizational competitive advantage, doi:10.2307/30040665.

Conover, M.D., Gonçalves, B., Ratkiewicz, J., Flammini, A., and Menczer, F. (2011) Predicting the political alignment of twitter users, in *Proceedings - 2011 IEEE International Conference on Privacy, Security, Risk and Trust and IEEE International Conference on Social Computing, PASSAT/SocialCom 2011*, doi:10.1109/PASSAT/SocialCom.2011.34.

Coviello, L., Sohn, Y., Kramer, A.D., Marlow, C., Franceschetti, M., Christakis, N.A., and Fowler, J.H. (2014) Detecting emotional contagion in massive social networks. *PLoS ONE*, **9** (3), e90 315, doi:10.1371/journal.pone.0090315.

Croitoru, A., Wayant, N., Crooks, A., Radzikowski, J., and Stefanidis, A. (2015) Linking cyber and physical spaces through community detection and clustering in social media feeds. *Computers, Environment and Urban Systems*, **53**, 47–64, doi:10.1016/j.compenvurbsys.2014. 11.002.

Ebner, M. and Reinhardt, W. (2009) Social networking in scientific conferences Twitter as tool for strengthen a scientific community, in *telearnnoekaleidoscopeorg*, vol. 2, vol. 2, pp. 1–8.

Eleta, I. and Golbeck, J. (2014) Multilingual use of Twitter: Social networks at the language frontier. *Computers in Human Behavior*, **41**, 424–432, doi:10.1016/j.chb.2014.05.005.

Feng, H., Tian, J., Wang, H.J., and Li, M. (2015) Personalized recommendations based on time-weighted overlapping community detection. *Information and Management*, **52** (7), 789–800, doi:10.1016/j.im.2015.02.004.

Fortunato, S. (2010) Community detection in graphs. *Physics Reports*, **486** (3-5), 75–174, doi:10.1016/j.physrep.2009.11.002.

Gong, M., Ma, L., Zhang, Q., and Jiao, L. (2012) Community detection in networks by using multiobjective evolutionary algorithm with decomposition. *Physica A: Statistical Mechanics and its Applications*, **391** (15), 4050–4060, doi:10.1016/j.physa.2012.03.021.

Granovetter, M.S. (1973) The strength of weak ties. *American Journal of Sociology*, **78** (6), 1360–1380.

Habibi, M.R., Laroche, M., and Richard, M.O. (2014) The roles of brand community and community engagement in building brand trust on social media. *Computers in Human Behavior*, **37**, 152–161, doi:10.1016/j.chb.2014.04.016.

Himelboim, I., Smith, M.A., Rainie, L., Shneiderman, B., and Espina, C. (2017) Classifying Twitter Topic-Networks Using Social Network Analysis. *Social Media + Society*, **3** (1), 205630511769 154, doi:10.1177/2056305117691545.

Hinton, G.E. and Salakhutdinov, R.R. (2006) Reducing the dimensionality of data with neural networks. *Science (New York, N.Y.)*, **313** (5786), 504–7, doi:10.1126/science.1127647.

Hossain, L., Kam, D., Kong, F., Wigand, R.T., and Bossomaier, T. (2016) Social media in Ebola outbreak. *Epidemiology and Infection*, **144** (10), 2136–2143, doi:10.1017/S095026881600039X.

Igawa, R.A., Barbon, S., Paulo, K.C.S., Kido, G.S., Guido, R.C., Júnior, M.L.P., and da Silva, I.N. (2016) Account classification in online social networks with LBCA and wavelets. *Information Sciences*, **332**, 72–83, doi:10.1016/j.ins.2015.10.039.

Johnston, J. (2017) Courts' use of social media: A community of practice model. *International Journal of Communication*, **11**, 669–683, doi:10.1021/am504320h.

Kramer, A.D.I., Guillory, J.E., and Hancock, J.T. (2014) Experimental evidence of massive-scale emotional contagion through social networks. *Proceedings of the National Academy of Sciences*, **111** (24), 8788–8790, doi:10.1073/pnas.1320040111.

Kundu, S. and Pal, S.K. (2015a) FGSN: Fuzzy Granular Social Networks - Model and applications. *Information Sciences*, **314**, 100–117, doi:10.1016/j.ins.2015.03.065.

Kundu, S. and Pal, S.K. (2015b) Fuzzy-rough community in social networks. *Pattern Recognition Letters*, **67**, 145–152, doi:10.1016/j.patrec.2015.02.005.

Kundu, S. and Pal, S.K. (2018) Double bounded rough set, tension measure, and social link prediction. *IEEE Transactions on Computational Social Systems*, **5** (3), 841–853, doi:10.1109/TCSS.2018.2861215.

Lakkaraju, H. and Ajmera, J. (2011) Attention prediction on social media brand pages, in *Proceedings of the 20th ACM international conference on Information and knowledge management - CIKM '11*, p. 2157, doi:10.1145/2063576.2063915.

Li, W. and Xu, H. (2014) Text-based emotion classification using emotion cause extraction. *Expert Systems with Applications*, **41** (4 PART 2), 1742–1749, doi:10.1016/j.eswa.2013.08.073.

Li, X., Du, N., Li, H., Li, K., Gao, J., and Zhang, A. (2014) A Deep Learning Approach to Link Prediction in Dynamic Networks, in *Proceedings of the 2014 SIAM International Conference on Data Mining*, Society for Industrial and Applied Mathematics, Philadelphia, PA, pp. 289–297, doi:10.1137/1.9781611973440.33.

Lima, A.C.E. and de Castro, L.N. (2014) A multi-label, semi-supervised classification approach applied to personality prediction in social media. *Neural Networks*, **58**, 122–130, doi:10.1016/j.neunet.2014.05.020.

Liu, C., Liu, J., and Jiang, Z. (2014) A multiobjective evolutionary algorithm based on similarity for community detection from signed social networks. *IEEE Transactions on Cybernetics*, **44** (12), 2274–2287, doi:10.1109/TCYB.2014.2305974.

Lo, Y.W. and Potdar, V. (2009) A review of opinion mining and sentiment classification framework in social networks, in *2009 3rd IEEE International Conference on Digital Ecosystems and Technologies, DEST '09*, pp. 396–401, doi:10.1109/DEST.2009.5276705.

McAuley, J. and Leskovec, J. (2012) Image labeling on a network: Using social-network metadata for image classification, in *Lecture Notes in Computer Science (including subseries Lecture Notes in Artificial Intelligence and Lecture Notes in Bioinformatics)*, vol. 7575 LNCS, vol. 7575 LNCS, pp. 828–841, doi:10.1007/978-3-642-33765-9_59. 1207.3809.

McGee, J., Caverlee, J., and Cheng, Z. (2013) Location prediction in social media based on tie strength, in *Proceedings of the 22nd ACM international conference on Conference on information & knowledge management - CIKM '13*, pp. 459–468, doi:10.1145/2505515.2505544. 1111.2904.

Narayanam, R. and Narahari, Y. (2011) A Shapley value-based approach to discover influential nodes in social networks. *IEEE Transactions on Automation Science and Engineering*, **8** (1), 130–147.

Nikfarjam, A., Sarker, A., O'Connor, K., Ginn, R., and Gonzalez, G. (2015) Pharmacovigilance from social media: mining adverse drug reaction mentions using sequence labeling with word embedding cluster features. *Journal of the American Medical Informatics Association*, **22** (3), 671–681, doi:10.1093/jamia/ocu041.

Ou, G., Chen, W., Wang, T., Wei, Z., Li, B., Yang, D., and Wong, K.F. (2017) Exploiting Community Emotion for Microblog Event Detection, in *Social Media Content Analysis*, pp. 439–456, doi:10.1142/9789813223615_0027.

Pal, S.K. and Kundu, S. (2017) Granular Social Network: Model and Applications, in *Handbook of Big Data Technologies* (eds A.Y. Zomaya and S. Sakr), Springer International Publishing, Cham, pp. 617–651, doi:10.1007/978-3-319-49340-4_18.

Pal, S.K., Kundu, S., and Murthy, C.A. (2014) Centrality measures, upper bound, and influence maximization in large scale directed social networks. *Fundamenta Informaticae*, **130** (3), 317–342.

Paluck, E.L., Shepherd, H., and Aronow, P.M. (2016) Changing climates of conflict: A social network experiment in 56 schools. *Proceedings of the National Academy of Sciences of the United States of America*, **113** (3), 566–71, doi:10.1073/pnas.1514483113.

Peled, O., Fire, M., Rokach, L., and Elovici, Y. (2016) Matching entities across online social networks. *Neurocomputing*, **210**, 91–106, doi:10.1016/j.neucom.2016.03.089.

Perozzi, B., Al-Rfou, R., and Skiena, S. (2014) DeepWalk: Online Learning of Social Representations. *Proceedings of the 20th ACM SIGKDD international conference on Knowledge discovery and data mining - KDD '14*, pp. 701–710, doi:10.1145/2623330.2623732.

Powell, W.W. and Brantley, P. (1992) Competitive Cooperation in Biotechnology: Learning through Networks?, in *Networks and Organizations: Structure, Form, and Action*, Harvard Business School Press, Boston, pp. 366–394.

Purushotham, S., Liu, Y., and Kuo, C.C.J. (2012) Collaborative Topic Regression with Social Matrix Factorization for Recommendation Systems, in *Proceedings of the 29th International Confer- ence on Machine Learning*, Edinburgh, pp. 759–766, doi:10.1016/j.jhydrol.2004.11.010. 1206.4684.

Qingfu Zhang and Hui Li (2007) MOEA/D: A Multiobjective Evolutionary Algorithm Based on Decomposition. *IEEE Transactions on Evolutionary Computation*, **11** (6), 712–731, doi:10.1109/TEVC.2007.892759.

Qiu, J., Tang, J., Ma, H., Dong, Y., Wang, K., and Tang, J. (2018) DeepInf: Social Influence Prediction with Deep Learning, in *Proceedings of the 24th ACM SIGKDD International Conference on Knowledge Discovery & Data Mining - KDD '18*, ACM Press, New York, New York, USA, pp. 2110–2119, doi:10.1145/3219819.3220077.

Rizman Žalik, K. (2019) Evolution Algorithm for Community Detection in Social Networks Using Node Centrality, pp. 73–87, doi:10.1007/978-3-319-77604-0_6.

Schirr, G.R. (2013) Community-Sourcing a New Marketing Course: Collaboration in Social Media. *Marketing Education Review*, **23** (3), 225–240, doi:10.2753/MER1052-8008230302.

Scott, J. (2000) *Social network analysis : a handbook*, SAGE Publications.

Shaji, A., Belfin, R., and Grace Mary Kanaga, E. (2018) *An innovated SIRS model for information spreading*, vol. **645**, doi:10.1007/978-981-10-7200-0_37.

Sitter, K.C. and Curnew, A.H. (2016) The application of social media in social work community practice. *Social Work Education*, **35** (3), 271–283, doi:10.1080/02615479.2015.1131257.

Song, Y., Lu, Z., Leung, C.W.k., and Yang, Q. (2013) Collaborative boosting for activity classification in microblogs, in *Proceedings of the 19th ACM SIGKDD international conference on Knowledge discovery and data mining - KDD '13*, p. 482, doi:10.1145/2487575.2487661.

Sparrowe, R.T., Liden, R.C., Wayne, S.J., and Kraimer, M.L. (2001) Social networks and the performance of individuals and groups. *Academy of Management Journal*, **44** (2), 316–325, doi:10.2307/3069458.

Statista.com (2018) Social Media Statistics & Facts | Statista. URL https://www.statista.com/topics/1164/social-networks/.

Tacchini, E., Ballarin, G., Della Vedova, M.L., Moret, S., and de Alfaro, L. (2017) Some Like it Hoax: Automated Fake News Detection in Social Networks. 1704.07506.

Tang, L. and Liu, H. (2011) Leveraging social media networks for classification. *Data Mining and Knowledge Discovery*, **23** (3), 447–478, doi:10.1007/s10618-010-0210-x.

Tucker, C.E. (2014) Social networks, personalized advertising, and privacy controls. *Journal of Marketing Research*, **51** (5), 546–562, doi:10.1509/jmr.10.0355.

Tuulos, V.H. and Tirri, H. (2004) Combining topic models and social networks for chat data mining, in *Proceedings - IEEE/WIC/ACM International Conference on Web Intelligence, WI 2004*, pp. 206–213, doi:10.1109/WI.2004.10025.

Vázquez, S., Muñoz-García, Ó., Campanella, I., Poch, M., Fisas, B., Bel, N., and Andreu, G. (2014) A classification of user-generated content into consumer decision journey stages. *Neural Networks*, **58**, 68–81, doi:10.1016/j.neunet.2014.05.026.

Verbeke, W., Martens, D., and Baesens, B. (2014) Social network analysis for customer churn prediction. *Applied Soft Computing Journal*, **14** (PART C), 431–446, doi:10.1016/j.asoc.2013.09.017.

Wang, C. and Blei, D.M. (2011) Collaborative topic modeling for recommending scientific articles, in *Proceedings of the 17th ACM SIGKDD international conference on Knowledge discovery and data mining - KDD '11*, p. 448, doi:10.1145/2020408.2020480. arXiv:1411.2581v1.

Wang, D., Irani, D., and Pu, C. (2014) SPADE: a social-spam analytics and detection framework. *Social Network Analysis and Mining*, **4** (1), 1–18, doi:10.1007/s13278-014-0189-1.

Wang, S. and Manning, C.D. (2012) Baselines and bigrams: Simple, good sentiment and topic classification, in *Proceedings of the 50th Annual Meeting of the Association for Computational Linguistics: Short Papers - Volume 2*, Association for Computational Linguistics, Stroudsburg, PA, USA, ACL '12, pp. 90–94.

Wanichayapong, N., Pruthipunyaskul, W., Pattara-Atikom, W., and Chaovalit, P. (2011) Social-based traffic information extraction and classification, in *2011 11th International Conference on ITS Telecommunications, ITST 2011*, pp. 107–112, doi:10.1109/ITST.2011.6060036.

Wilson, G. and Banzhaf, W. (2009) Discovery of email communication networks from the enron corpus with a genetic algorithm using social network analysis, in *2009 IEEE Congress on Evolutionary Computation, CEC 2009*, pp. 3256–3263, doi:10.1109/CEC.2009.4983357.

Yang, M., Kiang, M., and Shang, W. (2015) Filtering big data from social media - Building an early warning system for adverse drug reactions. *Journal of Biomedical Informatics*, **54**, 230–240, doi:10.1016/j.jbi.2015.01.011.

Ye, M., Shou, D., Lee, W.C., Yin, P., and Janowicz, K. (2011) On the semantic annotation of places in location-based social networks, in *Proceedings of the 17th ACM SIGKDD international conference on Knowledge discovery and data mining - KDD '11*, p. 520, doi:10.1145/2020408.2020491.

Zhang, X., Tokoglu, F., Negishi, M., Arora, J., Winstanley, S., Spencer, D.D., and Constable, R.T. (2011) Social network theory applied to resting-state fMRI connectivity data in the identification of epilepsy networks with iterative feature selection. *Journal of Neuroscience Methods*, **199** (1), 129–139, doi:10.1016/j.jneumeth.2011.04.020.

Zhou, W., Jin, H., and Liu, Y. (2012) Community discovery and profiling with social messages, in *Proceedings of the 18th ACM SIGKDD international conference on Knowledge discovery and data mining - KDD '12*, p. 388, doi:10.1145/2339530.2339593.

Zhu, Y., Wang, X., Zhong, E., Liu, N., Li, H., and Yang, Q. (2012) Discovering spammers in social networks, in *Association for the Advancement of Artificial Intelligence*, pp. 171–177.

5

Predicting Students' Grades Using CART, ID3, and Multiclass SVM Optimized by the Genetic Algorithm (GA): A Case Study

Debanjan Konar, Ruchita Pradhan, Tania Dey, Tejaswini Sapkota, and Prativa Rai

Department of Computer Science and Engineering, Sikkim Manipal Institute of Technology, Sikkim Manipal University, India

5.1   Introduction

Recent years have witnessed the popularity of data mining techniques among potential researchers. To analyze data for classification and predictions, data mining approaches like decision trees, fuzzy rules, etc., have been increasingly employed in the field of education technology. Educational data mining (EDM) is gaining popularity among researchers in the educational ecosystem because of its contribution and potential benefit in education and e-learning technologies. With an increase in the availability of educational data, there is a need to analyze big data in the student information systems [1] of educational institutions to enhance evaluation, assessments, planing, and decision-making processes in its educational programs. Student performance analysis is an essential part of any educational institute [2, 3]. It is always a herculean task to predict students' performance because of the large amount of data related to students. The final performance plays an important role in pursuing higher studies and also in placement opportunities. Therefore, predicting students' performance is important for mentors to obtain early feedback that allows them to take necessary action to improve a student's performance [4]. Educational data mining explores hidden patterns in the academic data and selects academic programs through prediction of student performance and academic behavior. These facts allow the administrations to allot resources and facilities in an efficient manner [5]. This also provides the necessary information to predict weak students and allocate suitable resources with precise approximation effectively.

In general, owing to unsatisfactory courses floated in engineering graduation programs, students sometimes withdraw from courses. The level of difficulty of an academic program is also a primary influencing factor according to Marra et al. [6]. In contrast, the relationships between student academic performance and the students those who successfully graduate, have been drawn by Mbuva et al. [7] investigating the relationship between the student academic program (SAP) and successful graduation. There are a few important parameters (previous academic grade, attendance percentage, total number of backlogs in the past, degree of intelligence, working nature, discipline, social activities, etc.) that guide us to predict the academic outcome of a student. These are incorporated into the prediction

Recent Advances in Hybrid Metaheuristics for Data Clustering, First Edition.
Edited by Sourav De, Sandip Dey, and Siddhartha Bhattacharyya.
© 2020 John Wiley & Sons Ltd. Published 2020 by John Wiley & Sons Ltd.

models and are essential for the effective and accurate prediction of student performance. In addition, student performance prediction relies on data pertaining to a student's subject knowledge, the proficiency in attempting a question, etc. There are numerous Learning Online Network with Computer Assisted Personalized Approach (LON-CAPA) models [8] to predict the final grade of the students that rely on features extracted from logged data in a higher educational web-based system. The higher educational institutions are using this LON-CAPA model to find out which parts of the education systems can be improved using data mining algorithms [9]. The model comprises mainly seven processes: evaluation, planning, registration, consulting, marketing, performance, and examination. To improve the quality of the management system, a decision tree is often introduced to predict the students' performance including successful students in specific subjects. The prediction of future outcome of the students allows instructor/faculty and managerial decision maker to take the necessary initiative, providing extra basic course skill classes, more academic counseling, financial aid help, etc.

The primary objective of the study on students' information was that it quantifies the association between different responsibility factors like student's attention during class lectures, hours spent in study on a daily basis after college, students' family income, students' mother's age, and mother's education. In addition, it also demonstrates the impact of factors affecting student performance using simple linear regression analysis. It has been reported from the analysis that factors such as mother's education and student's family income are predominantly correlated with the student academic performance.

With the growing popularity in e-learning platforms (Massive Open Online Courses (MOOCs)), education technology is enabling students to learn from a large number of contributors. However, in the last few years, with the rapid increase in the number of seats at universities and institutions with large class sizes and with MOOCs, it is a daunting task for the instructor and teaching assistants to keep track of an individual student's grade. The early prediction of the student performance can obviate poor students failing examinations, and excellent students can perform better, which leads to maximum benefit. Promotional and remedial activities often help the students improve their performance in examinations [10].

As shown in this chapter, student performance analysis has been studied using CART, ID3, and multiclass SVM on the dataset available from previous-year grade assessments at the Sikkim Manipal Institute of Technology. Now we will summarize a study on students' past performance that tried to predict the success rate of engineering students and forecast their grades in each subject, therein an attempt to drive the individual student toward the most successful academic path. Establishing the factors affecting student academic performance is the primary goal of this study. The research was solely centered on classroom teaching, and online courses are not included in this study.

The rest of the chapter is organized as follows. A literature review is provided in Section 5.2. A brief introduction about decision tree algorithms (CART and ID3) are in Section 5.3. Section 5.4 throws light on multiclass SVM optimized by the genetic algorithm. A vivid explanation about dataset preparation is included in Section 5.5. In addition, the experimental procedures, outcome on grade prediction, and discussions are reported in Section 5.6. Finally, Section 5.7 discusses insights from the studies and the new horizon of research.

5.2   Literature Review

The primary aim of the data mining algorithms is to provide assistance in fetching important information relevant to students' previous performance from the academic records located in institutional or university repositories [11]. A trustworthy and repeatable forecast method of the students' grades empowers the institution authorities to assist the students more efficiently. By predicting a student's grade, the advisors and students can take appropriate measures to improve a student's academic performance [12–14]. Furthermore, administrative staff can use this predictive model to choose the classes students should take. A student is more likely to continue a major if satisfied with the services the institution offers.

Various data mining approaches have been employed over the years by universities to analyze student performance. In last decade, a plethora of data mining approaches such as clustering, classification, association rules, etc., have been introduced that are suitable for educational data. These approaches expose the hidden data relevant to student performance and useful information. S. B. Kotsiantis et al. [15] predicted student performance relying on the naive Bayes classifier and Ripper. An extensive review of machine learning approaches (decision tree, k-nearest algorithms, rule induction, naive Bayes, and artificial neural networks) has been included to predict the students' performance by Raheela Asif et al. [16]. Yannick Meier et al. proposed a novel algorithm to predict the final grade of a student, relying on the student's past records [17]. A wide number of data mining approaches (tree classifier, Bayesian classifiers, $k - NN$ Classifier, etc.) are also involved in student grade prediction, and 1-NN and naive Bayes classifier have been reported promising results [18, 19].

A class imbalance problem relevant to student performance prediction is manifested by Shaleena et al. [20]. The results reported in the research article show that the decision tree (J48) classifier outperforms Jrip learner and $k - NN$ classifier. A compact study was performed using decision trees, random forests, neural networks, and support vector machines for both classification and regression by Paulo et al. [21] and found the most influencing factors affecting the grades. Baradwaj et al. [22] employed the ID3 decision tree classification algorithm to predict student performance. At the Hellenic Open University, a model is described by Kotsiantis et al. [15] to predict the performance of students for a distance learning course relying on the machine learning algorithms (C4.5, Nave Bayesian Network (NBN), Back Propagation (BP), 3-Nearest Neighborhood (3-NN), and Sequential Minimal Optimization (SMO)). It has been observed from the study of 510 students that the naive Bayes classifier outperforms with an accuracy of 72.48%. A similar type of work was also performed by Acharya et al. [23] to predict a student's performance, and the $k - NN$ classifier reported accuracy with 79% during training and 66% during testing. Behrouz et al. [8] also employed the quadratic Bayesian classifier, Parzen-window, 1-NN, KNN, multilayer perceptron, and decision tree to predict the final grade of the students, and it is evident from the outcome that kNN dominates over other machine learning algorithms with an accuracy of 82.3%.

A hybrid fuzzy neural network classifier [24] has been employed to target model students' academic profiles, relying on inexact information. The proposed hybridized neural network outperforms statistical models and multilayer neural networks in terms of predicting the students' academic grades. In addition, a comparison between the efficiency of the neural network and multiple linear regression approaches in predicting student academic achievements in e-learning courses was carried out by Lykourentzou et al. [25]. On the contrary, using student social and personal attributes to assist a Bayesian network framework was developed by Bekele et al. [26] to predict student performance and reported 64% accuracy. E-learning system–guided data mining techniques were compared to predict the final outcome of the students [27], and it was found that decision tree (CART) is superior in predicting students' grades. Recently, Kumar et al. [28] developed a *C*4.5 and *ID*3 decision tree to predict the success of the students, and it was reported that *C*4.5 performs better in the prediction of students' grades. According to the experiments conducted by Osmanbegovic et al. [29] in 2012 using three data mining algorithms, naive Bayes, decision tree, and neural networks, naive Bayes predominantly performed well when compared to other state-of-the-art methods.

The majority of past studies focus on classification for prediction relying on student past performance for a few courses, grade inflation, anticipated percentage of failing student, etc. However, a suitable study on classifications to predict student final performance based on the grades of all subjects is not reported. The study on various machine learning approaches for analyzing all the courses was done to identify the courses with a high impact on the final grade performance of the students. To obtain better classification accuracy in predicting students' grades, the suitable selection of parameters (model selection) in a support vector machine classifier is a crucial factor. In this chapter, a multiclass support vector classifier is modeled to rely on a well-known metaheuristic genetic algorithm striving to automate the model selection of SVM. The parameters are learned by the combined kernels in a data-driven fashion [30]. This chapter also contributes to utilizing classification to predict the final outcome of the students' performance guided by all courses. Insights of the current study yield important information and hidden patterns relevant to students and allow the instructor and university administration to decide on future suitable actions leading to better-quality education. In this chapter, datasets have been collected from the Sikkim Manipal Institute of Technology's (Sikkim Manipal University) website. The students, grades are calculated depending on the students' session marks, quiz performance, attendance, lab grades, and assignments, which form the total internal marks and are added to their external examination marks that sum up to the final grade.

5.3 Decision Tree Algorithms: ID3 and CART

In the field of data mining and induction research, decision tree algorithms are widely employed for classification and prediction. The CART and ID3 algorithms are popular decision tree algorithms [31] proposed by Ross Quinlan [32]. In the decision tree method, the property of each generated node is evaluated based on information gain theory and attributed with the highest information gain in terms of entropy reduction in the level of maximum. This property enables researchers to partition the training sample subset with containment of the current node and yields mixture degrees of different types for all the generated sample subsets to reduce to a minimum.

Consider a set A that comprises d number of data samples with n attribute values set corresponding to n distinct classes $C_i, \forall i = 1, 2, 3, ..., n$. Assuming d_i is the sample number of C_i, the amount of information required for the classification of a given data is as follows:

$$In(d_1, d_2, \ldots d_n) = -\sum_{i=1}^{n} s_i \log(s_i) \tag{5.1}$$

where the probability of the data sample subset contained in class C_1 is defined as $s_i = d_{ij}/d_i$. Let us consider P is a property with m number of distinct values $p_1, p_2, p_3, \ldots p_m$. The set S can be segmented into m number of subsets $A_1, A_2 \ldots A_m$ where A_j is containing data samples whose attribute P is equal to p_j in set A. To partition the current sample, if property P is selected, the required information entropy is defined as follows:

$$Ent(P) = -\sum_{j=1}^{m} \frac{A_{1j} + A_{2j} + A_{3j} + \ldots A_{mj}}{A} * In(A_{1j} + A_{2j} + A_{3j} + \ldots A_{mj}) \tag{5.2}$$

$A_{i,j}$ denotes the sample dataset of class C_i in subset A_j.
Information gain is obtained on the current branch node corresponding to the set partitioning sample dataset as follows:

$$Gn(P) = In(d_1, d_2, \ldots d_n) - Ent(P) \tag{5.3}$$

In the ID3 algorithm, the possible decision space is traversed in a top-down greedy search fashion and never traced back. To select the best attribute in the course of the growth of the tree, an information gain metric is introduced.

The ID3 algorithm for generating a decision tree and training using the given dataset is as follows [31]:

ID3 Algorithm
Input: Training dataset, candidate attribute list, test dataset

1. Create a root node N.
2. If all of the nodes belong to a class C, then return N as a leaf node. All the training samples are designated by the beginning root node.
3. If the attribute list is empty, then return N as a leaf node and save the node in a class with the maximum number of samples contained in the class.
4. Select the test attribute with the maximum information gain Gn from the attribute list and save node N with the test attribute.
5. The node N containing the sample dataset is partitioned for each given value of test attribute p_i
6. A branch related to test attribute p_i is generated from node N to exhibit test conditions satisfying test attribute p_i.
7. Set A_i as the sample dataset obtained under the condition of test attribute p_i. Save the corresponding leaf node in the class with the maximum categorized sample set, if A_i is empty. Else, it will be saved with the return value.

The ID3 algorithm follows a top-down divide-and-conquer iterative approach to construct a decision tree in a greedy search manner. The recursive algorithm is terminated once all samples within a node belong to the same class. If there is no attribute to be employed to a partition of the current sample dataset, then to make it a compulsory leaf node, the indexvoting principle is preferred. Save the corresponding leaf node in the class with the maximum categorized sample set. If none of the conditions of test attribute p_i is satisfied, then a leaf node is created and saved as the corresponding leaf node in the class with the maximum categorized sample set.

Quinlan et al. [32] proposed the successor of the ID3 classification algorithm referred to as the $C4.5$ decision tree algorithm suitable for fast classification. The $C4.5$ algorithm incorporates the concept of an information gain ratio instead of information gain unlike ID3 and continuous attributes. In addition, ID3 employs tree pruning in a more efficient manner and also deals with the vacancy of an attribute value to ID3. Various pruning algorithms are introduced in $C4.5$ to obviate the inherent problem of over-fitting in ID3. The rule of production can be generated from the knowledge representation of the $C4.5$ algorithm, which is a decision-making tree.

$$GnR(P) = \frac{Gn(P)}{Splt(P)} \tag{5.4}$$

where

$$Splt(P) = -\sum_{i=1}^{n} s_i \log(s_i) \tag{5.5}$$

5.4 Multiclass Support Vector Machines (SVMs) Optimized by the Genetic Algorithm (GA)

Support vector machine (SVM) is introduced as a supervised classifier targeting to solve linear and nonlinear classification. SVM was initially employed in binary classification problems [33] and later extended for multiclass classification [34]. Consider there are n training data sample for $(x_1, t_1), (x_2, t_2), \dots (x_i, t_i) \dots (x_n, t_n) \, \forall i \in R^n$ and $t_i \in 1 \dots n$ is the class of $x_i \in X$. The primary objective of support vector classification is to separate the data samples in terms of maximal marginal hyperplane [35]. The SVM classifier is built on minimizing the norm of weight vector $\mathbf{w}$ under the constraint that the training patterns of each class reside on the reverse side of the class margin, as shown in Figure 5.1. In this chapter, the multiclass SVM is implemented for student grade prediction assisted by a *one-against-all* procedure, as shown in Figure 5.2. It comprises m SVMs (ensemble of SVMs), which is the same as the number of classes. Each one of m SVMs is trained with all samples with positive classes and the rest with negative classes. The constraint can be defined formally for binary classification $t_i \in \{-1, 1\}$ as follows:

$$t_i(w^T \phi(x_i) + b) \geqslant 1, \forall i = 0, 1, 2 \dots m \tag{5.6}$$

The data points satisfying the equality condition of Eqn. 5.6 are said to be support vectors, and also they define the orientation of the hyperplane. To keep track of misclassified points, SVM introduces slack variables $\xi_i \in \Re$ [35] in the formulation of soft margins. Any one of kth SVMs solve the following convex quadratic programming problem to construct the maximum margin classifier.

$$\min_{w^k, b^k, \xi^k} \frac{1}{2}(w^k)^T w^k + C \sum_{i=1}^{n} \xi_i^k$$

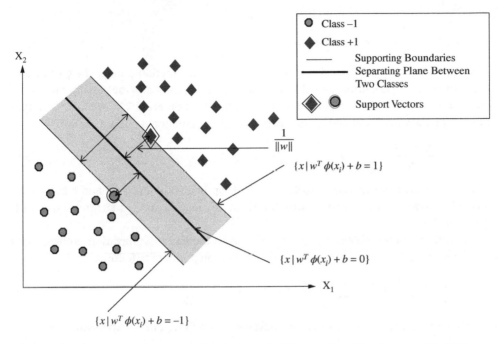

Figure 5.1 Linear separation of two classes −1 and +1 in two-dimensional space with SVM classifier

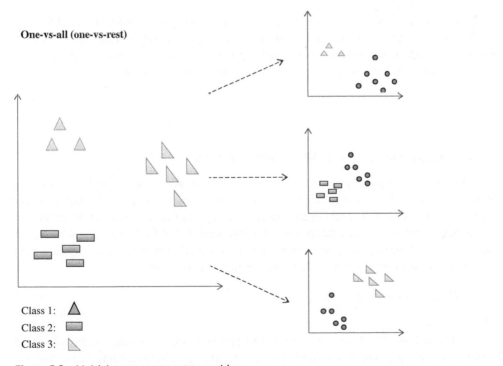

Figure 5.2 Multiclass support vector machine

s.t

$$(w^k)^T \phi(x_i) + b^k \geqslant 1 - \xi_i^k, \text{if } t_i = k \tag{5.7}$$

$(w^k)^T \phi(x_i) + b^k \leqslant -1 + \xi_i^k, \text{if } t_i \neq k, \xi_i^k \geqslant 0, i = 1 \dots n$. The function ϕ maps the given training samples to a higher-dimensional sample space, and C designates the penalty parameter, which can maximize the margin without miss-classification error. The geometric margin of the SVM classifier is defined as the normalization of functional margins as follows:

$$\gamma = \frac{\mathbf{w}.\mathbf{x} + b}{\|\mathbf{w}\|} \tag{5.8}$$

To obtain a maximum margin classifier in SVM, optimal values of $\gamma, \mathbf{w}$ and b need to be chosen intuitively and so as to maximize the geometric margin $\max_{\mathbf{w},b} \gamma$ s.t $t_i(w^T \phi(x_i) + b) \geqslant \gamma \|\mathbf{w}\|$ and $\|\mathbf{w}\| = 1$.

This optimization problem can be formulated as a convex optimization problem, and hence it leads to SVMs being a constraint optimization problem as follows:

$$L(\mathbf{w}, b) = \frac{1}{2}\|\mathbf{w}\|^2 - \sum_i \mu_i[t_i(w^T \phi(x_i) + b) - 1] \tag{5.9}$$

On solving Eqn.5.9, the dual form of support vector machine can be expressed as follows:

$$L(\mathbf{w}, b) = \sum_i \mu_i - \frac{1}{2} \sum_{i,j} \mu_i \mu_j t_i t_j (\phi(x_i)\phi(x_j)) \tag{5.10}$$

s.t $\sum_i \mu_i t_i = 0$ and $0 \leqslant C \leqslant 1$ where μ_i denotes the Lagrangian constraints. In this transformed feature space $\phi(x)$, construction of a separating hyperplane leads to a nonlinear decision boundary in the input space. To obviate the expensive calculation of dot products on high-dimensional feature space, the concept of kernel function K is employed as follows:

$$K(x_i, x_j) = \phi(x_i).\phi(x_j)) \tag{5.11}$$

5.4.1 Genetic Algorithms for SVM Model Selection

With the increasing popularity of metaheuristics techniques, researchers often rely on the genetic algorithm (GA) in conjunction with support vector machines (SVMs) on several occasions such as SVM kernel constructions [36, 37], SVM parameters optimization [38], and feature selection [39]. In this chapter, the GA is employed to leverage the SVM parameters for a fixed kernel, and a data driver kernel construction is introduced. Hence, a combination of base kernels is incorporated in this model as follows:

$$K_{Equiv} = K_1 \otimes K_2 \otimes \dots \otimes K_n \tag{5.12}$$

where $\otimes \in +;.$

The GA-optimized SVM construction is an iterative procedure starting with a randomly generated initial population that comprises genotypes (a well-defined combined kernel coding scheme) and is illustrated in Figure 5.3.

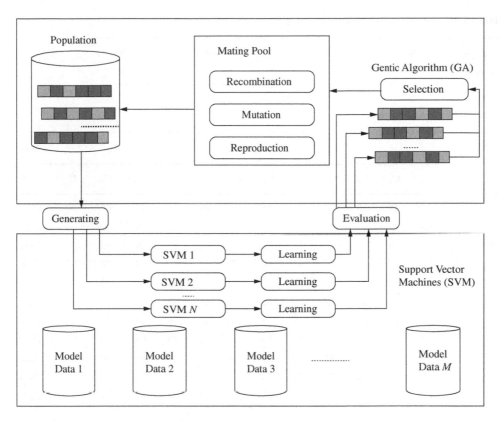

Figure 5.3 SVM optimized by genetic algorithms

5.5 Preparation of Datasets

The dataset used in this project was collected from the Sikkim Manipal Institute of Technology (SMIT) website (https://results.smu.edu.in/smit/). It comprises marks obtained in all subjects by 2016 – 2019 students from the third semester onward. The students' grades at SMIT are based upon the students' sessional marks, quizzes, attendance, lab grades, and assignments, which form the total internal marks and are added to their external examination marks, which sum up to the final grade. The data repository of the university contains a voluminous amount of data relevant to the analysis task that was retrieved from the website. Here, it includes the information of 1,543 students and their final grades in 46 subjects for B.Tech in CSE. For these 46 subjects the practical labs are also included. The grade is a numerical value; however, it has seven categories, as shown in Table 5.1. The marks obtained in each subject are the cumulative marks obtained for attendance, quizzes, programming assignment, and internal and external examinations both. The dataset that is generated is used for the system to learn the rules for the prediction of classes and is called the training data. The dataset is divided randomly on a 1:4 ratio of test to training data. The sample input binary and multiclass datasets are provided in Tables 5.2 and 5.3, respectively.

Table 5.1 Classification of Student Grades

Range	0 – 4	4 – 5	5 – 6	6 – 7	7 – 8	8 – 9	9 – 10
Grade	F	E	D	C	B	A	S

Table 5.2 Binary Dataset

Students	Courses												Grade
	C_1	C_2	C_3	C_4	C_5	C_6	C_7	C_8	C_9	C_{10}	C_{11}	C_{12}	
S_1	56	49	55	28	50	46	65	45	41	48	66	54	**Pass**
S_2	88	80	82	37	72	61	51	84	71	68	72	55	**Pass**
S_3	54	56	46	10	36	31	69	44	50	49	53	55	**Fail**
S_4	69	58	33	17	52	48	45	48	45	54	56	65	**Pass**
S_5	82	88	74	62	85	82	71	95	74	96	75	60	**Pass**
S_6	82	87	63	57	72	75	65	83	68	62	64	74	**Pass**
S_7	12	18	37	10	35	25	66	13	36	46	57	84	**Fail**
S_8	73	67	40	31	48	45	16	52	45	59	62	51	**Pass**
S_9	69	62	58	38	69	55	50	41	48	59	50	57	**Pass**
S_{10}	81	63	61	44	76	74	74	91	50	73	72	66	**Pass**
S_{10}	83	88	68	48	64	67	55	79	64	81	71	68	**Pass**

Table 5.3 Multiclass Dataset

Students	Courses									Grade
	C_1	C_2	C_3	C_4	C_5	C_6	C_7	C_8	C_9	
S_1	24	56	54	57	53	56	78	63	65	B
S_2	44	82	70	56	82	56	86	74	76	A
S_3	42	65	64	61	64	49	78	71	52	B
S_4	46	63	68	57	75	53	80	68	78	B
S_5	28	50	46	65	45	41	48	66	54	D
S_6	37	72	61	51	84	71	68	72	55	A
S_7	11	36	31	69	44	51	49	53	66	E
S_8	17	52	43	45	48	45	54	56	65	D
S_9	62	85	82	71	95	74	96	75	60	S
S_{10}	57	72	75	65	83	68	62	64	74	A
S_{11}	10	35	25	65	05	36	46	57	84	E
S_{12}	31	48	45	16	52	45	59	62	51	C

5.6 **Experimental Results and Discussions**

Rigorous experiments have been performed using the binary classification algorithms: ID3 and CART [32]. Figures 5.4, 5.5 and 5.6 show the accuracy obtained from the experiments. All students with a final grade above *E* have been declared *Pass*, while those with the grades *E* and *F* have been declared *Fail*. It has been observed that CART outperforms the ID3 algorithm with an accuracy of 87.1%, while ID3 has reported an accuracy of 83.9%. Since predicting the grade of a student is a multiclass problem, the multiclass SVM-optimized GA [30] has been used. An accuracy of 87% is obtained, while the crossover and mutation rate are set to 0.6 and 0.2, respectively. The test set to training set ratio is 1:4. For the multiclass problem, the CART and ID3 algorithms reported an accuracy of only 35.8% and 38.71%, respectively, in a multiclass problem.

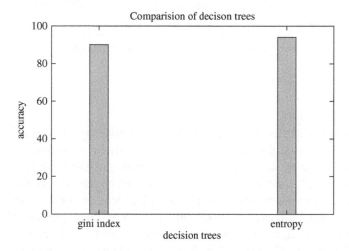

Figure 5.4 Bar graph showing accuracy of CART and ID3 on binary dataset

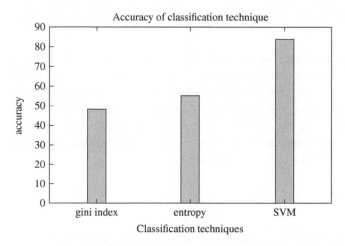

Figure 5.5 Bar graph showing accuracy of CART, ID3, and SVM on multiclass dataset

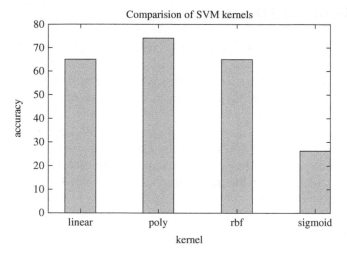

Figure 5.6 Bar graph showing accuracy of different SVM kernels on multiclass dataset

5.7 Conclusion

The performance prediction of students enables the instructor and university administration to identify dropouts ahead of time so that suitable counseling and special attention can be provided. Authors have investigated student performance in employing three efficient decision tree algorithms (ID3, CART, and multiclass SVM-optimized by the GA) on the binary and multiclass datasets extracted separately from the Sikkim Manipal Institute of Technology (SMIT) website. A case study of SMIT in educational data mining is presented was this chapter. It shows the potential of data mining to improve students' performance and predicting students' grades in the early stages. Classification techniques, decision trees, and SVMs are employed to discover classification rules to predict final grades based on scores of the mandatory subjects studied throughout the course. Different accuracy values are generated by the different kernel types, and the polynomial type kernel reported the highest accuracy.

The performance of the students who are pursuing their B.Tech in the CSE department has been predicted using various classification techniques such as ID3, CART, and SVM. Predicting the performance of students pursuing all the other courses in the various departments at SMIT hasn't been studied yet. In addition, the CGPA has been scaled to grades (discrete values), which gives a rough estimate of a student's final GPA. To get a more accurate idea of a student's future performance, the current work can be extended to predict the actual GPA (continuous values) using regression algorithms.

References

1 M. Al-Razgan, A. S. Al-Khalifa and H. S. Al-Khalifa, "Educational data mining: A systematic review of the published literature 2006-2013," *Proc. the 1st International Conference on Advanced Data and Information Engineering*, pp. 711–719, 2013.

2 K. B. Eashwar, R. Venkatesan and D. Ganesh, "Student Performance Prediction using SVM", *International Journal of Mechanical Engineering and Technology (IJMET)*, volume **8**, no. 11, pp. 649662, 2017.

3 H. Al. Shehri, "Student performance prediction using Support Vector Machine and K-Nearest Neighbor," *2017 IEEE 30th Canadian Conference on Electrical and Computer Engineering (CCECE)*, DOI:10.1109/CCECE.2017.7946847, 2017.

4 R. S. J. Baker, "Data Mining for Education in International Encyclopedia of Education," pp. 112–118, 2010.

5 F. Siraj and M. A. Abdoulha, "Mining Enrollment Data using Predictive and Descriptive Approaches", *Knowledge-Oriented Applications in Data Mining*, pp. 53–72, 2007.

6 M. R. Marra, A. K Rodgers, D. Shen and B. BogueB, "Leaving Engineering: A MultiǦYear Single Institution Stud", *Journal of Engineering Education*, vol. **101**, no.1, pp. 6–27, 2012.

7 J. M. Mbuva, "An Examination of Student Retention and Student Success In High School, College, and University", *Journal of Higher Education Theory and Practice*, vol. **11**, pp. 92–101, 2011.

8 B. Minaei-bidgoli, D. A. Kashy, G. Kortemeyer and W. F. Punch, "Predicting Student Performance: An Application Of Data Mining Methods With The Educational Web-Based System", *33rd ASEE/IEEE Front. Educ. Conf.*, vol. **1**, pp. 1-6, 2003.

9 N. Delavari, M. R. Beikzadeh, S. Phon-Amnuaisuk, "Application for Enhanced Analysis Model for Data Mining Processes in Higher Educational System," *6th International Conference on Information Technology Based Higher Education and Training*, DOI: 10.1109/ITHET.2005.1560303, 2005.

10 C. Tekin, J. Braun, and M. Schaar, "Etutor: Online learning for personalized education," *In Proc. 2015 IEEE Int. Conf. Acoustics, Speech and Signal Processing (ICASSP)*, 2015.

11 O. Taylan and B. Karagözoğlu, "An adaptive neuro-fuzzy model for prediction of student's academic performance", *Computers and Industrial Engineering*, vol. **57**, no. 3, pp. 732 741, 2009. http://dx.doi.org/10.1016/j.cie.2009.01.019.

12 G. Lassibille and L. N. Gomez, "Why do higher education students drop out?," *Evidence from Spain, Education Economics*, vol. **16**, no.1, pp. 89–105, 2007.

13 J. Nolan, "A Prototype Application of Fuzzy Logic and Expert Systems in Education Assessment," *AAAI Proceedings*, pp. 1134–1139, 1998.

14 D. F. Specht, "Probabilistic neural networks for classification mapping, or associative memory," *In Proceedings of IEEE International Conference on Neural Networks*, Vol. **1**, 1988.

15 S. B. Kotsiantis, C. J. Pierrakeas, I. D. Zaharakis and P. E. Pintelas, "Efficiency Of Machine Learning Techniques In Predicting Students' Performance In Distance Learning Systems", *Applied Artificial Intelligence*, volume **18**, no. 5, pp. 411–426, DOI: https://doi.org/10.1080/08839510490442058, 2004.

16 R. Asif, A. Merceron and M. K. Pathan,"Predicting Student Academic Performance at Degree Level :A Case Study," *I.J. Intell. Syst. Appl.*, pp. 4961, 2015.

17 Y. Meier, J. Xu, O. Atan, and M. Schaar, "Predicting Grades", *EEE Transactions on Signal Processing*, vol. **64**, no. 4, pp. 959–972, 2016.

18 A. M. Shahiri, W. Husain, N. A. Rashid, "A Review on Predicting Student's Performance using Data Mining Techniques", *Proc. of The Third Information Systems International Conference, Procedia Computer Science*, vol. **72**, pp. 414–422, 2015.

19 D. Kabakchieva, "Predicting Student Performance by Using Data Mining Methods for Classification", *Cybern. Inf. Technol.*, vol. **13**, no.1, pp.61–72, 2013.

20 K. P. Shaleena and S. Paul, "Data mining techniques for predicting student performance," *In Proc. of 2015 IEEE International Conference on Engineering and Technology (ICETECH)*, 2015, DOI: 10.1109/ICETECH.2015.7275025.

21 P. Cortez and A. Silva, "Using Data Mining to Predict Secondary School Student Performance," *In A. Brito and J. Teixeira Eds., Proceedings of 5th FUture Business Technology Conference (FUBUTEC 2008), Porto, Portugal, April, 2008, EUROSIS*, pp. 5–12, 2008, ISBN: 978-9077381-39-7.

22 B. K. Baradwaj and S. Pal, "Mining Educational Data to Analyze Students' Performance", *Int. J. Adv. Comput. Sci. Appl.*, vol. **2**, no. 6, pp. 63–69, 2011.

23 A. Acharya and D. Sinha, "Early Prediction of Students Performance using Machine Learning Techniques", *Int. J. Comput. Appl.*, vol. **107**, no. 1, pp. 37–43, 2014.

24 N. Arora, J. K. R. Saini, "A Fuzzy Probabilistic Neural Network for Student's Academic Performance Prediction", *International Journal of Innovative Research in Science*, vol. **2**, no. 3, pp. 4425–4432, 2013.

25 I. Lykourentzou, I. Giannoukos, G. Mpardis, V. Nikolopoulos, V. Loumos, "Early and dynamic student achievement prediction in e-learning courses using neural networks", *Journal of the American Society for Information Science and Technology*, vol. **60**, no. 2, pp. 372–380, 2009.

26 R. Bekele and W. Menzel, "A Bayesian approach to predict performance of a student (BAPPS): A case with Ethiopian students," *In Artificial Intelligence and Applications*, pp. 189–194, 2005.

27 C. Romero, S. Ventura, P. G. Espejo and C. Hervs, "Data mining algorithms to classify students," *International Conference on Educational Data Mining(EDM). Montreal*, pp. 8–17, 2008.

28 S. A. Kumar and M. N. Vijayalakshmi, "Efficiency of Decision Trees in Predicting Student's Academic Performance," *First International Conference on Computer Science, Engineering and Applications, Dubai*, pp. 335–343, 2011.

29 M. S. Edin Osmanbegovic, "Data Mining Approach For Predicting Student Performance", *Journal of Economics and Business*, vol. **10**, no. 1, pp. 3–12, 2012.

30 S. Lessmann, R. Stahlbock, S. F. Crone1, "Genetic Algorithms for Support Vector Machine Model Selection," *2006 International Joint Conference on Neural Networks Sheraton Vancouver Wall Centre Hotel, Vancouver, BC, Canada*, pp. 3063–3069, 2006.

31 C. Jin and L. De-lin, "An Improved ID3 Decision Tree Algorithm," *In. Proceedings of 2009 4th International Conference on Computer Science and Education*, pp. 127–130, 2009.

32 J. R. Quinlan, "Induction of Decision Trees," *Mach. Learn.*, pp. 81–106, 1986.

33 C. Cortes and V. Vapnik, "Support-vector network", *Mach. Learn.*, vol. **20**, pp. 273–297, 1995.

34 C. W. Hsu and C. J. Lin, "A Comparison of Methods for Multi-class Support Vector Machines", *EEE Transactions on Neural Networks*, vol. **13**, no. 2, pp. 415–425, 2002.

35 N. Cristianini and J. Shawe-Taylor, "*An introduction to support vector machines and other kernel-based learning methods*," *Cambridge University Press*, 2000.

36 F. Friedrichs and C. Igel, "Evolutionary Tuning of multiple SVM parameters", *Neuro-computing*, vol. **64**, pp. 107–117, 2005.

37 H. N. Nguyen, S. Y. Ohn, and W. J. Choi, "Combined Kernel Function for Support Vector Machine and Learning Method Based on Evolutionary Algorithm," *Proc. of the 11th Intern. Conf. on Neural Information Processing, Calcutta*, India, 2004.

38 B. Samanta, "Gear fault detection using artificial neural networks and support vector machines with genetic algorithms", *Mechanical Systems and Signal Processing*, vol. **18**, pp. 625–644, 2004.

39 L. Li et al, "A robust hybrid between genetic algorithm and support vector machine for extracting an optimal feature gene subset", *Genomics*, vol. **85**, pp. 16–23, 2005.

6

Cluster Analysis of Health Care Data Using Hybrid Nature-Inspired Algorithms

Kauser Ahmed P, Rishabh Agrawal

School of Computer Science and Engineering, VIT, Vellore, India

6.1   Introduction

The k-means algorithm and the firefly algorithm are used to develop a hybrid algorithm in this chapter to improve the quality of the cluster. Clustering is a technique to form a group of similar objects. The applications are endless, from machine learning to artificial intelligence. For example, it can be used to review several handwritten numbers and cluster similar ones together to do handwriting detection. There are several ways to do clustering, and it is not contained in a single domain. Different types of clustering algorithms can reveal different types of results for the same dataset. Also, clustering can be applied to the error detection methods or evaluation methods used to evaluate the clusters. They differ based on different criteria, so it is essential to know what type of evaluation method you will be using to get the results for your cluster because choosing the right method can make a massive difference when stating if the algorithm used to form a cluster gave a satisfying result or not. Then comes the nature-inspired algorithms, which are inspired by the events happening in nature. The original method that was used in optimizing the clustering algorithm is the firefly algorithm. The firefly algorithm is solely dependent on the fact that fireflies glow, and each firefly glows with a different intensity, and the less glowing firefly is attracted to the more glowing firefly and moves towards it.

There are various cluster models used by researchers to form clusters, and some of them are connectivity models, centroid models, distribution models, density models, and group models. There are also clustering algorithms for which a particular author does not define models.

A hybrid algorithm is an algorithm that consolidates at least two different algorithms that tackle a similar issue, either picking one (contingent upon the information) or exchanging between them through the span of the algorithm. This is by and large done to join wanted highlights of every algorithm, with the goal that the general algorithm is superior to the individual components. The hybrid algorithm does not allude to just consolidating various algorithms to take care of an alternate issue—various algorithms can be considered as mixes of less difficult pieces—however just to consolidating algorithms that take care of a similar issue yet vary in different qualities, mainly performance.

Recent Advances in Hybrid Metaheuristics for Data Clustering, First Edition.
Edited by Sourav De, Sandip Dey, and Siddhartha Bhattacharyya.
© 2020 John Wiley & Sons Ltd. Published 2020 by John Wiley & Sons Ltd.

Optimization means optimizing a currently available algorithm using different techniques, be that in the initial stages of that algorithm or after that algorithm does its work, but these techniques or algorithms are used to gain optimal results on the present algorithms and thus increase their efficiency.

The paper is organized as follows. Section 6.2 discusses the related work and introduces *k*-means clustering and the firefly algorithm. Section 6.3 discusses the proposed methodology. Results and discussion are highlighted in Section 6.4. Concluding remarks are given in Section 6.5.

6.2 Related Work

6.2.1 Firefly Algorithm

The firefly algorithm was proposed by Yang in 2008 [10] and is a computationally efficient, nature-inspired, population-based metaheuristic and multi-objective optimization algorithm that derives its solution approach from the social flashing behavior of fireflies. The main steps of the firefly algorithm start from initializing a group of fireflies, each of which is determined by the flashing light intensity. During the loop of pairwise comparison of light intensity, the firefly with the lower light intensity will move toward the higher one. The flashing light helps fireflies find mates, attract their potential prey, and protect themselves from their predators. The moving distance depends on the attractiveness. During the moving stage, the new group of fireflies is compared for light intensity, and the best iterated solution is updated after evaluation. The swarm of fireflies will move to brighter and more attractive locations by the flashing light intensity associated with the objective function of the problem considered in order to obtain efficient optimal solutions. The loop of the pairwise comparison process is repeated until the termination criteria are satisfied. Finally, the best-so-far solution is visualized.

The development of the firefly-inspired algorithm uses three main basic rules:

i) Evaluate the light intensity of all the fireflies.
ii) Attractiveness is proportional to their brightness of intensity of light and decreases as the distance among them increases.
iii) The brightness of the flashing light can be considered as the objective function to be optimized.

The firefly algorithm is applicable to job scheduling, network analysis, dispatch problems, structural optimization, continuous optimization, discrete optimization, vector quantization, price forecasting, load forecasting, the traveling salesman problem, non-linear optimization, and dynamic environment problems. Major important applications of firefly algorithm with excellent performance are classifications and clustering. For example, [9] provided an extensive performance study by comparing the firefly algorithm to 11 different algorithms and concluded that the firefly algorithm can be efficiently used for clustering. In most cases, the firefly algorithm outperforms all 11 algorithms. However, the firefly algorithm has two major advantages over other nature-inspired algorithms: automatical subdivision and the ability to deal with multimodality. The basic flow of firefly algorithm is depicted in Figure 6.1.

Figure 6.1 Flow diagram of the firefly algorithm

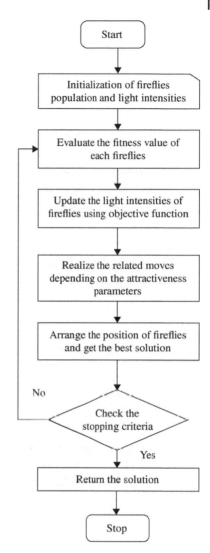

6.2.2 *k*-means Algorithm

The *k*-means algorithm is a typical partition-based clustering method. Given a pre-specified number K, the algorithm partitions the dataset into K disjoint subsets, which optimize the following objective function given in Eqn. 6.1.

$$J = \sum_{j=1}^{k} \sum_{i=1}^{n} \| x_i^{(j)} - c_j \|^2 \tag{6.1}$$

where J = objective function, k = number of clusters, n = number of cases, $x_i^{(j)}$ = case i, and c = centroid for cluster j.

The *k*-means algorithm is simple and fast. The time complexity of *k*-means is $O(l * k * n)$, where l is the number of iterations and k is the number of clusters. However, it also has several drawbacks as a data-based clustering algorithm. First, the

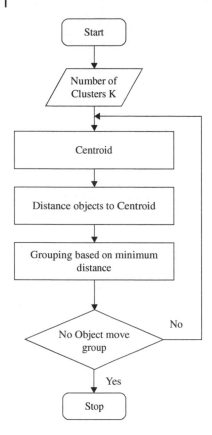

Figure 6.2   Flow diagram of the *k*-means algorithm

number of data clusters in a dataset is usually unknown in advance. To detect the optimal number of clusters, users normally run the algorithms repeatedly with different values and compare the clustering results. The basic flow of the *k*-means algorithm is depicted in Figure 6.2.

A brief review of literature is given in Table 6.1.

6.3   Proposed Methodology

The proposed model in Figure 6.3 focuses on the two ways we can go about constructing the said algorithm. The clustering algorithm can be used to gain initial clusters, and then the nature-inspired algorithm can be used to optimize the said clusters to get better cluster formations. The same can be done in reverse. The other method that is to be used is that both the algorithms can be hybridized in such a way that we use the favorable steps of both algorithms to get the better algorithm by leaving out the negative steps of each algorithm. The proposed system has been tested using the *k*-means algorithm for the clustering algorithm and the firefly algorithm for the nature-inspired algorithm. As a result, the *k*-means clustering depends solely on the distance between elements and the cluster. This sometimes negatively affects the outcome as two perfect clusters may clash. The results of before and after the *k*-means clustering are interesting. We can see that what should have been two

Table 6.1 Summary/Gaps Identified in the Survey

S.NO	Title	Technique Used	Advantages	Disadvantages
1	Efficient genetic k-means clustering for health care knowledge discovery [1]	k-means clustering using the self-organizing map	Scalable, better than known techniques at the time, works with other topics also.	Could be improved using other techniques like hybridization.
2	A New Approach for Data Clustering Based on PSO with Local Search [2]	k-means, particle swarm optimization algorithm	Very fast compared to other algorithms if the parameters are set right, gave best results on the dataset that it worked with.	Does not work well with various datasets, as it is robust finding the right parameters for different dataset may be time-consuming.
3	Automatic clustering using nature-inspired metaheuristics: A survey [3]	Compares already present techniques to find the best automatic clustering techniques	MOCK, mMOCK, MOPSOSA, and Gen-ClustMOO algorithms gave better results than the others.	Unable to compare all algorithm at once to find the one average algorithm, which gives fairly good result on all datasets.
4	A New Hybrid Approach for Data Clustering using Firefly Algorithm and k-means [4]	Firefly algorithm, k-means	Firefly algorithm gives better refined centroid to use as clusters, which cuts down processing time and gives more concrete clusters. Better than PSO, KPSO, and k-means.	Gives average results for all datasets but never exceeds the best result for that particular dataset for different algorithm.
5	Stock Market Prediction Using Clustering with Meta-Heuristic Approaches [5]	PSO, BAT algorithm, firefly	Comparing various meta heuristic approaches, the firefly method was proven to be the best among them.	Only certain datasets used and so we do not know how will its performance with other datasets.
6	An Effective Clustering Algorithm With Ant Colony [6]	Ant colony optimization, clustering validity analysis, sacc algorithm	E-sacc has proved better than saac.	Takes too much time and can be improved further with more work.
7	Hybrid PSO and GA models for Document Clustering [7]	Particle swarm optimization, genetic algorithm, stagnation	Better than relative local search heuristics as it gives better ability to cope with local optima.	Was not used against other algorithms to compare so cannot say it would work for all types of data or not.
8	Application of Particle Swarm Optimization in Data Clustering: A Survey [8]	Particle swarm optimization, k-means clustering PSO	Gives a better result when hybridized with other algorithms rather than using it for optimization.	Not all methods with all attributes were tried so the possibility for much improvement in the future.

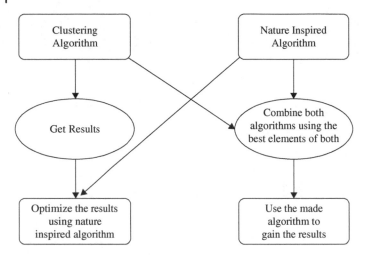

Figure 6.3 Proposed methodology

perfectly divided clusters are now coinciding in each other. This happened because of the lack of foresight in k-means as it evaluates solely based on the distance. We can use the firefly algorithm to use the intercluster distances and the intracluster element distances to get a comprehensible algorithm and density-distance relationship to determine whether the firefly head over to a new cluster or stay in the same one. We define it as the glowing coefficient only for the clusters centers in Eqn. 6.2.

$$GL = Density_{c(j)}/D_{(i,Ci)} \qquad (6.2)$$

where D is the distance between particle and cluster center j; and the $Density_{c(j)}$ is the number of elements in the cluster j, $i \in$ all elements, and $j \in$ all clusters. The glowing coefficient would be taken of all the particles with the cluster centers; and the one with the lowest glowing coefficient will be taken, and the output would be calculated. Similarly, all the particles would be assigned new clusters, or some may remain in their old ones. This will keep going until the threshold values are achieved; in other words, k-means and the glowing function would keep on iterating in series.

The centroid stabilizes, and we get our respective clusters. The proposed k-means firefly algorithm pseudocode is given in Figure 6.4.

6.4 Results and Discussion

The main sample case that was used for this purpose is the diabetes dataset. The other dataset used for analysis purpose has iris data. The diabetes dataset is the most extensive one with more than 10,000 instances and 179 different attributes, and as the algorithm is most effective on datasets that are large in size, it is perfect for this purpose. The others will serve as to set a benchmark for the main dataset.

The proposed datasets were tested over different clusters values, and the Davies-Bouldin index was calculated for each of them. First, they were calculated on the original simple

```
1       GENERATE K random cluster centroid
2     repeat
3         for all instance i in S do
4             shortest <- 0
5             membership <- null
6             for all Centroid c do
7                 distance <- Distance(c)
8                 if dist < shortest then
9                     shortest <- dist
10                    membership <- c
11                end if
12            end for
13        end for
14        Recalculate Centroids(c)
15
16        for all instance i in S do
17            shortest <- 0
18            membership <- null
19            for all Centroid c do
20                GL <- Total Members(c) / Distance(c)
21                if GL < shortest then
22                    shortest <- dist
23                    membership <- c
24                end if
25            end for
26        end for
27        Recalculate Centroids(c)
28    until convergence
29    end procedure
```

Figure 6.4 *k*-means firefly algorithm pseudocode

k-means clustering algorithm, and then the data was drawn on a graph. Then the same dataset was run on the *k*-means firefly algorithm, and then the results after evaluating using the Davies-Bouldin method were plotted on the graph on which we plotted the previous results. The entire process was done for the diabetes and iris datasets. It can be seen in Figure 6.5 that the value of evaluation for the dataset cluster after the *k*-means firefly was used is much less in comparison than the one with only the simple *k*-means applied to it. The evaluation of the Davies-Bouldin index takes into account both the distance of the element from the cluster and the intercluster distance to give an accurate measure of the error evaluation index. This means sacrificing the error measure of the square root detection method because this rates clusters solely based on their distance between the points inside the cluster and not regarding the fact that clusters can be different sizes and thus ending up giving an error index that truly favors the clustering algorithm that assigns the clusters based upon the distance of the particles.

As we can clearly see in Figure 6.5 after incorporating the firefly algorithm into the original *k*-means, the formation of two perfect clusters is shown. That proves our original

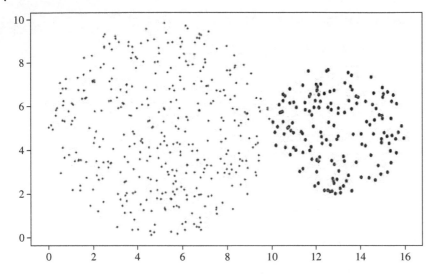

Figure 6.5 Circles cluster after *k*-means firefly algorithm

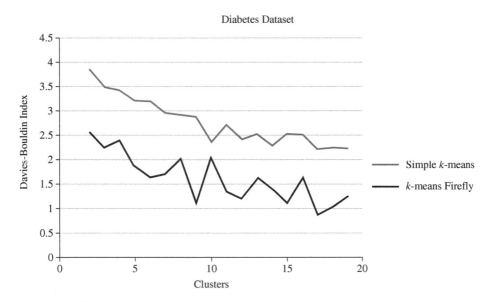

Figure 6.6 Diabetes Davies-Bouldin graph before verses after

assumption that *k*-means really was not giving accurate results, whereas because of the addition of the glowing index of the firefly algorithm, we now get cluster formations as they should have been from the beginning. So now we can apply it to some real datasets so that we can get results in real time. As you have seen, our main type of problem can be resolved using the algorithm made by the combination of the *k*-means and firefly. Figure 6.6 gives the analysis of our prime dataset, i.e., diabetes, using both the old and new algorithms with a different number of clusters.

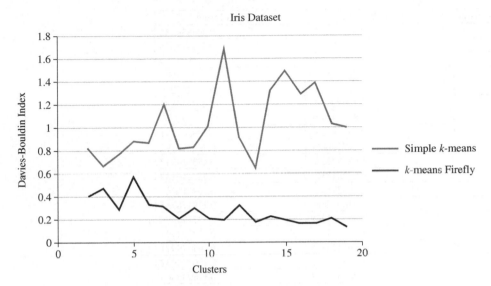

Figure 6.7   Iris Davies-Bouldin graph before versus after

Clusters	Simple *k*-means	*k*-means Firefly
2	3.850727766	2.546664505
3	3.5147365	2.236913561
4	3.416544944	2.389102819
5	3.214822627	1.842481249
6	3.192403864	1.636899643
7	2.952389859	1.705848023
8	2.922510646	2.012751061
9	2.870189125	1.086601769
10	2.344497389	2.034504567
11	2.711487515	1.339573445
12	2.41055976	1.186199471
13	2.530643363	1.607230156
14	2.288508315	1.393259955
15	2.522721881	1.097642295
16	2.50857728	1.64230359
17	2.203269192	0.866847726
18	2.251539357	1.03495922
19	2.228267331	1.246235285

Figure 6.8   Diabetes dataset Davies-Bouldin index

As seen in Figure 6.7, our new algorithm not only gives better results than the original simple *k*-means but also works on different types of dataset. Seeing as how diabetes and iris datasets gave positive improvement in results, we can safely assume that it could work with several other health-related datasets and give positive results (Figure 6.8 and Figure 6.9). The 2-D dataset represents two circles that we randomly generated to get a visual representation of the improvement that our algorithm provides so we know how the algorithm forms clusters and if the formed clusters are accurate or not.

Clusters	Simple *k*-means	*k*-means Firefly
2	0.815163522	0.404834136
3	0.666072158	0.471911535
4	0.775080743	0.27834299
5	0.887285999	0.575054937
6	0.868472014	0.328203275
7	1.199729392	0.308345681
8	0.815418159	0.201546707
9	0.833358856	0.29847631
10	1.017138064	0.208369492
11	1.686975839	0.183714947
12	0.908018803	0.322416437
13	0.65295032	0.169015164
14	1.316528683	0.219178785
15	1.494331338	0.187174596
16	1.281701923	0.162594991
17	1.391172345	0.164679911
18	1.033224045	0.200475032
19	1.006658211	0.126033866

Figure 6.9   Iris dataset Davies-Bouldin index

6.5 Conclusion

The *k*-means firefly algorithm on average is 54% better than the simple *k*-means algorithm when considering the Davies-Bouldin index. With this kind of improvement, it can right away be put to use in real-time applications in the place of the traditional algorithms for better output and efficiency. The limitation is still that, no matter what, any algorithm as of now can't improve both the *k*-means and Davies-Bouldin index because satisfying the criteria of both the evaluation techniques, i.e., one that favors purely distance and one that weighs the intercluster distance, is still a work in progress. Nevertheless, the improvement that we visually saw for the two-dimensional data was convincing enough to use the new algorithm over the old one. Another limitation is that the dataset needs to be correctly cleaned and integrated to be used here becuase the nominal data may create problems for us as the difference between nominal categories can't be displayed as mere numerical data and thus poses a challenge for us to solve in the future. The scope for future work is that we need to find a way to form clusters that could be accepted over a variety of evaluation index, and for that we need to try different optimization and hybridization methods and other different ways to overcome this particular barrier so that we can finally achieve our main goal, i.e., to find a clustering algorithm to form perfect clusters. We could also use this opportunity to take already diagnosed patients with diseases and use their initial stages data to form a dataset with a result through which we could form clusters and then use the data of a new patient with it to find and detect the traces of a disease in its early stages, which could lead to early detection of the disease and thus help prevent it.

References

1 Alsayat, A., & El-Sayed, H. (2016, June). Efficient genetic *k*-means clustering for health care knowledge discovery. In 2016 IEEE 14th International Conference on Software Engineering Research, Management and Applications (SERA) (pp. 45–52). IEEE.

2 Premalatha, K. and Natarajan, A.M. (2008). A New Approach for Data Clustering based on PSO with Local Search. *Computer and Information Science* **1** (4): 139–145.

3 Jose-Garcia, A. and Gómez-Flores, W. (2016). Automatic clustering using nature-inspired metaheuristics: A survey. *Applied Soft Computing* **41**: 192–213.

4 Hassanzadeh, T. and Meybodi, M.R., 2012, May. A new hybrid approach for data clustering using firefly algorithm and *k*-means. In Artificial Intelligence and Signal Processing (AISP), 2012 16th CSI International Symposium on (pp. 007–011). IEEE.

5 Prasanna, S. and Ezhilmaran, D. (2015). Stock Market Prediction Using Clustering with Meta-Heuristic Approaches. *Gazi University Journal of Science* **28** (3): 395–403.

6 Liu, X. and Fu, H. (2010). An Effective Clustering Algorithm With Ant Colony. *JCP* **5** (4): 598–605.

7 Premalatha, K. and Natarajan, A.M. (2010). Hybrid PSO and GA models for document clustering. *Int. J. Advance. Soft Comput. Appl* **2** (3): 302–320.

8 Sarkar, S., Roy, A., and Purkayastha, B.S. (2013). Application of particle swarm optimization in data clustering: a survey. *International Journal of Computer Applications* **65** (25): 38–46.

9 Senthilnath, J., Omkar, S.N., and Mani, V. (2011). Clustering using firefly algorithm: performance study. *Swarm and Evolutionary Computation* **1** (3): 164–171.

10 Yang, X.S. (2009, October). Firefly algorithms for multimodal optimization. In: *International symposium on stochastic algorithms*, 169–178. Berlin, Heidelberg: Springer.

7

Performance Analysis Through a Metaheuristic Knowledge Engine

Indu Chhabra[1] and Gunmala Suri[2]

[1]*Department of Computer Science and Applications, Panjab University, Chandigarh, India*
[2]*University Business School, Panjab University, Chandigarh, India*

7.1   Introduction

Different types of data in different formats in the physical and management sciences have posed a "data rich and information poor" challenge for the IT industry to model and investigate these complex systems for the behavioral understanding of human nature. Today, online discussions, blogs, chats, Flickr, and WhatsApp all work because of behavioral features of human beings. Facebook makes groups of like-minded people by using their subjective features. It recommends people "you may know." This data is vital to predicting new business strategies. Because of this kind of social networking, the total data generation in the world, which was 4.4 zettabytes in 2013, will rise steeply to 44 zettabytes by 2020 [1].

Because of social networking through audio and video online services of news, movies, and research resources, data mining systems are intended to address the information explosion by finding a small set of user items and meeting their personalized interests. For example, Amazon uses collaborative filtering to generate high-quality products to recommend online customers. As businesses gather raw facts and observations on consumer trends and preferences through these heterogeneous sources, data mining aids in filtering the ambiguity to approximate the partial truth into computationally knowledgeable solutions.

Business intelligence is one of the well-discussed applications of data mining. The massive amounts of data velocity and derived generalized metaheuristics to draw business intelligence are some of the major concerns for enterprises today. Traditional (OLTP) systems are not modeled for the incremental databases to evolve based on the customers' changing interests, but data mining paradigms analyze the data from different perspectives. The integration across heterogeneous, interdependent complex data resources for real-time decision-making, streaming data, collaboration, and ultimately value co-creation is the main benefit for the complex computing process. Utilizing computing infrastructure, various mining paradigms have been found to represent abstracted knowledge, user involvement, and data investigation such as association rule mining for metaheuristic development and validation, machine learning, statistics, and neural networks. Different studies based on consumer purchasing behaviors have been presented and used in real problems [2].

Data mining tools have great preprocessing, mining, and implementation capabilities for examination and result visualization. They follow the process of knowledge discovery through association mining. In real-life scenarios, data mining has enabled retail and marketing organizations to find the implicit relationships among the various market dynamics of cost, price, and shelf-organization to predict the most favorable market directives. To solve the real-life customer behavior problems, association rule learning standards like frequent pattern matching, market basket analysis, and a priori algorithms assure a promising solution to convert the qualitative subjectivity of consumer interest into a quantitative real-time generalized model so that market laws and policies can be framed for business expansion. Formulating business heuristics to predict user buying behavior is the main focus of this study. Association rule mining through market basket analysis is explored for the frequency and accuracy estimation of the mined rules.

7.2 Data Mining and Metaheuristics

Data mining, a kind of knowledge discovery in databases, acts as an organization's memory. It creates intellect from this memory by finding novel, useful, and previously unknown patterns. Data mining is the process of extracting previously unknown patterns from data to recognize past patterns and trends for business intelligence. It applies various statistical, neural computing, intelligent agents, genetic algorithms, and case-based reasoning techniques to resolve the iterative and scalable problems of scalable problems of classification, clustering, association, sequencing, regression, and forecasting. Amazon.com performs text mining to find hidden contents, determine relationships, and group relationships by themes. For profile practices, surveillance, and scientific discovery where the datasets are too small for reliable statistical inferences of new patterns, the data mining techniques are used to create new hypotheses for those discovery-driven systems.

In computer science, *heuristic* (from Greek εὑρίσκω "I find, discover") is a technique designed to resolve a problem more wisely when classic methods are not that efficient. This is achieved by trading optimality through frequency, accuracy, and completeness. A literature review on metaheuristic optimization suggests that it was Fred Glover who coined the word [3].

Metaheuristic is a higher-level process to select a heuristic to provide a sufficiently good solution for implicit or incomplete information with limited computation capacity. Technically the target is the efficient exploration of search space. Metaheuristics does not always guarantee that a globally optimal solution can be found on some class of problems. So as to find near-optimal solutions, we need to guide the search process. As these metaheuristics are not problem-dependent, its techniques range from simple local searching to complex learning procedures. Trade-off criteria for applying heuristics to the specific problem include the following:

- **Optimality**: Out of several alternative solutions, will heuristics guarantee an optimal solution? Is the optimal solution is the best?

- **Completeness**: Heuristics must be able to find several realistic solutions for the underlying problem. Are all solutions are needed? Many heuristics processes are meant to find only a few optimal solutions.
- **Accuracy and precision**: To provide accuracy, heuristics provides a confidence interval. Are the limits for solutions unreasonably large?

The objective of a heuristic is to produce a solution that is logically and technically good enough for the given problem. This solution may not be the best of all the solutions to this problem, or it may simply approximate the exact solution. But it is still valuable because finding it does not require a prohibitively long time and specific hardware and software like PolyAnalyst's Market Basket Analysis professional software. Heuristics may produce final results by itself and may act as intermediates processors for the other optimization algorithms to improve their performance like to generate good seed values. For example, antivirus software often uses heuristic rules for locating malware and viruses. Heuristic scanning checks for code patterns shared by the class of malware, through different rule-combinations. If a scanned document is suspected to contain matching code patterns, then that file is declared to be an infected file.

7.3 Problem Description

Various data mining methodologies based on data scalability and knowledge levels are applied to analyze user association in buying habits. The purpose of research is to imitate the empirical knowledge of these issues to create actual model that measures the impact of interesting parameters on system performance when they actually interact with the real system. The dilemma of quantification of customer behavior, meaning how and why one purchases a group of items, is explored through association analysis. Present research infers and delineates the hidden facts of implicit behavioral actions of the customer at the time of purchase. The traditional legacy systems lack in efficiently computing the item set purchased due to the flaw in candidate creation process so practically cannot harmonize the complexity of a data scenario. Hence, a proficient automatic data investigation and prediction tool is required that can quantify the real-factual patterns. To get a better understanding of different interesting factors that play important role in improving performance and how they behave in partitioning the database collection into subparts, a test set collection is analyzed for selective search and efficiency evaluation. The general model framework through market basket analysis is presented to experiment and estimate the effect of these factors.

The research contribution is structured in the form of first summarizing the key challenges for technology; some major research initiatives and projects; different issues from technical, developer, and user perspectives; and the present system evaluation and automation for the knowledge discovery. For the efficacy analysis of this pattern-discovery model, a database study of 10 baskets having 31 item patterns pertaining to 10 users is inspected for 5 different items. Then they are framed based on the vigilance parameters of support and confidence as well as the indicator matrix inferences so that general rules can be outlined for the future market concerns.

After summarizing the major association rule challenges in Section 7.4, we highlight the major research initiatives and projects in this field. Section 7.5 performs the literature analysis of the journey from traditional mining to advanced data mining. Section 7.6 elaborates on the framework of methodology adopted to automate the process. After implementing the system for market basket analysis through the case study of 31 service-set basket combinations in Section 7.7, we describe the research contributions and future work in Section 7.8. Section 7.9 concludes the finding of the study.

7.4 Association Rule Learning

In business, for timely product promotions, association rule mining is applied. Technically it searches for relationships between variables. It prunes the nonfrequent patterns as they represent the already known facts and hence lock out novelty. For example, a supermarket might gather data on customer purchasing habits. Using association rule learning, the supermarket can determine which products are frequently bought together and can use this information for marketing purposes.

Association rule is a probabilistic statement $X \to Y$ about the co-occurrence of certain subsequences and substructures within multidimensional relational databases. It searches for recurring relationships and derives correlations among the database attributes to produce if-then statements. For the process of automation, it depicts a relationship between X and Y through quantifiers of support and confidence. An association rule $X \Rightarrow Y$ holds with confidence c if $c\%$ of transactions in D containing Y confirms the happening of X. The $s\%$ of transactions in D support X if X is present in D and s is greater than and equal to the user-defined threshold, which is a fraction between [0,1].

7.4.1 Association Mining Issues

The following are association mining issues:

1) In real scenarios, there are always some additional variables that may influence the automatic system but are not derivable from the dataset during the modeling process like rare combinations. The reasons are different and range from high complexity to feature modeling to not visualizing the importance of some factors. So, the mining must be capable of handling the unobserved input Z besides the independent input variable X and dependent variable Y.
2) Data changing over time can be stored in many different kinds of database and information warehouses. The purpose is to map the heterogeneous repositories to a unified data mining schema of multidimensional views to facilitate in-depth analysis.
3) Because data is made up of different types and may be probabilistic in nature and from questionable sources, generating a hypothesis and supporting evidence for rule mining requires considerable skill for model management.

7.4.2 Research Initiatives and Projects

Certain database technology invented in the 1960s has evolved into the latest advanced spatial, scientific, and engineering data mining systems used in early 2000s. To create meaning from the huge amounts of daily emerging data, many official organizational efforts have been made globally.

- During 2012–2014, the National High Technology Research and Development Program was executed by the China government for the data mining extraction-transformation-loading process. The goal was the derivation of multigranularity knowledge while retaining the quality from massive facts.
- In October 2012, for civil society needs, the NDSAP of India launched a site for the visualization of public funds.
- Based on an announcement made by President Obama and Prime Minister Shri Manmohan Singh during the Indo-US talks in 2010, the OGD platform was jointly developed by India and the US government in 2013. It was intended to access datasets and services published by the government of India.
- To implement data mining systems in R&D, the Department of Science and Technology in the government of India launched a big data scheme in 2016 and the Data Science Research initiative in 2017. The purpose was the use of data science technology in practical, real scenarios for quality assessment.
- In 2018, the OGD platform was expanded to include the best features of India.gov.in and the US data.gov project.

Other than these research initiatives, various issues pertaining to government and semi-government databases are handled such as categorizing the type of access granted and not compromising on national security by maintaining individual privacy. Based on quality metadata, the dataset apps were created to prioritize the time sensitive data. To contribute to open-list datasets, the data was made available in different formats such as comma-separated value (CSV), spreadsheet (Excel), Extensible Markup Language (XML), and Resource Description Framework (RDF).

7.5 Literature Review

The versatility of data mining has encouraged academia research and motivated the business community to reap its benefits [4]. How the data mining domain and organizational intelligence can be applied to business growth is well illustrated through the complete human and machine cooperated system [5]. These systems provide better prediction accuracy than a random guess and bring significant business values to developers [6]. The dataset includes 10,974 articles published between 1995 and 2010 and examines them for knowledge management (KM) [7]. The results are validated through the application of KM techniques from the fields of knowledge management diagnostics and software engineering to a broad spectrum of other disciplines such as distributed databases and machine learning. Decision-making is a knowledge-concentrated activity where knowledge is both its raw material and finished goods. In 1998 Delphi Group survey instituted the role of knowledge management by validating that 50% respondents report KM efforts as a strategic issue, whereas 80% understand KM as significant contributor to business practices [8]. Data mining as a decision support tool extracts useful marketing insights of customers and their purchase patterns. Hence, proficiency in KM is crucial to be remain competitive [9]. However, the evolving quantitative database size can be reduced to retain only qualitative data, which is rationalized through the mining algorithm of filtering large databases [10].

Various KM techniques to process descriptive, procedural, and reasoning knowledge are applied to build automatic decision support systems. A systematic methodology is proposed to manage and support marketing decisions. This methodology can be the basis for enhancing customer experience. The role of knowledge management is justified through real-data empirical evidence of 1,743 surveys [11]. A hypothesis was formed from structural equation modeling with the findings validated through knowledge management for better resource utilization. This paper [2] reviews "how data mining techniques have evolved in the time span of 2000 to 2011" with respect to their architecture and knowledge analysis. The discussion revealed how data mining can be applied in expertise orientation for human behavior analysis. Inter-disciplinary research in the context of various methods and techniques has been carried out for different educational sources [12]. These techniques were used to investigate the data for unknown patterns surfaced after the investigations. This survey paper pictures the evolution of educational data mining by bringing to light the aspects and outcomes of various studies carried out from 2001 to 2015. The concept of repetitive purchasing and compulsive buying was combined with decision-making to study the consumer behavior of social media users. The findings were that compulsive shopping is more emotional than rational [13].

The comparative analysis of practical performance of well-known algorithms for solving the parameter estimation is well presented in the context of dynamic systems [14]. A case study of finite small-dimensional nonlinear programming problems was surveyed to approximate the metaheuristics effect on the global solution. The research was concerned with applying data mining clustering algorithms to derive graph cuts and partitions [15]. To produce high-quality partitions, two controlling thresholds of lower and upper bounds were studied. As observed in this paper, most of the k-way algorithms found in literature used a correspondence between the vertices as well as the rows of eigenvectors' matrix of G. To perform linear ordering and k-means clustering, an association between graph vertices and eigenvectors' matrix rows of G was utilized. A few other works use eigenvectors grouping. Experimentation has given new insights into the choice of controlling parameter k, the optimized number of clusters.

How these techniques can be used for many real-life and classical optimization problems has been well analyzed through a few important combinations [16]. In this regard, the alternatives may be other supporting metaheuristics, with AI constraint programming, and with techniques. They are applied with data mining approaches in a case study of risk prediction of hospital readmissions. Two controlling parameters, low quality of care in the hospital and poor arrangement of the discharge process, are analyzed. The purpose was to help the common man through the launching of readmission penalty program for hospitals by the government. Data mining along with swarm intelligent heuristics are applied to predict the risks [17]. As the final outcome is based on the applied methodology, various metaheuristic optimization algorithms have been introduced and utilized to find the optimal solutions with justified logical computation time [18]. The controlling parameters of support and confidence are competent enough to threshold their rating according to the interesting echelon of the generated rules. Directness and analytical precision are the parameters that can be evaluated in combination for association rule framing [19].

The innovative element of this project [20] is the application of data mining for psychometrics to clarify the consumer's emotional decision-making. Five scales are created through the Google Forms service, collected through questionnaires, and implemented through the R package machine learning algorithm. Results conclude that emotion envisages consumer performance rather than cognitive ability and hence is more important in predicting consumer behavior. The more influential top 10 data mining algorithms [21] including including k-means, SVM, apriori, AdaBoost, and kNN are identified are identified. The algorithms are inspected for their description and impact for further research. To fill the existing gap between academic researches and real-world business problems, how data mining improves the operations of conventional data mining is well analyzed. The paper [22] suggests solutions by reviewing and studying the latest methodological, technical, and practical processes as well. Several efficient rule mining methods to discover interesting and unpredicted rules from a large customer dataset are described for their comparative analysis [23].

Introduced by Agarwal and Srikant [24], association rule mining is a knowledge deriving technique used for sequential item sets to show how different rules are mined while preserving the sequences and subsequences within those item sets. The performance issues for predicting future stability are analyzed to generalize the metaheuristic mining process [25]. The existing association rule mining techniques in context of their theoretical and implementation issues are investigated for the efficiency of association mining at a reduced computational cost [26]. The four methods are as follows: reducing the number of passes over the database, sampling the database, adding extra constraints on the structure of patterns, and using parallelization. In recent years, much progress has been made in all these directions. To justify the expectations of industries for association rule mining, Seyed et al. [27] tried to understand and improve the processes of gaining new customers and of increasing the loyalty of existing ones. for overall growth and expansion.

The pitfalls of the existing techniques of association rule mining and future direction was also analyzed for the present perspective [28]. To achieve a high degree of privacy, data utility, and time efficiency, the frequent item set mining algorithm was improved through a novel smart splitting method to inspect the database for frequent pattern growth [29]. To limit the level of interestingness in the derived date [30], the support and confidence metrics were computed. Using these parameters resulted in finding only those interesting patterns that can improve comprehensibility and predictive accuracy.

7.6 Methodology

To fix the candidate diagnostic process, the results are generated and filtered to choose the best one. For this, first the data patterns are examined based on the computational value of interesting parameters to select only those item-combinations whose frequency and accuracy are high. After the three-phase analysis, this newly generated arrangement is confirmed through the threshold values so that the generalized formal automatic

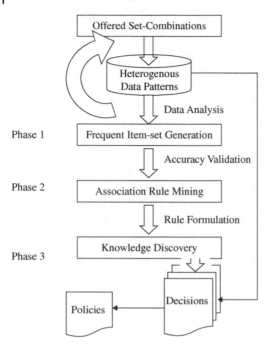

Figure 7.1 Knowledge discovery paradigm

marketing system can be developed. For the methodology, the user hypothesis is analyzed to determine the data to be examined. To discover the previously unknown frequent facts, association rule discovery is well implemented through the algorithm of market basket analysis. The flowchart of the solution derivation is shown in Figure 7.1. The working process goes through these various phases:

- Pattern search
- Rule mining
- Knowledge derivation as shown in Figure 7.1

7.6.1   Phase 1: Pattern Search

This candidate generation stage for frequent item sets quantifies the extent to which one variable is dependent on another related variable, through interestingness measures of frequency, accuracy, rarity, consistency, and periodicity. To prune the non-frequent patterns as they represent the common already known knowledge and lack novelty, the interestingness measures of support and confidence are computed to quantify the frequency and accuracy of only those items that "go together."

7.6.2   Phase 2: Rule Mining

Frequency: This means how often the number of instances in the complete database for which the association rules and corresponding metaheuristics can predict correctly. It computes how often X and Y occur together by calculating the percentage of transactions in the database (D) containing both X and Y in support of rule $R_i : X \rightarrow Y$. Hence,

$$Support = \frac{No.\ of\ occurrences\ of\ Rule\ R_i}{All\ occurrences\ of\ all\ Rules}$$

Accuracy: This means confidently measuring the accuracy and reliability of instances that the association rules predict correctly among all instances the rules are applied to. It calculates how much a particular item Y is dependent on another X by computing the percentage of transactions in the database (D) containing X, which also contains Y. Hence

$$Confidence = \frac{No.\ of\ occurrences\ of\ Rule\ R_i}{Rules\ supporting\ X\ only}$$

7.6.3 Phase 3: Knowledge Derivation

After deriving strong frequent patterns, knowledge derivation preserves only those associations of the database that have high support and confidence as validated by the metaheuristic application. Based on these identified relationships for various categories, the knowledge paradigm practically helps in framing future business rules and policies.

7.7 Implementation

To solve the common problem of dimensionality reduction in customer analysis, support and confidence are the metrics that are utilized to threshold the level of interestingness in the formulated heuristics. These parameters help discover the interesting patterns that are capable of improving the working machinery with respect to comprehensibility and predictive accuracy.

The prediction of previously unknown user preferences will help retailers improve their marketing strategies such as placing reliable item sets in close proximity to promote the sale of those items together. The various associated issues to be adhered to for the technical implementation are tabulated in Table 7.1. This practical scenario for association rule mining summarizes the data from different dimensions.

7.7.1 Test Issues

Based on the tabulated domain information, the derived analytics from this prototype study provide clear answers to the critical questions in Table 7.1 of the various competitive threats for technicians and developers.

7.7.2 System Evaluation

The data mining model of "Consumer Behavior Analysis for Efficient Cloud Services" is investigated. The prime concern is to inspect and evaluate the algorithm in such a way that it is capable of locating the most frequent but cost-effective item patterns to answer this question: "How can the services be well-rendered to cover the future market risks?" For

Table 7.1 Technical Scenario

User Satisfaction	Developer Perspective	System Processes
Which consumer trends and why?	Are there sufficient database observations to communicate user preferences?	Are the processes of design methodology and test execution followed properly?
Which item basket combination is bought most often?	Can you find the most frequent item sets through various interestingness measures?	Do the selected metrics measure the system effectively?
How do the customer preferences affect future postulates?	Are the applied data validation rules adequate enough to ensure the accuracy of data?	Does the database design have comprehensive and realistic observations of the requested needs?
Are the user support activities such as data entry and access, the GUI, and manual usage validated properly?	Are the selected techniques and tools adequate enough to ensure the integrity and consistency of datasets and are they selected in a logical manner?	Do the system quality reports, libraries, and help manuals summarize all the instructional Information and services with relevant details?

the efficacy analysis of the knowledge discovery paradigm, a database study of 10 cloud service combinations, pertaining to 10 users, was conducted for these five factors: efficiency, security, storage, data, and application. Market-basket association rule mining was applied to study the preferences of the users. Conclusions were formulated based on the an inferences of an indicator matrix [Table 7.2] so that general rules could be framed for timely service endorsement and future market stakes.

7.7.2.1 Indicator Matrix Formulation

Each row of this matrix indicates a user transaction of the service basket selected by a single customer, whereas the columns depict the service itself within the selected basket.

Table 7.2 Indicator Matrix

Basket-ID	Efficiency	Security	Storage	Data	Application
B_1	1	1	1		1
B_2			1	1	
B_3	1		1	1	
B_4	1	1	1		
B_5	1			1	
B_6		1			
B_7	1		1		
B_8		1			1
B_9	1	1	1		1
B_{10}				1	

7.7.2.2 Phase 1: Frequent Pattern Derivation

The controlling parameters of support and confidence are calculated to mine the most favorable rules according to If $((T_{i1} = 1) \wedge (T_{i2} = 1) \wedge \ldots \wedge (T_{ik} = 1))$ with $1 \leq ij \leq p$ for all j where T_{ij} is user transaction depicting that user i has chosen service j in the respective cloud service combination. Hence *Support* $= fr(\theta \wedge \psi)$ means ψ different customers in the database have demanded θ service-combinations. *Confidence* $= C(\theta \wedge \psi) = \frac{fr(\theta \wedge \psi)}{fr(\theta)}$ with $fr(\theta)$ = Total number of cases that favor the supported θ service set.

Results: With a support threshold of 0.30, only six are the found frequent basket combinations: ({Efficiency}, {Security}, {Storage}, {Data}, {Efficiency, Storage}, {Security, Storage}) filtered from the database of 31 service set combinations.

7.7.2.3 Phase 2: Association Rule Framing

Rule1: $(Effi \rightarrow Strg) = \frac{fr(Effi \wedge Strg)}{fr(Effi)} = \frac{\text{No. of cases of Strg in the database which satisfy Effi also}}{\text{Total cases favoring Effi only}} = \frac{5}{6} = 0.833$

Rule2: $(Secr \rightarrow Strg) = \frac{fr(Secr \wedge Strg)}{fr(Secr)} = \frac{\text{No. of cases favoring both Secr and Strg}}{\text{Total cases favoring Secr only}} = \frac{3}{5} = 0.60$

Results: As the confidence threshold is 0.75 and out of derived metaheuristics, Rule1 yields a value of 0.833, which is greater than the recommended threshold, and the Rule2 value of 0.60 does not satisfy the threshold, so the resulted observation is the {Efficiency, Storage} service combination should be the prime consideration for better cloud services.

7.7.2.4 Phase 3: Knowledge Discovery Through Metaheuristic Implementation

A metaheuristic implementation yields new knowledge that can be practically acted upon with better performance and greater efficiency. The generalization about user behavior is validated through association mining results, as listed in Table 7.3.

Results: Reduced cost of resource availability and less communication in terms of cloud infrastructure and computing cost. This knowledge results in the following recommendations:

1) Connecting new kinds of things like fog computing with cloud computing can create new business opportunities.
2) Resolving efficiency results in a storage trade-off.
3) Including machine as a service and pay-as-you-drive services can result in better reliability and efficiency.

Table 7.3 Association Rules (By Market Basket Analysis)

Services Demanded	Also Demanded Follow-Up Services	Confidence Threshold	Confidence
Efficiency	Storage	0.75	0.833
Security	Storage	0.75	0.60

7.8 Performance Analysis

The modeling technique called market basket analysis (MBA) works to answer the question, "Why do users give preference to certain group of items over others?" Data mining through MBA finds implicit relationships among the patterns. To find out what items are purchased together, it applies intelligent heuristics for user baskets and preserves only those that generalize which combinations are usually sold and in which specific areas. These results act as assets to businesses like Amazon, which can utilize this knowledge to design their catalog and order type and to build a policy for their preferred customers like an extra 5% off the price. Researchers use market basket analysis as a data analytical tool. It is a technique of knowledge discovery based on the co-occurrence of categorical items. It derives associations among datasets through the inputs of data transactions and the computation of multiple associations. Based on the controlling parameters, it outputs the optimized result as knowledge discovery.

1) The strength of market basket analysis over other data mining tools is its data-driven approach. For example, by using a computer, a developer may not find a reason for all the database products consumers logically buy together, but the basket data will speak for itself.

2) The basket analysis algorithm does not form groups that have less support than the user-provided support. So raising and lowering the support threshold will result in different product groups, which all may be appropriate but for different purposes.

3) MBA improves the efficacy of marketing tactics by developing a customer indicator matrix from the real online data. Hence, the efficiency is enhanced regardless of previous polices like Flipcart that may offer new value-added services or an extra benefit for a specific combination.

4) The higher confidence for a heuristic indicates a better rule for real-world applications. Yet, if the confidence threshold is set too high, a developer might find no association rules providing such confidence. So, the minimum confidence should be experimentally determined. Usually the default value is 0.65.

5) Market basket analysis eliminates the problem of potentially insignificant trivial results because a rule holding for one store may not hold for another because of different clientele, so it results in knowledge like "Item displays should be designed in more lucrative way."

6) Regarding its of complexity, MBA has the best results when the item set happens to be in roughly the same number of transactions in the data. This implicit fact of the indicator matrix will prevent heuristics from being dominated by the most common items.

By the time the frequent data clusters are produced for analysis, the chance to work on them may be gone. For computation and storage of decentralized selected data for historical analysis, efficient communication between the data source and the mining paradigm is required to preserve the benefits of knowledge discovery. Also for long-term storage, user-oriented decentralized logic can be designed to help retain customers.

To troubleshoot these performance issues, the problem diagnostic analytics are designed. The data patterns are analyzed in the database of 31 service packages to locate those service combinations whose confidence and accuracy are high for a given application. As a solution, the effective service combinations, which are in great demand, are validated through the support and confidence parameters as well as the corresponding factors. Inducing this new knowledge in the prevailing system will fetch new customers and retain old ones for the cloud services. For the defined processes of

M1: Customer Transactions   M2: Measuring Interestingness
M3: Metaheuristic rules application   M4: Derived Knowledge

Metaheuristics facilitates the following:

M1: Due to its data-driven approach, the likely complications based on certain combinations can be cross verified directly with the user transactional indicator matrix for the small datasets.

M2: In addition, two significance measures are provided; the support indicates in what percentage all transactions these combinations occur. Another confidence metric is computed to validate the accuracy of the applied heuristics.

M3: Metaheuristics computes how much better this rule is than random chance. It corresponds to the exploitation of the association heuristics for the minimum future improvement like hotel rooms booked on credit cards provide insight into the next product the user may purchase such as a rental car.

M4: Not all the created heuristics are equal. The confidence percentage shows how reliable a heuristic is, that is the percentage of chance for a user to go for the next item, if they already purchased a particular group of items. Unusual combinations of medical claims can be a sign of fraud. So, this knowledge will infer a general observation of "Require further investigation."

Case study: In our case, in the first row in Table 7.3, the users whose prime concern is the efficiency will prefer storage as the next item in the basket as computed and validated by a confidence of 83.30%. This is supported by 50% of the transactions, as indicated by Table 7.2.

7.9 Research Contributions and Future Work

The relevance and possible outputs of this study are useful for those who intend to improve the quality of business services. The discovery of such associations can help retailers to develop marketing strategies by gaining insight into which items are frequently purchased together by customers and which items can bring them better profits when placed in close proximity.

For assuring mined patterns, this work has covered interesting measures of support and confidence only. In the future, present implementation can be improved with other controlling measures of completeness and precision to achieve more optimization. Researchers may improve upon the quality of association rule mining for business development by incorporating the influential factors such as value (utility), quantity of items sold (weight), and more for the mining of association patterns.

7.10 Conclusion

Data mining and the knowledge discovery paradigm are evolutionary algorithms that are implemented in the versatile fields of computer science, applied mathematics, neuro and social informatics for the association rule. In the present study, association rule mining based on market basket analysis is performed where the quality data patterns are first identified and then verified and validated through the interestingness measures of support and confidence and corresponding heuristics to optimize the application for its improved performance. The current research aims at evaluating various quality service patterns as predicted by these controlling parameters and rules. Those service combinations that give better customer service are suggested. For the efficacy analysis, the complete dataset of 10 basket combinations, pertaining to 10 users, was inspected for five different services. The present implementation evaluated two quality factors capable of tracking the most frequent data patterns of dynamic customer purchasing patterns. The interestingness measures of support and confidence were computed to assure the quality and optimization of the rendered services. The data patterns were further scanned to formulate the key for the knowledge database. This work is useful for those who intend to lay out the failsafe rules about customer buying perspectives. Metaheuristic policy analytics are framed based on these valued data patterns as knowledge discovery. In the future, the implementation may be tested for the different learning environments of neural networks so that this supervised mechanism can be explored to capture the fuzziness in the unpredictable behavior of the customer. Moreover, the introduction of more vigilance parameters of consistency and rarity for pruning and selection can produce more combinations of data patterns to handle exceptions. The rule discovery can further be analyzed to optimize the resulted predictive and prescriptive behavior of the user.

References

1 "IBM What Is Big Data: Bring Big Data to the Enterprise," http://www-01.ibm.com/software/data/big data/, IBM, 2012.

2 S. Liao, P. Chu, and P. Hsiao, Data mining techniques and applications - A decade review from 2000 to 2011, *Expert Systems with Applications, Elsevier*, 39: 2012.

3 F. Glover, Future paths for integer programming and links to Artificial Intelligence, *Computers and Operations Research*, **13**: 533–549, 1986.

4 H. Varian, *Intermediate Microeconomics*, W.W. Norton, New York, 1996.

5 L. Cao and Y. Zhao, *Data mining for Business Applications*, Springer, New York, 2009.

6 J. Bughin and J. Manyika, *Clouds, Big Data, and Smart Assets: Ten Tech-Enabled Business Trends to Watch*, McKinSey Quarterly, 2010.

7 R. Lee and T. T. Chen, Revealing research themes and trends in knowledge management: From 1995 to 2010, *Knowledge Based Systems, Elsevier*, April 2012.

8 C. Holsapple, Knowledge Management Support of Decision Making, **31**: 1–162, May 2001.

9 J. Shaw and E. Welge, Decision Support System, *Elsevier*, May 2001.

10 P. S. Bradley and R. Ramakrishnan, Scaling Mining Algorithms to Large Databases, *Communications of the ACM*, August 2002.

11 J. Darroch, Knowledge management, innovation and firm performance, *Journal of Knowledge management*, **9**: 101–115, 2005.

12 K. Sukhija, N. Aggarwal, and M. Jindal, The Recent State of Educational Data Mining: A Survey And Future Visions, *IEEE 3rd International Conference On Moocs, Innovation And Technology In Education*, October 2015.

13 E. Gkintoni and C. Halkiopoulos, Using Data Mining Techniques to explore Shopping Addiction and Emotion Based Decision making, *5th Intenational Conference on Contemporary marketing Issues, Greece*, June 2017.

14 C.V. Ramadas and M. Fernanda, On Metaheuristics for Solving the Parameter Estimation Problem in Dynamic Systems: A Comparative Study, *Journal of Optimization*, 1–21, January 2018.

15 C.V. Nascimento and L.F. André, Spectral methods for graph clustering - A survey, *European Journal of Operational Research, Elsevier*, 221–231, 2011.

16 E. G. Talbi, *A Unified Taxonomy of Hybrid Metaheuristics with Mathematical Programming, Constraint Programming and Machine Learning*, Hybrid Metaheuristics, Springer, 3–76, 2013.

17 B. Zheng and J. Zhang, Predictive Modeling Of Hospital Readmissions Using Metaheuristics And Data Mining, *Expert Systems With Applications*, 2015.

18 K. Hussain, M. Salleh, and C. Shi, Metaheuristic research: a comprehensive survey, *Artificial Intelligence Review*, January 2018.

19 P. Sandhu, S. Dalvinder, and S. N. Panda, Mining utility oriented association rules: An efficient approach based on profit and quantity, *International Journal of the Physical Sciences*, **6**: 301–307, Jan 2011.

20 C. Papavasileiou, H. Antonopoulou, and G. Stamoulis, Decision Making With Machine Learning Techniques In Consumer Performance: Empathy, Personality, Emotional Intelligence As Mediators, *5th International Conference On Contemporary Marketing Issues, Greece*, June 2017.

21 X. Wu, Z. Zhou, and D. Hand, *Top 10 algorithms in data mining, Knowledge and Information Systems*, Springer, **14**: 1–37, January 2008.

22 A. Adejuwon and A. Mosavi, Domain Driven Data Mining - Application To Business, *International Journal Of Computer Science*, **7**: 41–44, July 2010.

23 B. Yildiz and B. Ergenc, Comparison of Two Association Rule Mining Algorithms without Candidate Generation, *International Journal of Computing and ICT Research*, 2010.

24 R. Agarwal and R. Srikant, Mining Sequential patterns, *ACM International conference on Data engineering*, 3–34, 1995.

25 R. Srikant and R. Agarval, Mining Generalized association Rules, *Future Generation Computer Systems*, December 1997.

26 S. Kotsiantis and D. Kanellopoulos, Association Rules Mining: A Recent Overview, *International Transactions on Computer Science and Engineering, GESTS*, **32**: 71–82, 2006.

27 J. Golchia and A. M. Seyed, Using Data Mining Techniques for Improving Customer Relationship Management, *European Journal of Natural and Social Sciences*, July 2013.

28 H. Kumar, S. Sharma and P. Mishra, Association Rule Mining: A Data Profiling and Prospective Approach, *International Conference on Futuristic Trends in Engineering, Science, Humanities, and Technology, Gwalior*, January 2016.

29 S. Bhise and S. Kale, Efficient Algorithms to find Frequent Item set Using Data Mining, *International Research Journal of Engineering and Technology*, **4**, June 2017.

30 K. Amandeep, Performance Efficiency Assessment for Software Systems, *Advances in Intelligent Systems and Computing*, 2018.

31 B. Leonora and J. Walter, A survey on metaheuristics for stochastic combinatorial optimization, *Natural Computing: An International Journal*, 239–287, 2009.

32 F. Glover and G. A. Kochenberger, *Handbook of metaheuristics*, Springer, International Series in Operations Research & Management Science, 2003.

33 E-G. Talbi, *Metaheuristics: from design to implementation*, John Wiley & Sons, Inc., Publication, 2009.

34 A. Heidari and H. Chen, Harris hawks optimization: Algorithm and applications, *Future Generation Computer Systems*, 849–872, 2019.

35 H. Mohammad and Y. W. Kuan, Simultaneous Selection and Scheduling with Sequence-Dependent Setup Times, Lateness Penalties and Machine Availability Constraint: Heuristic Approaches, *International Journal of Industrial Engineering Computations*, **7**: 147–160, 2016.

36 X. S. Yang, *Metaheuristic optimization*, Scholarpedia, 2011.

8

Magnetic Resonance Image Segmentation Using a Quantum-Inspired Modified Genetic Algorithm (QIANA) Based on FRCM

Sunanda Das[1], Sourav De[2], Sandip Dey[3], and Siddhartha Bhattacharyya[4]

[1]*Department of Computer Science and Engineering, National Institute of Technology, Durgapur, India*
[2]*Department of Computer Science and Engineering, Cooch Behar Government Engineering College, India*
[3]*Department of Computer Science, Sukanta Mahavidyalaya, Jalpaiguri, India*
[4]*Department of Computer Science and Engineering, CHRIST (Deemed to be University), Bangalore, India*

8.1 Introduction

As medical science becomes more advanced, it leads to a wide scope of research that tries to improve the quality of medical science. Magnetic resonance image segmentation is a popular field. The magnetic resonance image (MRI) processing technique is used to produce noninvasive high-quality images to represent the inner anatomical structure of the human body for medical analysis and to visualize the function of some organs and tissues. A MR image mainly contains gray matter (GM), white matter(WM), celebrospinal fluid (CSF), and some other in vasive and noninvasive tissue cells. Proper image analysis, rather, proper MR image segmentation, is needed for better treatment. MR image segmentation is mainly used to identify tumors, classification of tissues and blood cells, multimodal registration, etc.

Image segmentation [1] is the process where an image is partitioned into some distinct regions containing each pixel with similar attributes such as color, texture, intensity, etc. There are many research works where different classical and nonclassical methods are used for segmentation purposes. In our proposed methodology, we chose a clustering process to segment grayscale MR images. Clustering is an unsupervised learning method where pixels having similar characteristics make up a group called a cluster. Clustering techniques can be divided into hard clustering [2] and soft clustering. Unlike hard clustering, in soft clustering each pixel exists in more than one cluster. The FRCM algorithm [3], a soft clustering technique, is popularly used for MR image segmentation. Though it overcomes the problem of hard clustering, it has some demerits as it does not consider the spatial information and is thereby highly sensitive to noise and imaging artifacts. There is another problem, which is that before starting this algorithm, we have to initialize the exact number of cluster, which is known as the number of clusters dependency problem. As a result, it may be stuck at a local minima point instead of obtaining a global optimal solution. Many meta-heuristics optimization-based evolutionary algorithms such as the genetic algorithm, particle swarm

Recent Advances in Hybrid Metaheuristics for Data Clustering, First Edition.
Edited by Sourav De, Sandip Dey, and Siddhartha Bhattacharyya.
© 2020 John Wiley & Sons Ltd. Published 2020 by John Wiley & Sons Ltd.

optimization, etc., are used for image segmentation purposes. The main aim of those algorithms are to use some probabilistic rules to search for a near-optimal solution from a global search space.

The concept of the genetic algorithm came from the natural evolution process. Genetic algorithms are commonly used to generate high-quality solutions to optimization and search problems by relying on bio-inspired operators such as selection, crossover, and mutation. The GA is an iterative process; in each iteration, a new set of population is created called a generation. From this population, based on some objective function, more fitted chromosomes are selected for crossover and mutation purposes. Crossover and mutation are also done based on crossover and mutation probability. The GA has a balanced exploration and exploitation capability.

Many research studies have been conducted to create a hybrid system to get the most optimal solutions. Different eminent works have been done in combination and with [4–6], etc. Sometimes of FRCM is used to create the population of the GA or PSO, and sometimes the GA is used. It is obvious that these hybrid methods give better results than the traditional version, but these hybrid concepts take much more computational time. To overcome this problem, a new quantum computing [7] concept can be incorporated in to these traditional hybrid methods.

In the last decade, quantum computing has become a popular research area in computer science. The idea of quantum computing comes from quantum mechanics. It directly uses quantum mechanics properties such as superposition, entanglement, interference, and orthogonality, and has embedded these properties into classical methods. When this quantum computing concept is used along with the classical methods, it is observed that it decreases the computational time in a sharply manner as well as increases the quality of the result compared to classical methods.

Our main aim in this article is to incorporate the quantum computing phenomena into the classical modified GA (MEGA)-based FRCM [8] to decrease the computational time and increase the quality of the segmented output result. Previously it was said that it suffers from the problem of being stuck to local the minima point because the initialization of the cluster center is not done in a proper way. But the GA can be used to overcome this problem as it has the capability to find the near optimal solution from a global search space. But the GA also has some drawbacks so that it may be stuck to the local minima. So a modified version of the GA has been introduced where the selection and crossover parts have some modifications. Now the quantum computing characteristics are included into this. After compiling the quantum-inspired MEGA algorithm, the output class levels or the cluster centers are fed to the initial class levels thus yielding the optimized segmented output result. These previously stated algorithm is applied on two standard MR images. Based on three standard quality evaluation metrics, this quantum-inspired modified genetic algorithm (QIANA)-based FRCM and the classical MEGA-based algorithm were compared and showed that the computational time decreases and the quality of the segmented output images increases in a drastic manner.

This chapter's contents are as follows. In Section 8.2 a literature survey is presented where different eminent works are briefly described. A brief description about quantum computing is introduced in Section 8.3. In Section 8.4, three quality measure metrics, $F(I)$ [41], $F'(I)$ [42], and $Q(I)$ [42], are discussed. After that, our proposed methodology is described in Section 8.5. A comparison-based result is demonstrated in Section 8.6, and Section 8.7 concludes the topic.

8.2   Literature Survey

Image segmentation is the most popular research-oriented field in image processing. Different eminent works on image segmentation have been published at different times. Aly et al. [9] and Dass et al. [10] presented their review paper in which different types of segmentation concepts and algorithms were elaborated. Malik et al. [11] proposed an algorithm to partition a grayscale image using a normalized cut into disjoint regions based on coherent brightness and texture. Nunes et al. [12] applied a multilevel thresholding technique for MR image segmentation. Samanta et al. [13] suggested multilevel threshold grayscale image segmentation using Cuckoo Search. Here Cuckoo Search (CS) is used to select the optimal threshold values. Ghamisi et al. [14] introduced a multilevel segmentation method using fractional order Darwinian particle swarm optimization. Fractional derivative plays a role here to control the convergence rate of particles. k-means clustering and fuzzy c-means clustering are widely used in image segmentation. Zhang et al. [15] proposed a neighborhood-constrained k-means approach to classify the high spatial resolution of hyper spectral images. To overcome the drawback that intraclass variation affects the classification accuracy for a very high spatial resolution hyper spectral image due to low SNR and high spatial heterogeneity, a pure neighborhood index is incorporated into traditional k-means. Khan and Ahamed [16] improved the conventional k-means algorithm by modifying the initialization of the cluster centers. The watershed segmentation algorithm has been incorporated into the traditional k-means algorithm [17] to segment the medical images. To overcome the difficulties in achieving the optimum quality requirements, automation, and robustness requirements, the k-means algorithm has been merged with the LoG filter and Prewitt filter [18]. Many research papers have been published in the image segmentation field where researchers tried their best to overcome the drawbacks of the FRCM and enhanced the efficiency of the FRCM. Ahmed et al. [19] proposed a modified FRCM where noisy images can be efficiently segmented. The term bias field is introduced here that allows labels in immediate neighbor pixels to influence its labeling. Yang et al. [20] presented a method where the spatial function is considered as the sum of all the membership functions within the neighborhood of the pixel under consideration. Zhang and Chen [21] proposed FRCM-S1 and FRCM-S2 in their article where they simplified the neighborhood term of the objective function of FRCM-S. A conditional spatial FRCM clustering was introduced by Adhikari et al. [22] for MR image segmentation. Here a conditional parameter was introduced that defines the belongingness of each pixel to each cluster. A modified fuzzy c-means algorithm, where new efficient cluster center initialization and color quantization allows faster and accurate convergence, was proposed for color image segmentation in [23]. An enhanced FRCM algorithm was generated to segment grayscale brain MR images where a rough set is mixed with the FRCM to speed up the segmentation process [24]. In [43], a new version of the FRCM considers the spatial neighbor pixels and also similar super-pixel information to handle the issue of sensitivity of noise for medical image segmentation. They have also used a crow search algorithm for optimizing the influential degree of neighbor pixels. Arora and Tushir

[44] have also proposed a new novel intuitionistic fuzzy *c*-means (S-IFCM) algorithm for image segmentation where spatial information is taken into account for noise reduction. To compute the hesitation degree of a pixel, rank is computed between two pixels using city-block distance. Yager's type of fuzzy complement is used to compute the nonmembership function and to further calculate the hesitation degree.

The segmentation problem can also be considered as an optimization problem because more optimal cluster centers provide a better-quality segmentation results. Different conventional optimization algorithms like the genetic algorithm (GA) [25, 26] and particle swarm optimization (PSO) [27] are used for image segmentation. Researchers have tried their best to produce different hybrid algorithmic methods to achieve more accurate and optimized results. To overcome the impact of isolated points, the GA is used in the *k*-means algorithm for proper initialization of a cluster center [28]. Castillo et al. [29] presented an optimization of the FRCM algorithm by using the GA and PSO. Their aim was to emphasize the cluster validation. Mukhopadhyay and Maulik [30] suggested a multiobjective real coded genetic fuzzy clustering algorithm for the segmentation of multispectral MR images of the human brain. Biju et al. [31] presented the GA-based fuzzy *C*–Means (GAFCM) technique, which is used to segment spots of complimentary DNA (c-DNA) microarray images to find gene expression. De et al. [32] proposed an algorithm to segment multilevel grayscale images where the GA is combined with the multilayer self-organizing neural network (MLSONN) architecture. Here the GA is applied to generate the optimized class level to design the optimized MUSIG (OptiMUSIG) activation function. Afterward, this OptiMUSIG activation function MLSONN is able to segment a grayscale image, inducing the image heterogeneity property. The variable threshold OptiMUSIG activation function is also efficient for grayscale image segmentation [33]. Das and De [8] suggested a modified GA (MEGA) FRCM algorithm to segment multilevel grayscale images. MEGA enhanced the efficiency of the traditional GA by modifying the population initialization and crossover part. This MEGA produces the optimized class levels that are employed to the FRCM as the initial class level. It actually overcame the local convergence problem of the FRCM.

Hybrid methods obviously perform better than traditional methods, but they take much computational time. To overcome this problem, quantum computing concepts are incorporated into the classical methods. Quantum computing phenomena are merged with the conventional GA to speed up its execution time [34]. The author used this algorithm to solve the TSP problem. Here a lookup table is maintained for rotational angle. Talbi et al. [35] proposed a quantum-inspired genetic algorithm for multiobjective grayscale. In this article, the result of the *k*-means algorithm is applied as the input to the evolutionary algorithm to create a nondominated solution set. Bhattacharyya and Dey [36] suggest another quantum-inspired genetic algorithm that is used to determine the optimized threshold intensities to segment grayscale images. This quantum-inspired GA used different random chaotic map models to influence the predominant interference operator. Bhattacharyya et al. [37] used random map–based quantum-inspired GA that is capable of achieving optimum threshold value for grayscale image segmentation. Quantum-inspired ant colony optimization and quantum-inspired simulated annealing [38] are also efficient for multilevel thresholding techniques. Yang et al. [45] proposed a new FLSM based on quantum particle swarm optimization (QPSO) for medical image segmentation. The QPSO-FLSM algorithm iteratively optimizes the contours of the image, and then the segmentation procedure is happened using the level set method. This algorithm exploits the global search capability of QPSO to obtain a stable cluster center and a pre-segmentation contour closer to the region of interest during the iteration.

8.3 Quantum Computing

In 1965 Intel cofounder Gordon Moore introduced Moore's law [40], which states that the number of transistors per square inch on integrated circuits will double every 18 months. Years later there are a huge number of circuits that are used for processing purposes. But the question now is whether these processing circuits, using a massive amount of processing power, can produce more accurate results with lesser speed. From here, the concept of quantum computing was invented by American computer engineer Howard Aiken in 1947. The basic idea behind quantum computing is the direct usage of the quantum mechanics phenomenon to perform some operations on data and generate the most accurate results with a very high-speed computational time over classical computing. In this section, we describe some quantum characteristics that are used in our methodology.

8.3.1 Quoit-Quantum Bit

A quoit-quantum bit is the smallest unit of information in quantum computing. In classical computing, a bit can be represented using either 0 or 1; but in a quoit, can be represented as a superposition of 0 and 1. Actually, quantum systems relate with the wave function $|\psi>$ that exists in a Hilbert space comprising a set of states. This can be represented such as:

$$| \psi >= \alpha | 0 > + \beta | 1 > \tag{8.1}$$

where $|0>$ and $|1>)$ represent the classical bit values 0 and 1, respectively; α and β are complex numbers such that

$$\alpha^2 + \beta^2 = 1 \tag{8.2}$$

8.3.2 Entanglement

Quantum entanglement is the physical phenomenon where a group of particles interact in such a way that the quantum state of each particle cannot be distinguished independently. Unlike a classical bit, quantum entanglement cannot represent a single value at a time as it consists of multiple states. Theoretically, it can be defined as the tensor product between these states, as given by $|\vartheta_1 > \otimes |\vartheta_2 >$.

8.3.3 Measurement

Quantum measurement is the process where entangled resource states are transformed into corresponding single states. It actually provides the probabilities of transformation for the different possible outcomes in an experiment. From Eqn. 8.1, we can say that $|\psi>$ can be transformed into $|0>$ and $|1>$ with the probability α^2 and β^2, respectively.

8.3.4 Quantum Gate

Like classical logic gates quantum gates, are made with some digital circuits. Unlike classical logic gates except NOT gates, all quantum gates are reversible in nature. Different types of quantum gates are in existence. In this article, we have used the quantum-inspired rotation gate to update the state of a single quoit. This rotation gate can be defined as follows:

$$\begin{bmatrix} \alpha'_i \\ \beta'_i \end{bmatrix} = \begin{bmatrix} \cos\theta_i & -\sin\theta_i \\ \sin\theta_i & \cos\theta_i \end{bmatrix} \begin{bmatrix} \alpha_i \\ \beta_i \end{bmatrix} \tag{8.3}$$

where (α_i, β_i) and (α'_i, β'_i) are the ith quoit before and after updating; and θ_i represents the rotation angle between α_i and β_i, which can be determined in different ways based on the experiment. In our proposed algorithm, we can calculate the rotation angle as follows:

$$\theta = \tan^{-1}\frac{\beta}{\alpha} \tag{8.4}$$

8.4 Some Quality Evaluation Indices for Image Segmentation

After applying different segmentation algorithms on an image, evaluation of the resultant image is very much necessary to judge which algorithm provides the best result. Different statistical measurements are used to ascertain the quality of the resultant segmented image. In this section, three image evaluation metrics (Empirical Measures) are discussed.

8.4.1 F(I)

$F(I)$ is proposed by Liu and Yang [41], which is defined as follows:

$$F(I) = \sqrt{N} \sum_{Re=1}^{N} \frac{e_{Re}^2}{\sqrt{S_{Re}}} \tag{8.5}$$

where N indicates the number of segmented regions; RE_{Re} signifies the number of pixels placed in region Re. S_{Re} is the area of the Re region; e_{Re}^2 represents the squared color error of region Re, which is given as follows:

$$e_{Re}^2 = \sum_{v\in(R,G,B)} \sum_{px\in RE_{Re}} (C_v(px) - \widehat{C_v(RE_{Re})})^2 \tag{8.6}$$

Here, $\widehat{C_v(RE_{Re})}$ is the average value of feature v (Red, Green or Blue) of a pixel px in region Re and is given by

$$\widehat{C_v(RE_{Re})} = \frac{\sum_{px\in RE_{Re}} C_v(px)}{S_{Re}} \tag{8.7}$$

where $C_v(px)$ denotes the value of component v for pixel px.

8.4.2 F'(I)

Borosotti et al. [42] proposed an evaluation function $F'(I)$, which is the modified version of $F(I)$. It is represented as follows:

$$F'(I) = \frac{1}{1000.S_M} \sqrt{\sum_{u=1}^{maxarea} [N(u)]^{1+\frac{1}{u}} \sum_{Re=1}^{N} \frac{e_{Re}^2}{\sqrt{S_{Re}}}} \tag{8.8}$$

where S_M is the area of an original image, *maxarea* is represented as the area of the largest region in the segmented image, and $N(u)$ refers to the number of regions in the segmented image having an area of exactly u.

8.4.3 Q(I)

Borosotti et al. [42] suggested another evaluation function $Q(I)$, which is defined as follows:

$$Q(I) = \frac{1}{1000.S_M} \sqrt{N} \sum_{Re=1}^{N} \left[\frac{e_{Re}^2}{1 + \log S_{Re}} + \left(\frac{N(S_{Re})}{S_{Re}} \right)^2 \right] \tag{8.9}$$

where $N(S_{Re})$ stands for the number of regions having an area S_{Re}.

8.5 Quantum-Inspired Modified Genetic Algorithm (QIANA)–Based FRCM

Das and De [8] have already proposed the MEGA-based algorithm to overcome the drawbacks of the GA. It is a heuristic search algorithm that mimics the natural selection procedure. It is a population-based optimization technique. It finds a near-optimal solution in a large, complex, and multimodal problem space. The GA maintains a fixed size of population. The population in the GA consists of a number of chromosomes. Each chromosome contains a set of cluster centroids that are randomly generated. In the GA, the performance of the entire population can be upgraded instead of improving the performance of the individual members in the population-based optimization procedure.

The modified genetic algorithm enhances the performances of the conventional GA by improving its population initialization and crossover section. Since the GA chooses its initial cluster centers in a random manner, it may happen that the difference between two consecutive cluster centers is too small to differentiate them as different clusters. To overcome this limitation in MEGA, a weighted mean formula is introduced that is able to consider the neighbourhood cluster centers. Another improvement is also done in the crossover portion. As we know, in the GA a fixed crossover probability is used all over the process; it also may happen that a good chromosome may be mated with a bad chromosome, and that good chromosome is not stored in the next stage. To overcome this drawback, the MEGA suggests a crossover probability that decreases as the iteration of algorithm increases. The MEGA runs in the same way as the conventional GA following steps like selection, crossover, and mutation. After the compilation of MEGA, we get the optimized class level or cluster centers. As the initial class levels cannot be assigned properly to FRCM, it reaches to the local minima point, and it highly affects, the segmentation result. So as an improvisation, the derived class levels by the MEGA is employed to the FRCM as the initial input class level, and we get a optimized satisfactory segmented output result.

This performs better than the conventional FRCM, but it is computationally intensive. To decrease this computational time in our proposed methodology, we incorporate the quantum computing concept into this MEGA-based algorithm. This not only decreases the computational time but also increases the efficiency and quality of the segmented output. Here a short description of our proposed quantum-inspired modified genetic algorithm (QIANA)–based FRCM is given. This algorithm starts with randomly selected pixel intensity values as the cluster centers from a grayscale MR image to create its first population. In the conventional GA, we choose N number of cluster centers to segment an image into N segments, but in the MEGA we select $N+1$ number of cluster centers to segment an image into N partitions. Now from these $N+1$ number of cluster centers, we able to create N number of actual cluster centers using a weighted mean formula. These cluster centers are now encoded with real numbers between 0 and 1 as per the quantum computing rule to create the population $\mathcal{P}'$. Each chromosome of the population $\mathcal{P}'$ is considered as α, and using the quantum orthogonality property, we create the population called $\mathcal{P}''$ where each chromosome is known as β. After that we use the quantum rotational gate for a quick convergence and create the ultimate population $\mathcal{P}^+$. From this $\mathcal{P}^+$ population using a roulette wheel selection procedure and based on the fitness function, more fit chromosomes are selected for crossover and mutation. Crossover and mutation are done depending on crossover and mutation probability. Here crossover probability decreases as the iterations increase so that best fit chromosomes always stay in the population. Now after the complete iteration of selection, crossover, and mutation, we get the best fit chromosomes. These child solutions are now mixed with the parent solution to form the next generation of population $\mathcal{P}'$ with a fixed population size. Again, populations $\mathcal{P}'$, $\mathcal{P}''$, and $\mathcal{P}^+$ are generated for the next generation, and the same procedure is iterated for a certain number of times. After completing the QIANA algorithm, we get optimized class levels that are fed into the FRCM as the initial class levels, where as after completion we get our desired optimized segmented output. The flow diagram of the proposed QIANA-based FRCM is depicted in Figure 8.1. The details of the QIANA-based FRCM algorithm is illustrated next:

8.5.1 Quantum-Inspired MEGA (QIANA)–Based FRCM

Input:

1) Population size: 50
2) Number of cluster into which image is segmented: 6 and 8
3) Number of iterations: 50
4) Maximum crossover probability and minimum crossover probability: 0.8 and 0.5, respectively
5) Mutation probability: 0.01
6) Error ϵ: $0.1 * 10^{-6}$

---

1) Population Initialization:

   In the very first stage we need to create population $\mathcal{P}$, which consists a set of chromosomes. To segment an image into N segments, it randomly chooses $N+1$ class levels, i.e., pixel intensity values. From $N+1$ class levels, the ultimate N number of class levels are generated using the weighted mean formula, which is given here:

   $$N_i = \frac{\sum_{j=R_i}^{R_{i+1}} f_j * I_j}{\sum_{j=R_i}^{R_{i+1}} f_j} \tag{8.10}$$

   where R_i and R_{i+1} are the temporary class levels, f_j is the frequency of the jth pixel, and I_j shows the intensity value of the jth pixel.

2) After population $\mathcal{P}$ is created, each chromosome of this population is encoded randomly with a real number between 0 and 1 according to the quantum computing property and the population $\mathcal{P}'$ is created.

3) The quantum orthogonality property is now used in population $\mathcal{P}'$ to produce the population called $\mathcal{P}''$.

4) Now the quantum rotational gate as given in Eqn. 8.3, is induced in each chromosome of $\mathcal{P}''$ for faster convergence, thus generating the ultimate population $\mathcal{P}^+$.

5) The fitness value of each individual is now calculated based on some fitness functions.

6) Selection:

   From $\mathcal{P}^+$ the best fit chromosomes are selected using the roulette wheel selection procedure, and those selected chromosomes take part in the crossover and mutation processes.

7) Crossover:

   The selected chromosomes are crossed over with each other to produce better offsprings. This procedure is performed based on a crossover probability. This crossover probability basically indicates how many couples are taken for mating purposes. Here the crossover probability is decreased as the number of iterations is increased, which ensures that better-fit chromosomes are retained in the population. The calculation of the crossover probability is given here:

   $$C_{prob} = C_{max} - \frac{C_{max} - C_{min}}{Iter_{max} - Iter_{current}} \tag{8.11}$$

   where C_{prob} refers to the crossover probability, C_{max} and C_{min} indicate the maximum and minimum crossover probabilities, and $Iter_{max}$ and $Iter_{current}$ refers to the maximum iteration number and the current iteration number, respectively.

8) Mutation:

   Newly created offsprings are mutated with the mutation probability for better fitness.

9) Now the newly created offsprings are mixed up with the parent solutions to create the next generation of populations called $\mathcal{P}'$.

10) The termination condition is checked. If it is satisfied then the evolution stops; otherwise it iterates from step 3 to step 9.

11) After the completion of QIANA algorithm, we get the best-fit chromosome, which is now decoded.

12) This decoded output is then applied to the initial input of cluster centers, and these centers are used to obtain the final segmented output.

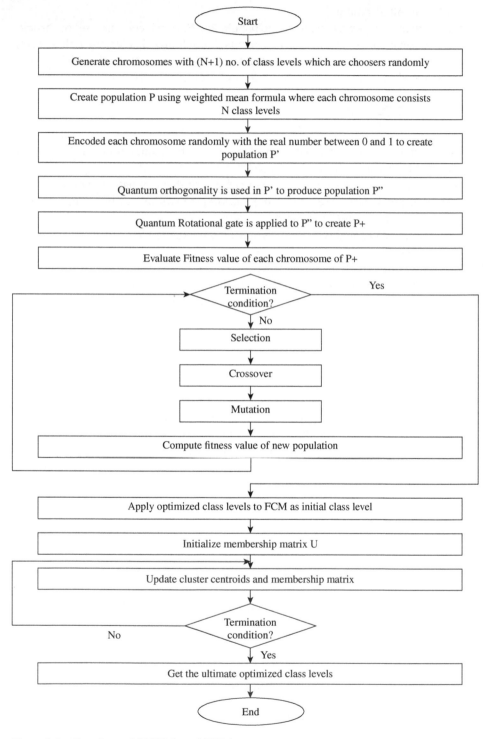

Figure 8.1 Flowchart of QIANA-based FRCM

8.6   Experimental Results and Discussion

In this section we demonstrated the experimental results of our proposed QIANA-based FRCM algorithm with the use of two multilevel grayscale MR images of size 256 × 256. As an MR image mainly contains gray matter (GM), white matter (WM), cerebrospinal fluid (CSF), and some other in vasive and noninvasive cells, it is convenient to segment an MR image into six to eight parts. So here we present our segmentation results based on the **K=(6,8)** class. Results are also reported for the segmentation of the multilevel grayscale MR images using the classical-based FRCM [5] and conventional FRCM [3] methods. To evaluate the quality of these algorithms, three quality evaluation metrics ($F(I),F'(I),Q(I)$), mentioned in Eqns. [8.5, 8.8, and 8.9], are used. Fig. 8.2 shows the test MR images under consideration.

The class levels generated are applied to the initial input class levels of values. At the very first stage, the MEGA randomly chose **(l+1)** number of class levels within the maximum and minimum range of intensity values. From **(l+1)** class levels, the actual **l** number of class levels is produced using the weighted mean formula (Eqn. 8.10). To speed up the convergence of this method, some quantum computing phenomena are employed. Each chromosome that consists of **l** number of class levels is now converted to the randomly created real number between the range of 0 and 1. Afterward, the orthogonality and quantum rotation properties are applied to each chromosome, and then they are ready for the selection, crossover, and mutation operations. Here the roulette wheel method is used to select the best-fit chromosome from the chromosome pool for crossover. In this technique, the crossover probability has been changed at each iteration to retain the good chromosomes in the chromosome pool based on the maximum and minimum crossover probabilities. Maximum crossover probability (C_{max}) and minimum crossover probability (C_{min}) are considered here as 0.8 and 0.5, respectively. The offsprings produced after mating are mutated using mutation probability 0.01. A population pool of 50 chromosomes are applied in both the classical and quantum-inspired algorithms.

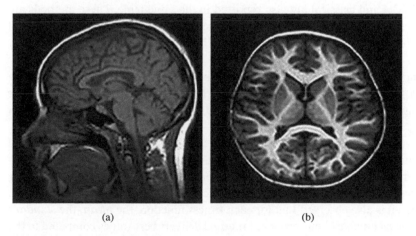

(a)   (b)

Figure 8.2   (a) MR image 1; (b) MR image 2.

Table 8.1 Class Boundaries and Evaluated Segmentation Quality Measures, *F(I)* by Different Algorithms for Different Classes of MR image1

Segments	Algorithm	Sl No.	Class Levels	Fit Value
6	FRCM	1	**1,30,55,83,111,234**	**7.89E+13**
		2	2,26,67,91,139,232	1.95E+14
		3	1,29,55,89,116,234	2.34E+14
	MEGA-based FRCM	1	**2,37,66,108,161,234**	**6.74E+12**
		2	1,30,54,83,110,234	1.16E+13
		3	1,29,53,81,109,233	6.79E+12
	QIANA-based FRCM	1	2,38,66,100,166,243	2.74E+12
		2	**2,37,63,100,165,244**	**1.00E+12**
		3	2,37,66,99,163,243	3.08E+12
8	FRCM	1	1,21,42,60,84,108,172,245	6.6E+14
		2	**1,18,38,54,72,91,111,216**	**3.4E+14**
		3	1,21,42,60,83,107,173,243	1.9E+15
	MEGA-based FRCM	1	1,16,34,50,68,95,122,236	2.96E+13
		2	0,15,32,47,62,85,110,235	3.81E+13
		3	**0,14,31,46,61,84,109,234**	**1.92E+13**
	QIANA-based FRCM	1	1,28,52,77,103,145,193,249	5.96E+12
		2	**2,39,68,98,128,175,216,252**	**5.401E+12**
		3	1,26,50,72,94,114,180,246	7.30E+12

We demonstrated in Tables 8.1, 8.2, and 8.3, the class levels generated by the proposed method based on three fitness functions $(F(I), F'(I), Q(I))$ for a different number of segments for MR image1. The table consists of number of segments, name of algorithm, serial number, class levels, and corresponding fitness values. The class levels generated by the conventional FRCM and classical are also reported in the same table. These methods are run several times, but only three good results in respect of each algorithm are tabulated here. We have highlighted the best results obtained by each process for each segment by **boldfacing**.

The *mean* and *standard deviation* are also computed for each algorithm of different segments for each fitness value, and they are reported in Table 8.4. The column *Mean time* refers the average convergence speed of FRCM reaching its optimal goal. Here it is shown in seconds.

If we consider Tables 8.1, 8.2, and 8.3, it is clear that our proposed quantum-inspired MEGA always performs better than the classical MEGA-based FRCM and also the conventional FRCM. From every table it is shown that our proposed QIANA-based FRCM always derives the better fitness values for each fitness function $F(I)$, $F'(I)$, and $Q(I)$. If we look at Table 8.4, then it is also observed that for each fitness function, the *mean*, the *standard deviation*, and the *mean time* of our proposed method delivers best values compared to the classical MEGA-based FRCM and conventional FRCM.

Table 8.2 Class Boundaries and Evaluated Segmentation Quality Measures, $F'(l)$ by Different Algorithms for Different Classes of MR image1

Segments	Algorithm	Sl No.	Class Levels	Fit Value
6	FRCM	1	1,30,55,83,111,234	7.09E+09
		2	1,29,52,84,117,234	2.69E+10
		3	**1,31,56,89,117,233**	**1.26E+10**
	MEGA-based FRCM	1	1,30,55,83,111,234	1.79E+09
		2	1,28,52,79,108,233	5.37E+08
		3	**1,31,53,81,109,235**	**5.21E+08**
	QIANA-based FRCM	**1**	**2,37,66,100,166,243**	**1.22E+08**
		2	1,30,55,83,111,234	1.41E+08
		3	1,35,59,96,153,238	5.93E+07
8	FRCM	**1**	**1,16,35,51,69,90,113,236**	**7.76E+09**
		2	0,16,34,50,68,88,111,234	1.16E+10
		3	1,21,42,60,83,107,173,245	2.54E+10
	MEGA-based FRCM	1	0,11,25,40,54,73,104,210	1.44E+09
		2	**1,18,37,54,93,73,115,235**	**9.82E+08**
		3	1,15,30,45,66,89,111,234	1.52E+09
	QIANA-based FRCM	1	1,28,52,77,104,143,196,249	8.41E+08
		2	1,30,56,81,111,159,201,253	4.96E+08
		3	**1,39,66,100,124,175,211,253**	**7.96E+08**

Table 8.3 Class Boundaries and Evaluated Segmentation Quality Measures, $Q(l)$ by Different Algorithms for Different Classes of MR image1

Segments	Algorithm	Sl No.	Class Levels	Fit Value
6	FRCM	1	1,30,55,83,11,234	11838.58
		2	**1,29,51,86,109,233**	**8653.50**
		3	1,30,59,88,111,234	9110.19
	MEGA-based FRCM	**1**	**1,29,53,81,109,233**	**7076.14**
		2	1,30,55,83,100,230	7564.77
		3	1,35,53,83,117,237	7903.81
	QIANA-based FRCM	**1**	**1,30,55,83,111,234**	**2060.29**
		2	2,31,55,84,111,235	2123.35
		3	2,37,66,100,165,243	2822.40
8	FRCM	1	1,21,42,60,83,107,173,245	62494.64
		2	1,16,35,51,68,88,111,233	38830.58
		3	**1,20,41,59,83,107,173,245**	**35577.55**
	MEGA-based FRCM	**1**	**0,13,28,42,58,80,107,231**	**12536.58**
		2	0,15,32,47,63,84,109,231	14195.46
		3	0,14,31,46,61,84,109,234	13963.00
	QIANA-based FRCM	1	1,28,52,77,103,144,197,249	4175.32
		2	**1,27,50,79,109,148,193,251**	**3215.58**
		3	2,29,53,78,105,139,196,248	4703.29

Table 8.4 Different Algorithm Based Mean and Standard Deviation Using Different Types of Fitness Functions and Mean of Time Taken by Different Algorithms for MR image1

Fit. Fn.	Segments	Algorithm	Mean ± Std. div.	Mean Time
$F(I)$	6	FRCM	1.68E+14± 7.72E+13	44
		MEGA-based FRCM	8.40E+12± 2.83E+12	34
		QIANA-based FRCM	**2.94E+12± 2.04E+12**	**15**
	8	FRCM	9.80E+14±6.35E+13	95
		MEGA-based FRCM	9.21E+13± 7.55E+13	43
		QIANA-based FRCM	**6.22E+12± 9.78E+11**	**39**
$F'(I)$	6	FRCM	3.33E+10±1.53E+10	49
		MEGA-based FRCM	1.52E+09± 1.25E+09	37
		QIANA-based FRCM	**1.16E+08± 4.6E+07**	**27**
	8	FRCM	1.18E+10± 7.93E+09	84
		MEGA-based FRCM	2.69E+09± 2.73E+09	39
		QIANA-based FRCM	**8.58+08± 4.9E+07**	**31**
$Q(I)$	6	FRCM	9929.74±1262.02	56
		MEGA-based FRCM	7397.55± 1432.51	48
		QIANA-based FRCM	**3606.46± 1180.83**	**26**
	8	FRCM	32571.40± 18174.39	74
		MEGA-based FRCM	9507.81± 3154.19	57
		QIANA-based FRCM	**4310.39± 1754.22**	**45**

The same procedure is applied to the MR image2 for the same number of times. The class boundaries and their corresponding fitness values are derived by the proposed method based on $F(I)$, $F'(I)$, and $Q(I)$ and are tabulated in Tables 8.5, 8.6, and 8.7, respectively. The same results for the conventional FRCM and classical methods are also reported in the same table. It is observed that our proposed method outperforms the other methods for both six and eight segments. The best results are also shown in **boldface**.

The *mean* and *standard deviation* for each process and for each segments of MR image2 are presented in Table 8.8. In this table, the execution times for FRCM are also reported. From this table it can be concluded that the QIANA-based FRCM always performs better than FRCM and QIANA-based FRCM methods.

We also present some segmented output images generated by some fitness functions. In Figure 8.3, the six segment output images based on $F(I)$ as a fitness function are presented in (a)-(c), (d)-(f), and (g)-(i), respectively.

In the same manner, the multilevel grayscale segmented output images for MR image2 are depicted in Figure 8.4 based on $Q(I)$ as the fitness function.

A statistical analysis called one-way is applied here for each image based on each fitness function and for each segment. The one-way analysis of variance (ANOVA) is used to determine whether there are any statistically significant differences between the means of

Table 8.5 Class boundaries and Evaluated Segmentation Quality Measures, $F(I)$ by Different Algorithms for Different Classes of MR image2

Segments	Algorithm	Sl No.	Class Levels	Fit Value
6	FRCM	**1**	**1,42,73,115,166,217**	**1.72E+14**
		2	1,45,77,111,166,219	2.19E+14
		3	1,45,69,115,173,217	1.93E+14
	MEGA-based FRCM	1	1,44,75,119,170,218	8.87E+12
		2	1,23,50,76,123,206	3.68E+12
		3	**1,35,62,96,144,211**	**1.36E+12**
	QIANA-based FRCM	**1**	**2,43,75,118,170,218**	**2.49E+11**
		2	1,48,83,131,183,223	3.54E+11
		3	1,48,85,133,186,225	5.22E+11
8	FRCM	1	1,13,35,54,78,119,177,220	9.69E+14
		2	**1,18,44,65,95,137,186,224**	**7.47E+14**
		3	1,23,49,72,102,141,188,224	8.57E+14
	MEGA-based FRCM	1	1,31,58,86,121,160,203,238	7.38E+13
		2	**0,17,42,62,89,127,173,218**	**3.33E+13**
		3	1,30,49,68,99,127,168,189,226	5.95E+13
	QIANA-based FRCM	1	1,37,64,97,134,171,209,243	7.63E+11
		2	1,26,66,97,132,177,216,246	5.45E+12
		3	**1,37,59,100,128,169,199,234**	**3.92E+12**

Table 8.6 Class Boundaries and Evaluated Segmentation Quality Measures, $F'(I)$ by Different Algorithms for Different Classes of MR image2

Segments	Algorithm	Sl No.	Class Levels	Fit Value
6	FRCM	**1**	**1,43,73,116,167,218**	**3.22E+10**
		2	1,44,75,119,170,218	4.79E+10
		3	1,42,73,118,170,219	5.58E+10
	MEGA-based FRCM	**1**	**1,46,80,127,179,221**	**3.68E+08**
		2	1,45,77,122,173,219	4.38E+08
		3	1,42,79,125,179,221	5.32E+08
	QIANA-based FRCM	1	2,50,87,136,189,227	4.52E+07
		2	**1,48,84,132,185,224**	**3.85E+07**
		3	2,48,85,133,187,226	4.36E+07
8	FRCM	1	1,31,58,87,122,160,203,239	2.45E+10
		2	1,32,59,88,124,162,204,240	1.49E+10
		3	**1,31,58,87,121,160,203,239**	**1.21E+10**
	MEGA-based FRCM	**1**	**0,4,21,45,65,94,141,211**	**1.39E+09**
		2	1,31,58,86,160,121,203,238	4.94E+09
		3	1,35,62,93,129,167,206,242	1.52E+09
	QIANA-based FRCM	1	1,41,69,101,141,182,210,250	5.34E+07
		2	1,37,59,100,128,169,201,231	5.02E+07
		3	**2,32,66,104,149,189,214,243**	**4.57E+07**

Table 8.7 Class Boundaries and Evaluated Segmentation Quality Measures, $Q(I)$ by Different Algorithms for Different Classes of MR image2

Segments	Algorithm	Sl No.	Class Levels	Fit Value
6	FRCM	1	1,40,75,121,173,219	10381.19
		2	1,42,72,115,166,216	9526.41
		3	**1,45,72,123,162,220**	**8767.01**
	MEGA-based FRCM	1	1,45,77,122,173,219	6442.74
		2	**1,42,78,122,169,222**	**5259.47**
		3	1,39,73,129,182,219	5260.27
	QIANA-based FRCM	**1**	**1,42,72,113,163,216**	**1211.66**
		2	1,46,81,127,179,222	4125.79
		3	1,43,79,121,168,214	5257.67
8	FRCM	1	1,32,59,88,123,161,204,239	59748.93
		2	1,31,58,86,121,160,203,239	63301.81
		3	**1,31,58,86,120,159,203,238**	**58977.87**
	MEGA-based FRCM	**1**	**1,30,57,85,120,159,202,238**	**40187.37**
		2	1,31,58,86,121,160,203,239	42318.93
		3	1,41,70,106,145,184,212,246	43108.12
	QIANA-based FRCM	1	1,43,72,108,146,185,208,243	41657.21
		2	**1,41,69,101,141,182,210,250**	**31325.13**
		3	1,45,77,109,143,182,218,246	44935.66

Table 8.8 Different Algorithm-Based Mean and Standard Deviation Using Different Types of Fitness Functions and Mean of Time Taken by Different Algorithms for MR image2

Fit. Fn.	Segments	Algorithm	Mean ± Std. div.	Mean Time
$F(I)$	6	FRCM	2.02E+14± 2.99E+13	37
		MEGA-based FRCM	8.72E+12± 4.96E+12	24
		QIANA-based FRCM	**2.94E+12± 4.57E+12**	**16**
	8	FRCM	9.49E+14± 8.83E+14	97
		MEGA-based FRCM	5.55E+13± 2.05E+13	54
		QIANA-based FRCM	**3.38E+12± 2.39E+12**	**31**
$F'(I)$	6	FRCM	4.42E+10±8.56E+09	54
		MEGA-based FRCM	1.07E+09± 1.26E+09	29
		QIANA-based FRCM	**4.75E+07± 1.23E+07**	**17**
	8	FRCM	2.17E+10±6.58E+09	79
		MEGA-based FRCM	3.25E+09± 2.09E+09	45
		QIANA-based FRCM	**5.33E+07± 7.78E+06**	**28**
$Q(I)$	6	FRCM	9043.64± 1213.71	48
		MEGA-based FRCM	6075.24± 1197.23	33
		QIANA-based FRCM	**3734.29± 1819.40**	**19**
	8	FRCM	57037.72±6465.00	76
		MEGA-based FRCM	53052.87± 22396.80	39
		QIANA-based FRCM	**51519.91± 17137.27**	**26**

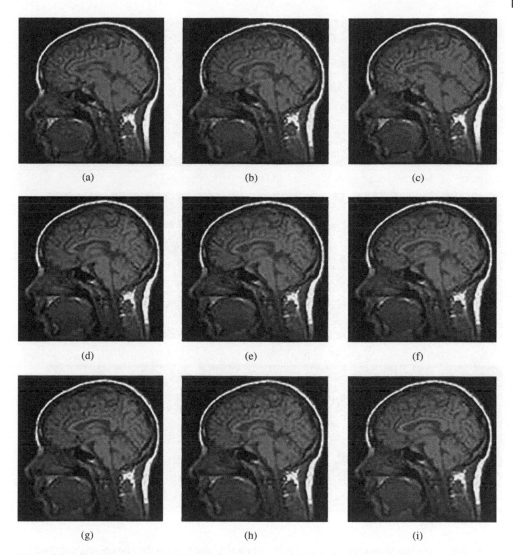

Figure 8.3 Six-class segmented 256 × 256 grayscale MR image1 with the class levels obtained by (a–c) FRCM (d–f) MEGA-based FRCM (g–i) QIANA-based FRCM algorithm of three results of Table 8.1 with $F(I)$ as the quality measure.

different independent (unrelated) groups. Though we have done this test for each image of each segment based on each fitness function, in this chapter we only demonstrate the result for six segments based on Q(I) as the fitness function for MR image1 and MR image2 in Table 8.9 and Table 8.10, respectively.

The ANOVA test tests the null hypothesis that samples in two or more groups are drawn from populations with the same mean values. Now if we consider the value of F and F_{crit} in both Table 8.9 and Table 8.10, then it is clearly shown that F $> F_{crit}$, which rejects the null hypothesis and indicates that the expected values in the groups are different. Here we use a 5% significance level.

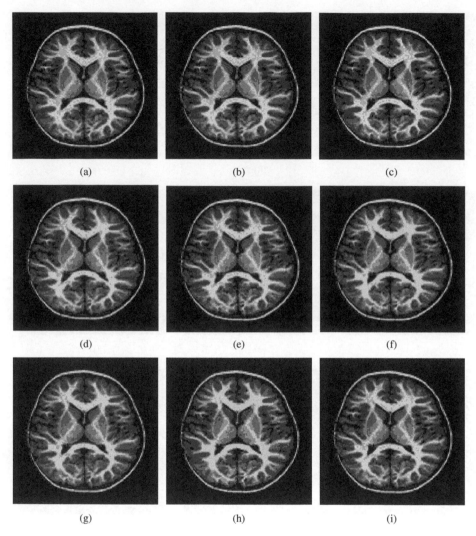

Figure 8.4 Six-class segmented 256 × 256 grayscale MR image2 with the class levels obtained by (a-c) FRCM (d-f) MEGA-based FRCM (g-i) QIANA-based FRCM algorithm of three results of Table 8.7 with $Q(l)$ as the quality measure.

Table 8.9 Single ANOVA Analysis Based on $Q(l)$ for MR image1

Groups	Count	Sum	Average	Variance		
QIANA-based FRCM	10	36064.62	3606.462	1394379.87		
MEGA-based FRCM	10	73975.56	7397.53	187067.50		
FRCM	10	99297.42	9929.74	1592701.80		
Source of Variation	**SS**	**df**	**MS**	**F**	**P-value**	F_{crit}
Between Groups	202560778.4	2	101280389.2	95.72	5.52E-13	3.35
Within Groups	28567342.25	27	1058049.71			
Total	231128120.7	29				

Table 8.10 Single ANOVA Analysis Based on $Q(l)$ for MR image2

Groups	Count	Sum	Average	Variance		
QIANA-based FRCM	10	37342.93	3734.29	3310252.54		
MEGA-based FRCM	10	60752.42	6075.24	1433378.34		
FRCM	10	90436.44	9043.64	1473108.77		
Source of Variation	**SS**	**df**	**MS**	**F**	**P-value**	F_{crit}
Between Groups	141602213.4	2	70801106.68	34.16	4.01E-08	3.35
Within Groups	55950657.01	27	2072246.55			
Total	197552870.4	29				

At the very end of the previously presented results, it can be concluded that our proposed quantum-inspired modified genetic algorithm (QIANA)–based FRCM is more efficient both qualitatively and quantitatively than the classical MEGA-based FRCM as far as the segmentation of images is concerned.

8.7 Conclusion

In this chapter, we have presented a QIANA-based FRCM algorithm for multilevel grayscale MR image segmentation. We compared this quantum version of the algorithm with respect to its classical version. It was already proven that the MEGA is more efficient than the conventional GA; and the MEGA-based FRCM performs better still. But if we consider the computational time of the classical MEGA-based FRCM, it seems that it will take a huge computational time. To overcome this drawback and also to improve the efficiency, some quantum computing principles were incorporated into this classical MEGA-based FRCM method. Now considering the performance result of both the MEGA-based FRCM and QIANA-based FRCM method, it shows our proposed QIANA-based FRCM method outperforms the other method both quantitatively and qualitatively.

References

1 R.C. Gonzalez, & R.E. Woods, *Digital image processing*, Upper Saddle River, NJ: Prentice Hall (2002).

2 J. MacQueen, Some methods for classification and analysis of multivariate observations, Fifth Berkeley Symposium on Mathematics,Statistics and Probability (1967) 281–297

3 J. Bezdek, *Pattern Recognition with Fuzzy Objective Function Algorithms*, Plenum Press, New York (1981)

4 A. Halder, S. Pramanik, A. Kar, Dynamic Image Segmentation using Fuzzy *C*-means based Genetic Algorithm, *International Journal of Computer Applications* (0975–8887), **28**(6) (August 2011) 15–20.

5 S. Jansi, P. Subashini, Modified FCM using Genetic Algorithm for Segmentation of MRI Brain Images, 2014 IEEE International Conference on Computational Intelligence and Computing Research, (2014), doi:10.1109/ICCIC.2014.7238461.

6 A. Mekhmoukh, K. Mokrani, Improved Fuzzy *C*-means based Particle Swarm Optimization (PSO) initialization and outlier rejection with level set methods for MR brain image segmentation, *Computer Methods and Programs in Biomedicine*, **122**(2) (2015) 266–281.

7 D. Mcmohan, *Quantum computing explained*, Hoboken, New Jersey:John Wiley & Sons, Inc.(2008).

8 S. Das, S. De, A Modified Genetic Algorithm based FCM Clustering Algorithm for Magnetic Resonance Image Segmentation, 5th International Conference on Frontiers of Intelligent Computing: Theory and applications (FICTA), 515 (2016) 435–443.

9 A.A. Aly, S.B. Deris, N. Zaki, Research review for digital image segmentation techniques, *International Journal of Computer Science & Information Technology (IJCSIT)*, **3**(5), Oct 2011.

10 R. Dass, Priyanka, S. Devi, Image Segmentation Techniques, *IJECT*, **3**(1), Jan. - March 2012, ISSN : 2230-7109 (Online) | ISSN : 2230–9543 (Print).

11 J. Malik, S. Belongie, T. Leung and J. Shi, Contour and Texture Analysis for Image Segmentation, *International Journal of Computer Vision*, Kluwer Academic Publishers, Manufactured in The Netherlands, **43**(1) (2001) 7–27 .

12 E.O. Nunes, M.G. Perez, Medical Image Segmentation by Multilevel Thresholding Based on Histogram Difference, IWSSIP, 17th International Conference on Systems, Signals and Image Processing (2010).

13 S. Samanta, N. Dey, P. Das, S. Acharjee, S.S. Chaudhuri, *Multilevel Threshold Based Gray Scale Image Segmentation using Cuckoo Search*, In proceedings of ICECIT, published by Elsevier (2012) 27–34.

14 P. Ghamisi, M.S. Couceiro, F.M.L. Martins, and J.A. Benediktsson, Multilevel Image Segmentation Based on Fractional-Order Darwinian Particle Swarm Optimization, *IEEE Transactions on Geoscience And Remote sensing*, **52**(5) (2014) 2382–2394, doi: 10.1109/TGRS 2013.2260552.

15 B. Zhang, S. Li, C. Wu, L. Gao, W. Zhang and M. Peng, *A neighbourhood-constrained k-means approach to classify very high spatial resolution hyperspectral imagery*, Remote Sensing Letters ISSN 2150-704X print/ISSN 2150-7058 online ©2012 Taylor & Francis.

16 S.S. Khan, A. Ahamed, Cluster center initialization algorithm for Kmeans clustering, *Pattern Recognition Letters*, **25**(11) (2004) 1293–1302.

17 H.P. Ng, S.H. Ong, K.W.C. Foong, P.S. Goh, W.L. Nowinski, Medical Image Segmentation Using *k*-means Clustering and Improved Watershed Algorithm, 2006 IEEE Southwest Symposium on Image Analysis and Interpretation, (2006) 61–65.

18 B. Subbiah and S. Christopher, Image Classification through integrated K- Means Algorithm, *IJCSI International Journal of Computer Science Issues*, **9**(2)2, March 2012 ISSN (Online): 1694–0814.

19 M.N. Ahmed, S.M. Yamany, N. Mohamed, A.A. Farag, T. Moriarty, A modified fuzzy *c*-means algorithm for bias field estimation and segmentation of MRI data, *IEEE Transactions on Medical Imaging*, **21**(3) (2002) 193–199.

20 Z. Yang, F.L. Chung, W. Shitong, Robust fuzzy clustering-based image segmentation, *Applied Soft Computing* ,**9**(1) (2009) 80–84.

21 D.Q. Zhang, S.C. Chen, A novel kernelized fuzzy *C*-means algorithm (FCM) algorithm with application in medical image segmentation, *Artificial Intelligence in Medicine*, **32**(1) (2004) 37–50.

22 S.K. Adhikari, J.K. Sing, D.K. Basu, M. Nasipuri, Conditional spatial fuzzy C-means clustering algorithm for segmentation of MRI images, *Applied Soft Computing*, **34** (2015) 758 –769.

23 H.L. Capitaine, C. Frelicot, A fast fuzzy c-means algoritm for color image segmentation, EUSFLAT-LFA-2011,aix-les-Bains,Frace, (2011) 1074 –1081.

24 W. Zhang, C. Li, Y. Zhang, A new hybrid algorithm for image segmentation based on rough sets and enhanced fuzzy c-means clustering, 2009 IEEE International Conference on Automation and Logistics, DOI: 10.1109/ICAL.2009.5262701.

25 S. Nie, Y. Zhang, W. Li, Z. Chen, A fast and automatic segmentation method of MR brain images based on genetic fuzzy clustering algorithm, Proc. of International Conference on Engineering in Medicine and Biology Society, (2007) 5628–5633.

26 L.O. Hall, I.B. Ozyurt, J.C. Bezdek, Clustering with a genetically optimized approach, *IEEE Trans. Evol. Comput.* **3** (2) (1999) 103–112.

27 L. Zheng, Q. Pan, G. Li, Improvement of Grayscale Image Segmentation Based on PSO Algorithm, 2009 Fourth International Conference on Computer Sciences and Convergence Information Technology, (2009) 442–446, doi: 10.1109/ICCIT.2009.68.

28 W. Min, Y. Siqing, Improved k-means clustering based on genetic algorithm, International Conference on Computer Application and System Modeling (ICCASM), IEEE, **6** (2010) 636–639.

29 O. Castillo, E. Rubio, J. Soria, E. Naredo, Optimization of the fuzzy Cmeans algorithm using evolutionary methods, *Eng. Lett.*, **20**(1) (2012).

30 U. Mukhopadhyay, A. Maulik, A multiobjective approach to MR brain image segmentation, Appl. *Soft Comput.*, **11** (2012) 872–880.

31 V.G. Biju, P. Mythili, A Genetic Algorithm based Fuzzy C Mean Clustering Model for Segmenting Microarray Images, *International Journal of Computer Applications*, **52**(110) (2012) 42–48.

32 S. De, S. Bhattacharyya, P. Dutta, Efficient grey-level image segmentation using an optimised MUSIG (OptiMUSIG) activation function, *International Journal of Parallel, Emergent and Distributed Systems*, **26**(1) (2010) 1–39.

33 S. De, S. Bhattacharyya and P. Dutta, *Multilevel Image Segmentation using OptiMUSIG Activation Function with Fixed and Variable Thresholding: A Comparative Study*. Applications of Soft Computing: From Theory to Praxis, Advances in Intelligent and Soft Computing, (eds. Mehnen, J., Koppen, M., Saad, A. and Tiwari,A.), Springer- Verlag, Berlin, Heidelberg, (2009)53–62.

34 H. Talbi, A. Draa, M. Batouche, A New Quantum-Inspired Genetic Algorithm for Solving the Travelling Salesman Problem, 2004 IEEE International Conference on Industrial Technology (KIT), 3 (2004) 1192–1197.

35 H. Talbi, M. Batouche, A. Draa, A Quantum-Inspired Evolutionary Algorithm for Multi-objective Image Segmentation, *International Journal of Mathematical, Physical and Engineering Sciences* **1**(2) (2007) 109–114.

36 S. Bhattacharyya, S. Dey, An Efficient Quantum Inspired Genetic Algorithm with Chaotic Map Model based Interference and Fuzzy Objective Function for Gray Level Image Thresholding, International Conference on Computational Intelligence and Communication Networks (CICN),(2011) 121–125.

37 S. Bhattacharyya, P. Dutta, S. Chakraborty, R. Chakraborty, and S. Dey, Determination of Optimal Threshold of a Gray-level Image Using a Quantum Inspired Genetic Algorithm with Interference Based on a Random Map Model, in Proc. 2010 IEEE International Conference on Computational Intelligence and Computing Research (ICCIC), (2010), doi:10.1109/ICCIC.2010.5705806.

38 S. Dey, I. Saha, U. Maulik, S. Bhattacharyya, New Quantum Inspired Meta-heuristic Methods for Multi-level Thresholding, 2013 International Conference on Advances in Computing, Communications and Informatics (ICACCI), At Mysore, (2013) 1236–1240, doi:10.1109/ICACCI.2013.6637354.

39 J.C. Dunn, A Fuzzy Relative of the ISODATA Process and Its Use in Detecting Compact Well-Separated Clusters, *Journal of Cybernetics*, **3** (1973) 32–57.

40 G.E. Moore, Cramming more components onto integrated circuits, *Electronics*, **38**(8) (1965) 114–117.

41 J. Liu, Y.H. Yang, Multi-resolution color image segmentation, *IEEE Transactions on Pattern Analysis and Machine Intelligence*, **16**(7) (1994) 689–700, doi:10.1109/34.297949.

42 M. Borsotti, P. Campadelli, R. Schettini, Quantitative evaluation of color image segmentation results, *Pattern Recognition Letters*, **19** (1998) 741–747, doi:10.1016/S0167-8655(98)00052-X.

43 S. N. Kumar, A. Lenin FredP, Sebastin Varghese, Suspicious Lesion Segmentation on Brain, Mammograms and Breast MR Images Using New Optimized Spatial Feature Based Super-Pixel Fuzzy *C*-means Clustering, *Journal of Digital Imaging*, **32**(2) (2019) 322–335, doi: 10.1007/s10278-018-0149-9.

44 J. Arora, M. Tushir, Robust spatial intuitionistic fuzzy *C*-means with city-block distance clustering for image segmentation, *Journal of Intelligent and Fuzzy Systems*, **35**(5) (2018) 1–10, doi: 10.3233/JIFS-169809.

45 L. Yang, Y. Fu, Z. Wang, X. Zhen, Z. Yang, X. Fan, An Optimized Level Set Method Based on QPSO and Fuzzy Clustering, *IEICE Transactions on Information and Systems*, E102.D(5) (2019) 1065–1072, doi: 10.1587/transinf.2018EDP7132.

9

A Hybrid Approach Using the k-means and Genetic Algorithms for Image Color Quantization

Marcos Roberto e Souza, Anderson Carlos Sousa e Santos, and Helio Pedrini

Institute of Computing, University of Campinas, SP, Brazil

9.1 Introduction

Color image quantization is a procedure used to reduce the number of colors in an image while maintaining a minimum degree of distortion so that the resulting image is similar to the original. This is an important stage for representing and displaying images on devices with limited computational resources, for instance, video memory requirements.

Typically, full-color RGB (Red-Green-Blue) images consist of approximately 16 million (2^{24}) colors, where each pixel is described by three 8-bit color components. The color quantization problem aims to divide the full color space into a small number of regions and assign a single representative color for each pixel that falls into a different region.

Several applications can benefit from color quantization, such as segmentation, compression, texture analysis, watermarking, and content-based retrieval. Although modern computers can currently display millions of colors at the same time, this is much more than can be distinguished by the human eye.

Color quantization can be considered as a lossy image compression method. Let I be a digital color image and n be the number of its colors. The quantization aims to select a set of $k < n$ representative colors to represent the image. In addition, the image quantization can be seen as a clustering problem.

Cluster analysis refers to the partitioning of given data points into different groups (clusters) such that the data points within the same group share more similar characteristics to each other than to those in other groups. More specifically, image clustering is a process of splitting unlabeled image data into clusters based on feature similarities. Several clustering algorithms have been proposed in the literature based on connectivity [1], centroid [2], distribution [3], density [4], and graph [5], among other models. A difficulty found in most of the clustering algorithms is the automatic determination of a proper number of clusters to result in a good data separation [6–10].

One of the most known clustering methods is the k-means algorithm, where n observations or data points are partitioned into k clusters, such that each observation is assigned to the cluster with the closest mean. The k-means algorithm is simple to implement, fast to

Recent Advances in Hybrid Metaheuristics for Data Clustering, First Edition.
Edited by Sourav De, Sandip Dey, and Siddhartha Bhattacharyya.

execute, and scalable to large datasets. Despite these advantages, a serious drawback of the k-means algorithm [11] is its high dependence of the location of the initial cluster centroids, which affects the quality of the final clustering. In addition, the algorithm may be very sensitive to noisy data and outliers. Since k-means is stochastic, the algorithm may converge to a local minimum solution for clustering. Therefore, it is important to develop an effective mechanism for reducing the adverse effects of initial conditions of the cluster centroids, improving the results of the k-means algorithm.

In this work, we propose and evaluate a hybrid method that combines k-means and genetic algorithm for image color quantization. The genetic algorithm aims to improve the quantized images generated by the k-means algorithm through a qualitative objective function, which considers the local neighborhood. Evolution is performed over a number of epochs. Crossover and mutation operators are applied, and the population is reinitialized during the process, except for the best individual. Experiments demonstrate that the proposed hybrid approach surpassed the color quantization based on the k-means clustering algorithm. Furthermore, it has been found that the use of pixel-by-pixel metrics is inefficient, either for an objective function or for quality evaluation of the quantization, even though these metrics are used in the majority of the methods available in the literature.

As the main contribution of this work, we have different crossover operators and the objective function based on the structural similarity index (SSIM) [12], which is a perceptual measure of image quality. In contrast to clustering methods, such as k-means, and other genetic algorithm-based approaches [13, 14], we consider the interactions in the pixel neighborhood to perform image color quantization with the SSIM objective function. In this sense, the motivation of this work is to develop a color quantization method that explores human visual perception. To the best of our knowledge, this is the first work that uses an SSIM-based metric for color quantization.

The remainder of the chapter is organized as follows. This section presented an introduction to this work. Section 9.2 describes some relevant concepts and approaches related to the topic under investigation in this work. The proposed methodology based on k-means and genetic algorithms is described in Section 9.3. Experimental results are presented and discussed in Section 9.4. Finally, Section 9.5 concludes the paper, followed by the references.

9.2 Background

Several color quantization approaches have been proposed in the literature over the last few years. In general, two steps are involved in the process. The first one partitions the color space into a small number of colors. The second one assigns these colors to each pixel in the image. In a general fashion, color quantization algorithms can be categorized as uniform and adaptive.

Uniform quantization divides the color space (for instance, represented by an RGB cube) into disjoint subspaces of equal size, such that the number of regions depends on the strategy for partitioning the color space. On the other hand, adaptive quantization divides the color space according to a certain criterion.

A known uniform quantization partitions the red (R) and green (G) axes of color space into 8 segments and the blue (B) axis into 4 segments, resulting in 256 (= 8 × 8 × 4) regions [15]. This scheme is simple and fast; however, the palette colors of the original and quantized images are usually very different.

The minimum variance quantization method [16, 17] partitions the color space into boxes (not necessarily cubes), where the sizes of the boxes depend on how the colors are distributed in the image. Pixels are associated into groups based on the variance between their pixel values. Statistical computations for color quantization are based on variance minimization [18].

The median cut method [17, 19] divides the color space into boxes with approximately the same number of pixels within each region. The boxes of the space are repeatedly partitioned into planes perpendicular to one of the color axes. The region with the most pixels is selected to be partitioned along the largest axis. The division process keeps half the pixels in each portion. The division process is applied until the desired number of boxes is achieved, which is the maximum number of color entries in the available colormap.

A color quantization based on the radius weighted mean cut was proposed to construct a color palette [20]. The method hierarchically divides the dataset into two subsets using the centroids of the cells.

Dynamic programming was used to construct a global optimal partitioning of the color space according to an ordering of the colors along their principal axis [21]. Some statistical computations and nearest-neighbor searching were also investigated.

The octree method [22] partitions the color space into octants, repeatedly selecting the color for the initial color space. Adjacent colors with the least amount of pixels are merged when the number of colors is higher than the desired number.

A color quantization approach based on the moment-preserving principle [23] initially divides the color histogram into smaller boxes, where two color values are assigned as two representative palette colors for every two nonadjacent boxes. The quantized image is partitioned into nonoverlapping square blocks, such that two representative colors for each block are selected by the moment-preserving thresholding.

A common technique for color quantization is to reduce the problem into a clustering scheme of points [24], where each point represents the color of an image pixel. For each cluster, a representative point is selected to create the color palette. The k-means clustering algorithm [25–30] is the most commonly used strategy to partition the image into a set of clusters.

Notwithstanding, the k-means clustering algorithm is highly dependent on the initial conditions. To address this problem, other strategies have been proposed, such as k-harmonic means [31], fuzzy c-means [32–35], and self-organizing maps [36–39].

Although the k-means clustering has some advantages, such as its convergence speed and implementation simplicity, it is sensitive to cluster initialization, which may converge to a local optimal solution. To address this drawback, evolutionary-based algorithms have been applied to the color quantization problem, for instance, particle swarm optimization (PSO) [40], differential evolution (DE) [41], genetic algorithm (GA) [13], ant colony optimization (ACO) [42], artificial fish swarm optimization (AFSA) [43], and artificial bee colony (ABC) [44].

A color quantization approach was proposed based on Gaussian PSO and k-means [45]. The reported results showed an improvement over the traditional PSO method. The mean squared error (MSE) is used as an objective function and as a metric to compare the different approaches.

Khaled et al. [46] proposed a color quantization algorithm based on the harmonic search. Two variations were examined: one with the harmonic search algorithm and a second with a hybrid method between harmonic search and k-means. The results presented were better than the other methods used for comparison in terms of PSNR.

A method for adaptive initialization of k-means subsampling and coreset construction was proposed to accelerate the execution of k-means for color quantization [47]. The results presented showed a faster algorithm with MSE values close to those obtained with conventional k-means.

Even the most recent approaches employ the MSE or peak signal-to-noise ratio (PSNR) metric both for the objective function and as a measure to evaluate the quality and compare different methods. However, these metrics are calculated pixel by pixel and do not consider the differences between the neighborhoods.

Thus, our work proposes a method based on a genetic algorithm for the quantization of images using a metric based on SSIM. The genetic algorithm applies mutation and crossover operators directly to the image, as already done in other applications such as noise removal [48, 49]. However, in our case, the method was developed for the clustering context, more specifically for the image quantization problem.

9.3 Color Quantization Methodology

An overview of the main stages of the proposed method for image color quantization, which combines k-means and genetic algorithms, is illustrated in Figure 9.1.

From a color image with a number of colors N, the first step of the algorithm is to calculate the initial quantization. To do this, we compute the quantized image with the k-means clustering method [11] with $k < N$ colors. With a certain probability (50%, in this work), one of the mutation operators presented in Section 9.3.2 can be applied to the original image, before the initial quantization.

In the k-means algorithm, the initial positions of the k cluster centers are determined randomly. Given a function $f : \mathfrak{R}^n \to \mathfrak{R}$ and set $S \subseteq \mathfrak{R}^n$, find $x^* \in S$ that $f(x^*) \geq f(x)$ for all $x \in S$. In our problem, the objective is to maximize the value of SSIM between the original image and the corresponding result from each thresholding approach. Most optimization methods are designed to find the local maximum, which may not be the global maximum. If $x^* \in S$ is a global maximum, then $f(x^*) \geq f(x)$ for all $x \in S$. If $x^* \in S$ is a local maximum, then $f(x^*) \geq f(x)$ for all feasible x in some neighborhood of x^*.

In addition to the k-means initialization, another individual of the population is initialized through a uniform quantization algorithm in one of the channels of the HSV (Hue-Saturation-Value) color space. To do this, a channel is randomly chosen to determine the regions. In the chosen channel, the indices of a uniform quantization are calculated and can be described as follows:

$$M(p) = \frac{I(p)}{\frac{255}{k}} \tag{9.1}$$

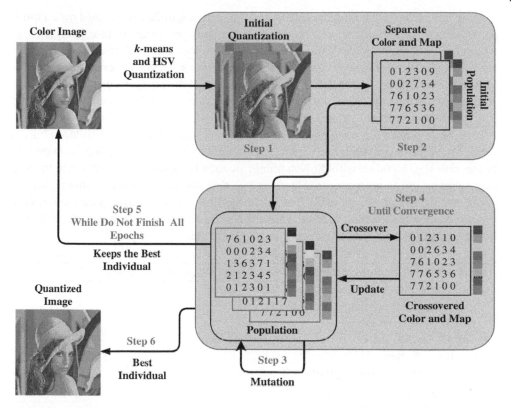

Figure 9.1 Main steps of the hybrid method of image color quantization based on k-means and genetic algorithms.

where $I(p)$ is the value of the pixel p in the chosen HSV channel. Thus, we will have an M image of labels in the range of 0 to $k - 1$. Finally, an RGB image is created in which the average of the original image pixel colors labeled with the label of p is assigned to the pixel p of the final image.

An $H \times W \times 3$ matrix, where H and W are respectively its height and width, is usually the structure used to store a color image. However, this structure may not be very useful to control the amount, tones, and location of colors in the genetic algorithm. Therefore, as a second step, we transformed the already quantized images, generated through k-means and quantization in HSV, into a color vector C with size $k \times 3$, which separates the colors from the map M of size $H \times W$. The value of $M(p)$ corresponds to the index of the vector C that contains the color referring to the pixel p.

An individual of the genetic algorithm consists of a tuple $I = (C, M)$. The population P is constructed, initially from the tuples I, J obtained from the quantized images generated by the k-means and the quantization in the HSV space. In addition, the other $\#P - 2$ tuples are resulted from the application of the mutation operators, presented in Section 9.3.2, in one of the generated previously tuples randomly chosen. The construction of the population is taken as the third step.

After generation of the initial population, the genetic algorithm is executed over a number of of epochs E. In each iteration, the fourth step is performed until convergence, in which two random individuals are selected and, from them, an individual child is generated through the crossover operators presented in Section 9.3.1. With a certain probability, a mutation operator can still be applied to the individual. If the fitness value of this new individual is better than the father with the worst fitness value, then the population is updated from the replacement of the father by its child.

To achieve population convergence, it is necessary that all individual children have a worse fitness value than their two parents after iterating across the population. After convergence, only the individual with the best fitness function keeps for the next season in the fifth step, whereas the others are replaced by a new initialization process, made from mutations of the original image, resuming the first step. Algorithm 9.1 presents the pseudocode of the proposed color quantization method, where the `crossover_ratio` parameter indicates how many times the population should be iterated to verify convergence.

Algorithm 1 Pseudocode of the proposed hybrid color quantization approach.

1: Input: original color image
2: Output: quantized image
3: initialize the population
4: **for all** $e = 1$ to E **do**
5:     **if** $e > 1$ **then**
6:         reinitialize the population
7:     **while** not converged **do**
8:         converged = true
9:         **for all** $i = 1$ to crossover_ratio(#P) **do**
10:             get two random parents p_1 and p_2
11:             child = crossover(p_1, p_2)
12:             **if** mutation **then**
13:                 mutate_map()
14:                 mutate_colors()
15:             get p_{worse} with worse fitness between p_1 and p_2
16:             **if** fitness(child) is better than fitness(p_{worse}) **then**
17:                 remove p_{worse} from the population
18:                 add child in the population
19:                 converged = false

From Algorithm 9.1, it is possible to observe that the computational time complexity is directly related to the number of epochs E, the size of the population, and the size of the image. The crossover operation is performed in $O(N)$, where $N = \max\{H, W\}$, such that H and W are the height and width of the input image, respectively. On the other hand, the mutation operation is performed, in the worst case, in the complexity order of the nonlocal means, that is, $O(HW(2T + 2)(2S + 1)^2)$, where T and S correspond to the size of the patches and the window search of the nonlocal means, respectively. Then, the complexity of the loop at line 9 is given as $O(PHW(2T + 2)(2S + 1)^2)$, which is the same for the population reset, where P corresponds to the population size. Therefore, the final complexity of the algorithm in a nonformal analysis is $O(EPHW(2T + 2)(2S + 1)^2)$.

9.3.1 Crossover Operators

The crossover in the color vector has only one point operator, which combines the colors of the two parents from a point $p \in [0, k]$, whereas the map has four operators, applied with the same probability. Figure 9.2 illustrates a graphical representation of the crossover operators applied to the index map.

The main steps involved in the application of the crossover operator are described as follows: (a)-(b) two parents; (c) one-point column: from the two parent maps, the child map can be calculated from the combination of the $[0, c]$ columns of the first parent and the columns in the range of (c, W) in the second, such that $c \in [0, W)$ is a random column; (d) one-point row: calculates the child map from the combination of the $[0, r]$ lines of the first parent and the (r, H) lines of the second, such that $r \in [0, H)$ is a random line; (e-1) point-point random: assigns randomly to each pixel of the child map $M_c(p)$, an equivalent

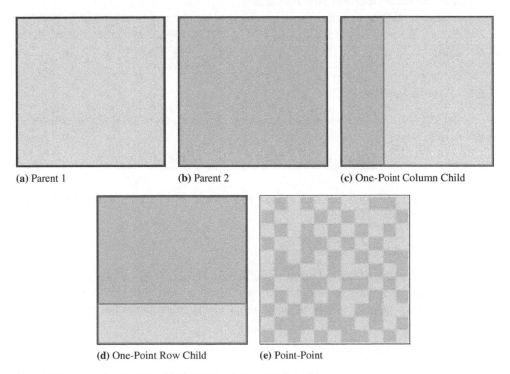

(a) Parent 1   **(b)** Parent 2   **(c)** One-Point Column Child

(d) One-Point Row Child   **(e)** Point-Point

Figure 9.2 Graphical representation of the crossover operator.

map pixel value of the first parent $M_1(p)$ or the second parent $M_2(p)$; (e-2) point-point best squared error: each pixel of the child map $M_c(p)$ receives the equivalent pixel value of the parent that minimizes the quadratic error between that pixel and the pixel of the original image.

9.3.2 Mutation Operators

Mutation operators are applied separately on the map and in the color vector. As map operators, we have:

- *Smoothing Operators*: One of the Gaussian filters, median filter, bilateral filter, and non-local means are applied to smooth map indices and render neighboring pixels with the same or more similar colors.
- *Uniform Noise*: A uniform noise is added in the image (map) to randomly change some of its indices. Thus, some variations are added to the image.

In the color vector, the mutations are applied in the HSV space, which are described as follows:

- *Brightness Change*: A random number $N \in [-20, 20]$ is added to all values of the color vector in the value channel of the HSV space.
- *Color Change*: All hue channel values are changed by adding a number $N \in [-20, 20]$.
- *Random Color Change*: A random value $N \in [0,255]$ is assigned to a random index in the hue channel.

9.3.3 Fitness Function

We model a fitness function to find the best values of the parameters for the image clustering problem as follows:

$$F^* = \underset{F \in \Omega}{\arg\max} \ \frac{\text{MSSIM}(\mathbf{f}_R, \mathbf{g}_R) + \text{MSSIM}(\mathbf{f}_G, \mathbf{g}_G) + \text{MSSIM}(\mathbf{f}_B, \mathbf{g}_B)}{3} \tag{9.2}$$

where Ω is the set of all possible solutions and the MSSIM between the two images channels $\mathbf{f}_c$ and $\mathbf{g}_c$ is expressed as follows:

$$\text{MSSIM}(\mathbf{f}_c, \mathbf{g}_c) = \frac{\sum^p |SSIM(x, y)|}{WH} \tag{9.3}$$

where W and H are the width and height of the images, respectively, the structural similarity index (SSIM) [12] is a quality measure calculated between two equivalent windows x and y around the pixel p, respectively, from the images $\mathbf{f}$ and $\mathbf{g}$, expressed as follows:

$$\text{SSIM}(\mathbf{x}, \mathbf{y}) = \frac{(2\mu_x\mu_y + C_1)(2\sigma_{xy} + C_2)}{(\mu_x^2 + \mu_y^2 + C_1)(\sigma_x^2 + \sigma_y^2 + C_2)} \tag{9.4}$$

where μ_x is the mean of $\mathbf{x}$, μ_y is the mean of $\mathbf{y}$, σ_x^2 is the variance of $\mathbf{x}$, σ_y^2 is the variance of $\mathbf{y}$, and σ_{xy} is the covariance of $\mathbf{x}$ and $\mathbf{y}$. The SSIM measure varies in the range of $[-1..1]$, such that closer it is to 0, the more dissimilar the windows $\mathbf{x}$ and $\mathbf{y}$ are. On the other hands, MSSIM varies in the range of $[0..1]$.

Since SSIM was proposed to deal only with the luminance, we calculated its average for the three RGB channels of the image. This approach proved to be adequate in our preliminary experiments. However, a deeper investigation could result in an objective function to deal with colors more effectively and produce an even better result.

9.4 Results and Discussions

In the experiments conducted in this work, we consider a database with 14 images, presented in Figure 9.3. Eleven of them are well known and commonly used as a benchmark in image processing tasks, whereas the remaining three images ("gradient," "jet," and "rgb") are synthetic. All images have 8-bit channels. We used a population of size of 15, 20% of mutation probability, and crossover_ratio equal to 2. All experiments were executed on an Intel(R) Core(TM) i7-3610QM @ 2.30GHz CPU with 8 GB RAM using Linux Mint version 19.1 and the C++ programming language.

Most of the approaches available in the literature use the MSE as the basis of the objective function. However, this measure does not consider the relationships between neighboring pixels and may produce undesired results. Figure 9.4 presents the results obtained with the MSE metric as an objective function.

We can see that the quantized images with the MSE have a significant difference between neighboring pixels. Thus, although metrics such as the MSE or PSNR, used in several methods in the literature to evaluate the results, have demonstrated superior results with optimization schemes, this does not necessarily indicate a visual improvement. On the other hand, as we will see next, the results achieved with the use of the SSIM metric as the basis of the objective function can bring a more satisfactory result. These results show the difficulty of a comparison with other methods of the literature.

Table 9.1 presents the results obtained through three executions with $k = 4$. From these results, we can notice that, already in the fifth epoch, there was an improvement with respect to the MSSIM metric when compared to the result obtained through the k-means algorithm. In addition, results continue to improve over time.

As expected, in most cases, the standard deviation decreases as we increase the number of epochs. This indicates that the larger the number of epochs performed a smaller variation between the images, indicating that the algorithm tends to converge.

Figure 9.5 presents the results obtained for the "fruits" image with four colors. In this case, we can see that the image obtained with the genetic algorithm ignores the yellow color adopted by the k-means algorithm. This caused the resulting image to have its details more clearly defined.

We can observe, by zooming the image as presented in Figure 9.6, that in the version of the genetic algorithm the details between the local pixels are visually better with smoother and well-defined variations. This result was observed throughout all the images, as shown in another example of Figure 9.7, where the neighboring pixels are smoother and the color tones are slightly altered. This was possible only because of the use of an objective function based on SSIM.

We can notice that although the outcomes of the color quantization were improved, the quality of the results of our method is quite dependent on the quality of the initialization of

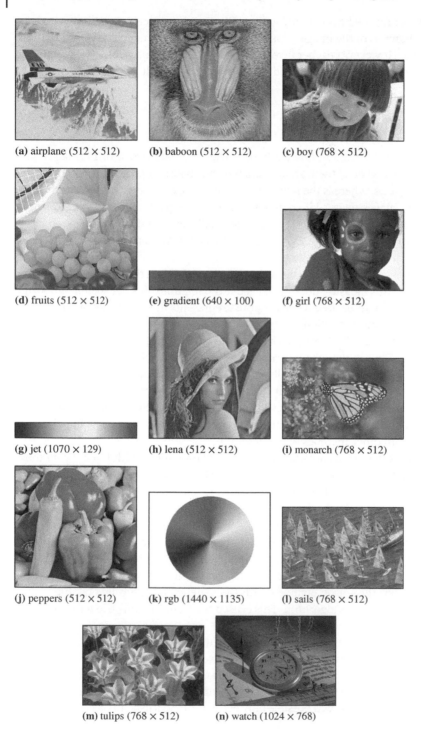

(**a**) airplane (512×512)   (**b**) baboon (512×512)   (**c**) boy (768×512)

(**d**) fruits (512×512)   (**e**) gradient (640×100)   (**f**) girl (768×512)

(**g**) jet (1070×129)   (**h**) lena (512×512)   (**i**) monarch (768×512)

(**j**) peppers (512×512)   (**k**) rgb (1440×1135)   (**l**) sails (768×512)

(**m**) tulips (768×512)   (**n**) watch (1024×768)

Figure 9.3 Images and their sizes used in the experiments to evaluate our color segmentation methodology.

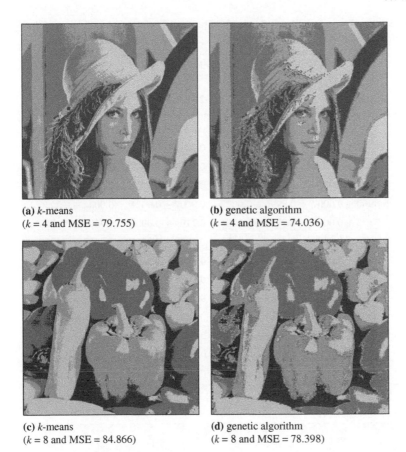

(a) k-means
($k = 4$ and MSE = 79.755)

(b) genetic algorithm
($k = 4$ and MSE = 74.036)

(c) k-means
($k = 8$ and MSE = 84.866)

(d) genetic algorithm
($k = 8$ and MSE = 78.398)

Figure 9.4 Results for k-means and genetic algorithms on "lena" and "peppers" images with MSE as the objective function.

the population. Thus, when the k-means algorithm generates a very bad result, our method fails to converge satisfactorily. Figure 9.8 illustrates an example of this situation.

For the case presented in Figure 9.8, the k-means algorithm selected two clusters of the same color. Thus, our method was not able to rearrange the map to avoid that local minimum.

Table 9.2 presents the results obtained in three executions with $k = 8$, which behave similarly to the results obtained with $k = 4$. In the fifth epoch, we can see an improvement in the terms of MSSIM, which is deepened with more epochs. Figure 9.9 presents an example of the result for the "girl" image, in which we can see that the interactions between the neighboring pixels have become smoother.

Table 9.3 presents the average and standard deviation values of the results obtained with 16 colors in 3 executions. In these results, we can observe that the genetic algorithm maintained its behavior, improving the results achieved by the k-means algorithm.

Figure 9.10 displays the result obtained for 16 colors in the "tulips" image. We can see that the k-means already produces satisfactory results in terms of softness of the pixels, due to the greater number of colors in the palette. However, when we look closely, we can see that

Table 9.1 Results of SSIM for Three Executions (Mean and Standard Deviations Are Shown) of the Genetic Algorithms with Four Colors

Images	k-means	Genetic			
		5 Epochs	15 Epochs	25 Epochs	35 Epochs
airplane	0.8143	0.8249 ± 0.0005	0.8279 ± 0.0008	0.8293 ± 0.0002	0.8299 ± 0.0005
baboon	0.6227	0.6333 ± 0.0024	0.6385 ± 0.0005	0.6390 ± 0.0003	0.6396 ± 0.0007
boy	0.5305	0.5446 ± 0.0011	0.5587 ± 0.0012	0.5604 ± 0.0002	0.5608 ± 0.0005
fruits	0.6554	0.6728 ± 0.0016	0.6881 ± 0.0003	0.6884 ± 0.0003	0.6888 ± 0.0006
gradient	0.8933	0.8960 ± 0.0007	0.8996 ± 0.0022	0.9002 ± 0.0021	0.9004 ± 0.0020
girl	0.7098	0.7175 ± 0.0026	0.7196 ± 0.0001	0.7199 ± 0.0000	0.7200 ± 0.0000
jet	0.8153	0.8274 ± 0.0079	0.8285 ± 0.0071	0.8358 ± 0.0052	0.8367 ± 0.0047
lena	0.7026	0.7225 ± 0.0029	0.7261 ± 0.0026	0.7277 ± 0.0007	0.7285 ± 0.0007
monarch	0.7881	0.7955 ± 0.0006	0.7980 ± 0.0016	0.7986 ± 0.0010	0.7994 ± 0.0001
peppers	0.5508	0.5783 ± 0.0003	0.5789 ± 0.0003	0.5790 ± 0.0003	0.5793 ± 0.0003
rgb	0.7475	0.7616 ± 0.0000	0.7617 ± 0.0000	0.7617 ± 0.0000	0.7617 ± 0.0000
sails	0.7626	0.7661 ± 0.0002	0.7668 ± 0.0007	0.7672 ± 0.0005	0.7674 ± 0.0007
tulips	0.5994	0.6064 ± 0.0004	0.6072 ± 0.0007	0.6077 ± 0.0007	0.6081 ± 0.0003
watch	0.8718	0.8729 ± 0.0007	0.8737 ± 0.0009	0.8743 ± 0.0001	0.8743 ± 0.0001

(a) original image   (b) k-means algorithm   (c) genetic algorithm

Figure 9.5 Results for the "fruits" image with $k = 4$.

the genetic algorithm was able to choose colors that were more suitable for some regions of the image, such as the brown tones obtained with the k-means algorithm around the flowers, which were changed to greenish tones.

To compare the results and the behavior of the genetic algorithm for different values of k, Figures 9.11 to 9.13 present comparative graphics for the images considered in this work. In the axis of abscissas, we have the number of epochs, whereas the values of the objective function are shown in the axis of ordinates. All 35 epochs are reported. The results of k-means with 4, 8, and 16 colors are presented, respectively, by straight blue, green, and

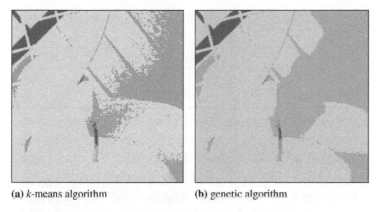

(a) k-means algorithm   (b) genetic algorithm

Figure 9.6 Zooming of the results for the "fruits" image with $k = 4$.

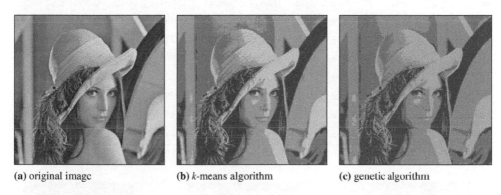

(a) original image   (b) k-means algorithm   (c) genetic algorithm

Figure 9.7 Results for the "lena" image with $k = 4$.

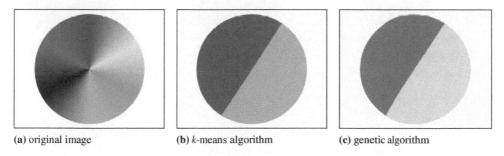

(a) original image   (b) k-means algorithm   (c) genetic algorithm

Figure 9.8 Results for the "rgb" image with $k = 4$.

purple. In turn, the average results for three executions of the genetic algorithm with 4, 8, and 16 colors are, respectively, shown through orange, red, and brown curves. The standard deviation values of the executions are presented by vertical lines superimposed on the average curves.

From the graphs presented in Figures 9.11 to 9.13, we can notice that there was a distinct behavior for some image groups. In the improvement of the genetic algorithm over the k-means algorithm, we can observe that there was a more significant improvement with

Table 9.2 Results of SSIM for 3 Executions (Mean and Standard Deviations Are Shown) of the Genetic Algorithms with 8 Colors

		Genetic			
Images	*k*-means	5 Epochs	15 Epochs	25 Epochs	35 Epochs
airplane	0.8585	0.8777 ± 0.0008	0.8783 ± 0.0006	0.8784 ± 0.0007	0.8786 ± 0.0005
baboon	0.7205	0.7248 ± 0.0005	0.7254 ± 0.0007	0.7257 ± 0.0008	0.7261 ± 0.0012
boy	0.6512	0.6577 ± 0.0026	0.6608 ± 0.0007	0.6615 ± 0.0003	0.6616 ± 0.0004
fruits	0.7370	0.7516 ± 0.0006	0.7528 ± 0.0005	0.7532 ± 0.0006	0.7535 ± 0.0003
gradient	0.9401	0.9435 ± 0.0007	0.9448 ± 0.0006	0.9452 ± 0.0007	0.9454 ± 0.0008
girl	0.7737	0.7891 ± 0.0038	0.7922 ± 0.0010	0.7940 ± 0.0013	0.7943 ± 0.0013
jet	0.8483	0.8582 ± 0.0066	0.8627 ± 0.0055	0.8661 ± 0.0089	0.8663 ± 0.0088
lena	0.7681	0.7790 ± 0.0010	0.7804 ± 0.0010	0.7824 ± 0.0012	0.7833 ± 0.0013
monarch	0.8155	0.8284 ± 0.0028	0.8306 ± 0.0017	0.8315 ± 0.0008	0.8319 ± 0.0010
peppers	0.6634	0.6846 ± 0.0031	0.6860 ± 0.0030	0.6881 ± 0.0026	0.6886 ± 0.0025
rgb	0.8236	0.8318 ± 0.0044	0.8348 ± 0.0005	0.8352 ± 0.0001	0.8353 ± 0.0001
sails	0.8315	0.8373 ± 0.0025	0.8387 ± 0.0011	0.8392 ± 0.0010	0.8395 ± 0.0011
tulips	0.7086	0.7172 ± 0.0005	0.7194 ± 0.0002	0.7199 ± 0.0004	0.7200 ± 0.0004
watch	0.9099	0.9116 ± 0.0006	0.9127 ± 0.0006	0.9130 ± 0.0007	0.9133 ± 0.0006

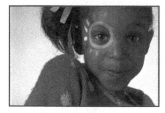  

(a) original image   (b) *k*-means algorithm   (c) genetic algorithm

Figure 9.9 Results for the "girl" image with *k* = 8.

four colors for the "fruits," "lena," and "peppers" images; however, the results of the genetic algorithm were considerably improved with 8 and 16 colors.

In other images, such as "baboon" and "boy," the improvement with 8 and 16 colors is relatively small compared to the improvement obtained with 4 colors. This seems to occur because, with $k = 4$, the genetic algorithm can choose a palette of colors that is globally better. However, with $k = 8$ or $k = 16$, the k-means color palette is not improved by the genetic algorithm. In addition, the genetic algorithm does not make very considerable changes in the image map, possibly because they have a more complex texture.

The "gradient" and "jet" images have an interesting feature of having a higher standard deviation with a lower number of colors. This shows a certain difficulty in converging the method, most likely because of the large number of color tones of the original image that

Table 9.3 Results of SSIM for 3 Executions (Mean and Standard Deviations Are Shown) of the Genetic Algorithms with 16 Colors

Images	k-means	Genetic			
		5 Epochs	15 Epochs	25 Epochs	35 Epochs
airplane	0.9095	0.9153 ± 0.0003	0.9155 ± 0.0001	0.9159 ± 0.0002	0.9164 ± 0.0003
baboon	0.8036	0.8068 ± 0.0002	0.8073 ± 0.0003	0.8076 ± 0.0004	0.8077 ± 0.0004
boy	0.7295	0.7313 ± 0.0004	0.7338 ± 0.0032	0.7362 ± 0.0029	0.7380 ± 0.0008
fruits	0.7877	0.7984 ± 0.0009	0.8016 ± 0.0009	0.8025 ± 0.0010	0.8034 ± 0.0003
gradient	0.9528	0.9546 ± 0.0001	0.9555 ± 0.0004	0.9563 ± 0.0004	0.9566 ± 0.0001
girl	0.8240	0.8293 ± 0.0021	0.8323 ± 0.0017	0.8341 ± 0.0017	0.8350 ± 0.0017
jet	0.9276	0.9320 ± 0.0028	0.9325 ± 0.0026	0.9354 ± 0.0005	0.9361 ± 0.0001
lena	0.8052	0.8120 ± 0.0031	0.8140 ± 0.0024	0.8149 ± 0.0023	0.8162 ± 0.0016
monarch	0.8619	0.8683 ± 0.0006	0.8705 ± 0.0016	0.8715 ± 0.0015	0.8720 ± 0.0012
peppers	0.7259	0.7391 ± 0.0012	0.7428 ± 0.0027	0.7458 ± 0.0003	0.7468 ± 0.0006
rgb	0.8751	0.8767 ± 0.0004	0.8802 ± 0.0035	0.8810 ± 0.0038	0.8812 ± 0.0036
sails	0.8975	0.8986 ± 0.0002	0.8993 ± 0.0003	0.8997 ± 0.0002	0.8999 ± 0.0003
tulips	0.7958	0.8012 ± 0.0010	0.8035 ± 0.0011	0.8042 ± 0.0006	0.8048 ± 0.0005
watch	0.9330	0.9337 ± 0.0006	0.9343 ± 0.0005	0.9345 ± 0.0003	0.9348 ± 0.0002

(a) original image   (b) k-means algorithm   (c) genetic algorithm

Figure 9.10 Results with zooming for the "tulips" image with $k = 16$.

need to be represented by a very small number of colors. In the "jet" image, the amount of color of the original image is larger. This behavior is also evident with $k = 8$.

There are also images, such as "airplane" and "girl," in which the improvement with eight colors is superior compared to the use of four colors. In these cases, the k-means algorithm seemed to generate a greater difference between neighboring pixels with $k = 8$. This effect was corrected by the genetic algorithm due to the use of the SSIM-based objective function. This correction allowed for a more significant improvement in the final result.

As reported in our experiments, our genetic method for image color quantization was compared to the k-means clustering algorithm using the same set of images. In addition, we compared our objective function based on SSIM against the traditional MSE metric.

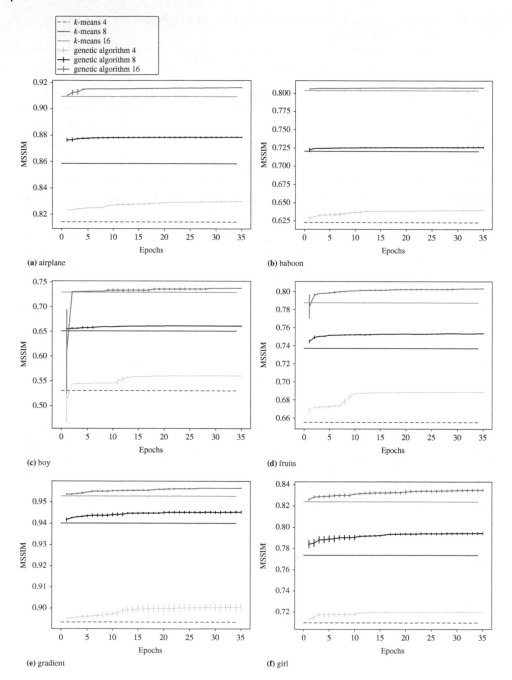

Figure 9.11 Comparative graphics of the results obtained for each of the images with different values of *k*.

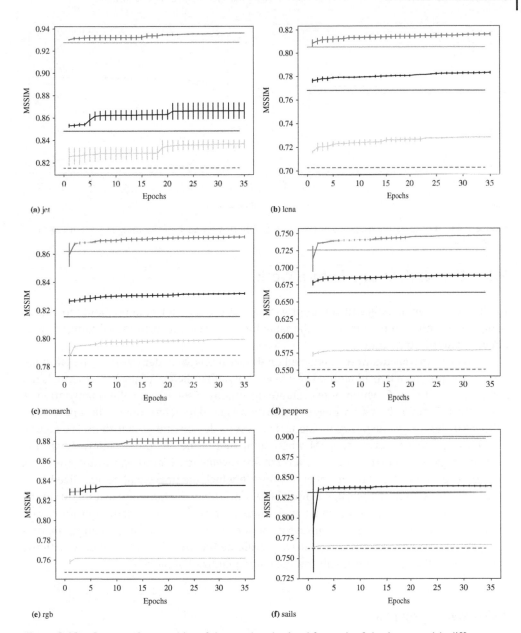

Figure 9.12 Comparative graphics of the results obtained for each of the images with different values of k.

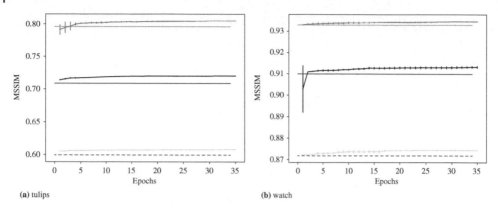

(a) tulips   (b) watch

Figure 9.13 Comparative graphics of the results obtained for each of the images with different values of *k*.

9.5 Conclusions and Future Work

In this work, we investigated the improvement of image color quantization approaches using genetic algorithms to enhance the capability of *k*-means algorithm in finding a proper cluster center initialization.

Extensive experiments were conducted on different images to demonstrate the effectiveness of the proposed hybrid method. We have shown that the use of the MSE metric is not indicated as a fitness function or to evaluate the quality of the image color quantization. A new fitness function based on image similarity was used to determine the best parameter values for the image clustering problem. The results demonstrated that there is a consistent improvement in terms of SSIM when compared to the outcomes obtained with the *k*-means algorithm. Furthermore, the level of improvement achieved significantly depends on the image content and the number of colors in which the image will be quantized.

As directions for future work, we intend to explore other evolutionary techniques in the context of image color quantization. Other strategies related to the genetic algorithm itself could be investigated in order to improve its performance when very large changes are necessary. Finally, we plan to more extensively evaluate the use of the SSIM metric with the color information, more specifically on the color quantization problem.

Acknowledgments

The authors thank FAPESP (grants #2014/12236-1 and #2017/12646-3), CNPq (grant #309330/2018-1), and CAPES for the financial support.

References

1 Bouguettaya, A., Yu, Q., Liu, X., Zhou, X., and Song, A. (2015) Efficient Agglomerative Hierarchical Clustering. *Expert Systems with Applications*, **42** (5), 2785–2797.

2 Hamerly, G. and Elkan, C. (2002) Alternatives to the *k*-means Algorithm That Find Better Clusterings, in *Eleventh International Conference on Information and Knowledge Management*, ACM, McLean, VA, USA, pp. 600–607.

3 Assaad, H.E., Samé, A., Govaert, G., and Aknin, P. (2016) A Variational Expectation-Maximization Algorithm for Temporal Data Clustering. *Computational Statistics & Data Analysis*, **103**, 206–228.

4 Ester, M., Kriegel, H.P., Sander, J., and Xu, X. (1996) *A Density-based Algorithm for Discovering Clusters in large Spatial Databases with Noise*, in *Second International Conference on Knowledge Discovery and Data Mining*, AAAI Press, pp. 226–231.

5 Hartuv, E. and Shamir, R. (2000) A Clustering Algorithm based on Graph Connectivity. *Information Processing Letters*, **76** (4-6), 175–181.

6 Sengupta, S., Basak, S., and Peters, R.A. (2018) Data Clustering using a Hybrid of Fuzzy *c*-means and Quantum-behaved Particle Swarm Optimization, in *IEEE 8th Annual Computing and Communication Workshop and Conference*, IEEE, pp. 137–142.

7 Omran, M.G., Engelbrecht, A.P., and Salman, A. (2005) A Color Image Quantization Algorithm based on Particle Swarm Optimization. *Informatica*, **29** (3).

8 Yang, F., Sun, T., and Zhang, C. (2009) An Efficient Hybrid Data Clustering Method based on K-Harmonic Means and Particle Swarm Optimization. *Expert Systems with Applications*, **36** (6), 9847–9852.

9 Emami, H. and Derakhshan, F. (2015) Integrating Fuzzy *k*-means, Particle Swarm Optimization, and Imperialist Competitive Algorithm for Data Clustering. *Arabian Journal for Science and Engineering*, **40** (12), 3545–3554.

10 Serapião, A.B.S., Corrêa, G.S., Gonçalves, F.B., and Carvalho, V.O. (2016) Combining *k*-means and K-Harmonic with Fish School Search Algorithm for Data Clustering Task on Graphics Processing Units. *Applied Soft Computing*, **41**, 290–304.

11 MacQueen, J.B. (1967) Some Methods for Classification and Analysis of MultiVariate Observations, in *Fifth Berkeley Symposium on Mathematical Statistics and Probability*, vol. 1 (eds L.M.L. Cam and J. Neyman), University of California Press, vol. 1, pp. 281–297.

12 Wang, Z., Bovik, A.C., Sheikh, H.R., and Simoncelli, E.P. (2004) Image Quality Assessment: From Error Visibility to Structural Similarity. *IEEE Transactions on Image Processing*, **13** (4), 600–612.

13 Taşdizen, T., Akarun, L., and Ersoy, C. (1998) Color Quantization with Genetic Algorithms. *Signal Processing: Image Communication*, **12** (1), 49–57.

14 Scheunders, P. (1996) A Genetic Approach towards Optimal Color Image Quantization, in *International Conference on Image Processing*, vol. 3, IEEE, vol. 3, pp. 1031–1034.

15 Hill, F.S. and Kelley, S.M. (2001) *Computer Graphics: Using OpenGL*, vol. 2, Prentice Hall Upper Saddle River, NJ.

16 Wan, S.J., Prusinkiewicz, P., and Wong, S.K.M. (1990) Variance-Based Color Image Quantization for Frame Buffer Display. *Color Research & Application*, **15** (1), 52–58.

17 Heckbert, P. (1982) Color Image Quantization for Frame Buffer Display. *Computer Graphics*, **16** (3), 297–307.

18 Wu, X. (1991) Efficient Statistical Computations for Optimal Color Quantization. *Graphics Gems II*, pp. 126–133.

19 Kruger, A. (1994) Median-Cut Color Quantization. *Dr. Dobb's Journal*, pp. 46–54.

20 Yang, C.Y. and Lin, J.C. (1996) RWM-Cut for Color Image Quantization. *Computers & Graphics*, **20** (4), 577–588.

21 Wu, X. (1992) Color Quantization by Dynamic Programming and Principal Analysis. *ACM Transactions on Graphics*, **11** (4), 348–372.

22 Gervautz, M. and Purgathofer, W. (1988) A Simple Method for Color Quantization: Octree Quantization, in *New Trends in Computer Graphics*, Springer, pp. 219–231.

23 Yang, C.K. and Tsai, W.H. (1998) Color Image Compression using Quantization, Thresholding, and Edge Detection Techniques all based on the Moment-Preserving Principle. *Pattern Recognition Letters*, **19** (2), 205–215.

24 Bing, Z., Junyi, S., and Qinke, P. (2004) An Adjustable Algorithm for Color Quantization. *Pattern Recognition Letters*, **25** (16), 1787–1797.

25 Santos, A.C.S. and Pedrini, H. (2016) A Combination of k-means Clustering and Entropy Filtering for Band Selection and Classification in Hyperspectral Images. *International Journal of Remote Sensing*, **37** (13), 3005–3020.

26 Celebi, M.E. (2011) Improving the Performance of k-means for Color Quantization. *Image and Vision Computing*, **29** (4), 260–271.

27 Hu, Y. and Lee, M.G. (2007) k-means-based Color Palette Design Scheme with the Use of Stable Flags. *Journal of Electronic Imaging*, **16** (3).

28 Hu, Y.C. and Su, B.H. (2008) Accelerated k-means Clustering Algorithm for Colour Image Quantization. *The Imaging Science Journal*, **56** (1), 29–40.

29 Kasuga, H., Hiroaki, Y., and Masayuki, O. (2000) Color Quantization using the Fast k-means Algorithm. *Systems and Computers in Japan*, **31** (8), 33–40.

30 Huang, Y.L. and Chang, R.F. (2004) A Fast Finite-State Algorithm for Generating RGB Palettes of Color Quantized Images. *Journal of Information Science and Engineering*, **20** (4), 771–782.

31 Frackiewicz, M. and Palus, H. (2011) KM and KHM Clustering Techniques for Colour Image Quantisation. *Computational Vision and Medical Image Processing*, pp. 161–174.

32 Kim, D.W., Lee, K., and Lee, D. (2004) A Novel Initialization Scheme for the Fuzzy c-means Algorithm for Color Clustering. *Pattern Recognition Letters*, **25** (2), 227–237.

33 G., G.S. and Zhou, H. (2009) Fuzzy Clustering for Colour Reduction in Images. *Telecommunication Systems*, **40** (1–2), 17–25.

34 Wen, Q. and Celebi, M.E. (2011) Hard vs. Fuzzy c-means Clustering for Color Quantization. *EURASIP Journal on Advances in Signal Processing*, **1**, 118–129.

35 Özdemir, D. and Akarun, L. (2002) A Fuzzy Algorithm for Color Quantization of Images. *Pattern Recognition*, **35** (8), 1785–1791.

36 Xiao, Y., Leung, C.S., Lam, P.M., and Ho, T.Y. (2012) Self-Organizing Map-based Color Palette for High-Dynamic Range Texture Compression. *Neural Computing and Applications*, **21** (4), 639–647.

37 Rasti, J., Monadjemi, A., and Vafaei, A. (2011) Color Reduction using a Multi-Stage Kohonen Self-Organizing Map with Redundant Features. *Expert Systems with Applications*, **38** (10), 13 188–13 187.

38 Chung, K.L., Huang, Y.H., Wang, J.P., and Cheng, M.S. (2012) Speedup of Color Palette Indexing in Self-Organization of Kohonen Feature Map. *Expert Systems with Applications*, **39** (3), 2427–2432.

39 Chang, C.H., Xu, P., Xiao, R., and Srikanthan, T. (2005) New Adaptive Color Quantization Method based on Self-Organizing Maps. *IEEE Transactions on Neural Networks*, **16** (1), 237–249.

40 Omran, M., Engelbrecht, A.P., and Salman, A. (2005) Particle Swarm Optimization Method for Image Clustering. *International Journal of Pattern Recognition and Artificial Intelligence*, **19** (03), 297–321.

41 Su, Q. and Hu, Z. (2013) Color Image Quantization Algorithm based on Self-Adaptive Differential Evolution. *Computational intelligence and neuroscience*, **2013**, 3.

42 Ghanbarian, A.T., Kabir, E., and Charkari, N.M. (2007) Color Reduction based on Ant Colony. *Pattern Recognition Letters*, **28** (12), 1383–1390.

43 Yazdani, D., Nabizadeh, H., Kosari, E.M., and Toosi, A.N. (2011) Color Quantization using Modified Artificial Fish Swarm Algorithm, in *Australasian Joint Conference on Artificial Intelligence*, Springer, pp. 382–391.

44 Akay, B. and Demir, K. (2019) Artificial Bee Colony Algorithm Variants and its Application to Colormap Quantization, in *Evolutionary and Swarm Intelligence Algorithms*,Springer, pp. 25–41.

45 Barman, D., Hasnat, A., Sarkar, S., and Murshidanad, M.A.R. (2016) Color Image Quantization using Gaussian Particle Swarm Optimization (CIQ-GPSO), in *International Conference on Inventive Computation Technologies*, vol. 1, IEEE, vol. 1, pp. 1–4.

46 Khaled, A., Abdel-Kader, R.F., and Yasein, M.S. (2016) A Hybrid Color Image Quantization Algorithm based on k-means and Harmony Search Algorithms. *Applied Artificial Intelligence*, **30** (4), 331–351.

47 Valenzuela, G., Celebi, M.E., and Schaefer, G. (2018) Color Quantization Using Coreset Sampling, in *IEEE International Conference on Systems, Man, and Cybernetics*, IEEE, pp. 2096–2101.

48 Toledo, C.F.M., Oliveira, L., Silva, R.D., and Pedrini, H. (2013) Image denoising based on genetic algorithm, in *IEEE Congress on Evolutionary Computation*, IEEE, pp. 1294–1301.

49 Paiva, J.L., Toledo, C.F.M., and Pedrini, H. (2015) A Hybrid Genetic Algorithm for Image Denoising, in *IEEE Congress on Evolutionary Computation*, IEEE, pp. 2444–2451.

Index

Recent Advances in Hybrid Metaheuristics for Data Clustering, First Edition.
Edited by Sourav De, Sandip Dey, and Siddhartha Bhattacharyya.
© 2020 John Wiley & Sons Ltd. Published 2020 by John Wiley & Sons Ltd.